OUR SAVAGE GOD

OUR SAVAGE GOD

The Perverse Use of Eastern Thought

by R. C. Zaehner

SHEED AND WARD, INC.
Subsidiary of Universal Press Syndicate
New York

Library of Congress Catalog Card Number 74-29644
ISBN: 0-8362-0611-8

For
Edward Hussey

CONTENTS

INTRODUCTION

This book is largely the result of chance or what C. G. Jung would have called 'synchronicity'. It was, I suppose, triggered off by a letter I received from an American professor which included an offprint of his, along with a typescript of an article he had written about the *Bhagavad-Gītā* which pointed out how dangerous this most highly esteemed of all the Hindu sacred books could be if literally interpreted. As witness for the prosecution he produced, among others, the sinister figure of Charles Manson who was responsible for the Sharon Tate murders which shocked the world in 1969. What was so peculiarly horrifying about these murders was that neither Manson nor his youthful accomplices, most of whom came from respectable middle-class homes, showed the slightest remorse at what they had done. How was this possible?

The generally accepted answer was that they had been turned on to murder by psychedelic drugs. This seemed interesting to me since I had already written two books on mysticism and drugs and the similarity that undoubtedly exists between certain mystical states and some drug-induced experiences. I therefore obtained two books on the Manson case which had been mentioned in the American professor's offprint. These were *The Family* by Ed Sanders and *Witness to Evil* by George Bishop. Both books seemed to show that it was not only drugs that launched Charles Manson on his murderous career but also some experience of what he took to be 'enlightenment' as preached by the religions of Indian origin. Could it, then, be that mystical experience or at least some types of it could lead not to a 'holy indifference' but to a diabolic insensitivity which was experienced as being beyond

9

good and evil? After all, there are plenty of texts, whether Hindu, Zen Buddhist or Taoist, which speak of a timeless state of being which transcends good and evil, right and wrong, and all the opposites and contradictions which bedevil our human life; and it is very easy to misinterpret them.

The connection between drug experiences and Eastern mysticism was first noted by Aldous Huxley in his little book, *The Doors of Perception* (1954), and it has been the subject of much debate since. I would not now dispute that similarities do exist between some types of the two groups of experience, as readers of my last book, *Drugs, Mysticism and Make-believe*, will probably have understood. That there are different types of mystical experience as there are of drug experience seems to me so obvious that it should no longer be necessary to labour the point. Unfortunately, however, there are still many rather simple intellectuals who prefer to treat mysticism as a single phenomenon, identical in all its manifestations and present everywhere in the world, though necessarily modified by the particular religious framework in which the mystic has grown up. That this is very far from the truth I have repeatedly argued because the evidence supplied by the mystics themselves compels me to do so. It is no use picking out the odd phrase, of say, St John of the Cross or Meister Eckhart and comparing it with the 'great sayings' of the Hindu Upanishads which *are* characteristic of early Hindu spirituality, and then going on to conclude that what each is trying to describe is one and the same. Each author or tradition must be studied in his or its entirety before the critic is entitled to express any valid opinion. Few writers on mysticism seem disposed to undertake this essential preliminary spadework, and can, therefore, scarcely claim to be taken seriously.

That there should be so much interest among the young in Eastern mysticism today is not only understandable but healthy. Our materially advanced but spiritually impoverished civilization has so little spiritual fare to offer. Official Christianity, forced by science to relinquish its dogmas one after another, is compelled to fall back on a purely 'social' gospel, thereby reducing itself to a vaguely deistic humanism, a ground on which it is singularly ill-equipped to meet its rivals. The Roman Catholic Church, in particular, which once maintained a precarious balance between the active and contemplative sides of religion, seems to have turned its back on contemplation as if it were in some way disreputable. This is surely absurdly short-sighted as well as one-sided and therefore 'heretical' (if by 'heretical' we mean *choosing* whatever aspect of the traditional faith we find most congenial or expedient). So one-sided indeed has the Catholic Church become that most people, not only outside the Church but also within it, do not seem to be aware that the mystical tradition of Christianity is at least as rich and variegated as is that of either Hinduism or Buddhism. Hence the young 'turn on' to Zen or one or other of the wide selection of Hindu guru-cults now so readily available to all and sundry in California and elsewhere. They do not give Christian mysticism a thought – for two reasons. First, through no fault of their own, they know nothing about it, and secondly, even if they did, they would probably find it much less attractive than the Hindu and Buddhist varieties presented to them in an endless outpouring of popular books which offers them something that corresponds to their mood and gives them a glimpse of another 'reality' which transcends our everyday world and claims to transport them into an eternal mode of existence where sorrow and anxiety are somehow transformed into an incomprehensible joy. In this other 'reality' the Lord God of Israel finds no place, for neither classical Hindu philosophy nor Buddhism in either its early Theravāda form or in its more popular Zen manifestation is at all interested in a sovereign God who directs and rules the universe with what seems to many of us an almost paranoiac severity. True, there *are* Christian mystics who play down this all too personal God and direct our gaze to the impersonal Godhead that transcends the triune God himself (Eckhart of course is always cited in this connection) or confuse him with the sum total of existence (Angelus Silesius is the most typical example here), but these are exceptions. The fact remains that Christian mysticism is overwhelmingly God-centred or Christ-centred, and both God and Christ have ceased to have any meaning for the young who see in religion neither dogma nor liturgy nor 'faith' nor social service but a direct apperception of that which *is* – the Eternal which remains changeless behind the ever-changing world now emptied of meaning.

The starting-point of this book was, as I have said, Charles Manson, not because he was responsible for a series of peculiarly shocking murders but because he claimed to have had an 'enlightenment' experience which transported him into an eternal Now in which time was transcended and in which, therefore, all the opposites which confront us on earth were seen to be either non-existent or identical. 'All is One, and One is All, and there is no difference anywhere', seems to have been his basic philosophy, and this is indeed what Aldous Huxley considered to be the kernel of what he called the 'perennial philosophy'. And he was right.

This philosophy has not only survived but thrived throughout the East, but it has atrophied in the West. Why?

The first point, perhaps, that needs to be made is that Western civilization is essentially not Judaeo-Christian but Greco-Roman, and Christianity only became acceptable to the pagan civilization of the Roman Empire once it started to express itself not in terms of Judaic prophecy but in those of Greek philosophy. Our civilization is rooted not in the prophetic tradition of Abraham and Moses but in those first attempts in the Greek world to find a rational principle behind the universe at large and the phenomenon of man in particular. These first thinkers are known as the Presocratics, and the manner of their thinking is strikingly, almost uncannily, similar to that of the Indian philosopher-sages who were their contemporaries. In Greece the great names were Heraclitus and Parmenides; in India, they are for the most part nameless, but their thoughts are collected in those strange treatises called the Upanishads. Here we find much that is not only totally incomprehensible to the modern mind but was also barely understood by the medieval Indian commentators on these sacred texts. But alongside this apparent gibberish we find the same philosophical gropings after coherence that are found among the ancient Greeks, the search for the changeless One which holds together and 'explains' the apparent incoherence of the ever-changing, ever-shifting many, or again for a One that flatly denies and negates the many and, astonishingly, is identical with the human soul as it really is in eternity.

These two philosophies, which can be summed up in the slogans 'One is All, and All is One' on the one hand, and 'The One IS: all else is illusion' on the other, have remained basic to the mainstream of Indian thought, both Hindu and Buddhist.

In Greece the Presocratics were superseded by Socrates himself and his pupil, Plato. Socrates is mainly remembered for his skilful use of the 'dialectical' method of argument, his willingness to question all accepted ideas and to rely on reason so far as he could. But, if Plato's account of him is at all true, there was another Socrates quite different from this, a deeply religious man with a firm belief in supernatural agencies which transcended reason and which it would be both foolish and dangerous to disregard. This was even more true of Plato whose vision of the 'Idea of the Good', the One supremely real, was necessarily expressed in terms of imaginative myth rather than those of rational argument. The West, too, then had its 'perennial philosophy' in rich abundance, but it was all reduced to order by the genius of Aristotle, the real 'father' of the West.

It seemed, then, almost providential that at about the time that I became interested in the Manson case my friend and

colleague, Edward Hussey, produced a book on the Presocratics in which, after years of reflection, he was able to
present the thought of these early thinkers with unusual
lucidity. Once again I was struck by the extraordinary resemblance between them and the early Indians. The reason
why Charles Manson and thousands of other young Americans
had to turn to the East in their search for a direct experience of
the Eternal then suddenly dawned on me. The 'perennial
philosophy' in Europe had been reduced to some sort of order
by Aristotle. He had not killed it nor did he wish to do so, for
he knew quite as well as his teacher, Plato, that the life of
active virtue that good men should pursue on earth must
culminate in the contemplation of the one changeless Reality
which he described as the Unmoved Mover and the 'Awareness of Awareness' or 'Thinking of Thought'.

It is, I suppose, generally admitted that Aristotle's analytic
mind and his insistence on definition and precision is ultimately responsible for the whole development of Western
thought and science, but it is not by any means realized that
he too had his mystical insights. The difference between him
and the recognized mystics, however, is that whereas these tend
to regard discursive thought as the arch-enemy of mystical
experience (and this is particularly true of modern Zen and
the modern Guru-cults which proliferate in California and
elsewhere), he regarded it as the necessary training for that
timeless act of contemplation which is the natural end and
goal of the enlightened human being, for in this act alone
does the 'social animal', man, become truly divine.

To anyone who reads this book it will very soon become
plain that its hero is Aristotle, but you cannot introduce the
proverbial 'intelligent layman' to Aristotle without saying
something about the philosophical milieu in which he had
grown up. In order to do this it seemed to me that a study in
some depth of early Greek thought was necessary, particularly
in view of the Indian parallels which have been mentioned. I
have assumed that the 'intelligent layman', who seems to be

able to swallow book after book on Mahayana Buddhism which, for sheer obscurity, leaves poor Heraclitus and Parmenides standing, might also have the patience to consider their European counterparts, but I have been repeatedly told that this is not so. And this presumably means that the 'intelligent layman' for whom publishers cater is not intelligent at all. If so, then perhaps he would do well to skip chapters 2 and 3 and simply take it on trust that the essence of Heraclitus is summed up in the formulas: 'All is One' and 'Justice *is* strife', both of which would have been readily understood by Charles Manson. As to Parmenides, you will either understand him or you will not. If you have the cast of mind that is attracted by the absolute monism (or non-dualism as it is more often called today) of the Indian idealists, then you will. Otherwise you will not; for what he is saying is that only Absolute Being *is*, everything else (including you and me) being pure imagination. He had his exact parallel in India, and the interest of the comparison is, of course, that whereas this absolute monism became the predominant trend in Indian philosophy and still is so, in the West Parmenides is no more than a name to most of us. That this is so is once again due to our 'father', Aristotle.

You do not have to be a logician to see that any philosophy that asserts that 'justice *is* strife', or that everything except the Absolute One does not in any meaningful sense exist, may result in such phenomena as Charles Manson, for whom killing and being killed were identical and the same. He is no doubt an exceptional case, but there have been other murderers since in California who have interpreted Eastern mysticism in just this way. Most people regret this, but there *is* a moral ambivalence both in Neo-Vedanta and Zen as there is in Heraclitus and Parmenides, and in our everyday world this ambivalence can have disastrous results.

It is not contemplation or 'enlightenment' that is wrong (from our everyday point of view) but the way in which some individuals interpret it. Aristotle too had his enlightenment, but he reached it *through* rational thought, not *against* it: and this is, I suppose, why I wrote the first half of this book which culminates in the apotheosis of Aristotle whose rational approach to contemplation seems to me what the modern world really needs.

The God of the philosophers, then, is the God of Aristotle as interpreted by St Thomas Aquinas, but not the God of the Bible or of the Reformers who sought to extricate the 'true' biblical God from the sweet reasonableness of his Aristotelian rival. As Pascal pointed out with absolute clarity, the God that *he* had experienced in mystical ecstasy was *not* the God of the philosophers and scientists but the God of Abraham, Isaac and Jacob, the God who speaks through the prophets and Jesus Christ. However, in these days of ecumenical 'dialogue', it is no longer possible to speak of the God of revelation, meaning the God of the Christian revelation alone. That this should have been possible at all seems strange, for this claim has been made by Muslims on behalf of their own sacred book, the Koran, ever since Muhammad made his stupendous claim to be the 'Seal of the prophets'. Hitherto few Christians have bothered to examine this claim at all seriously. But we must. For if it is no longer possible to find God by reason leading to contemplation, then surely we must consider him as he reveals himself, at least in part, in all those scriptures where he speaks in the first person. In the Indian tradition he does so, unequivocally, only once, and that is in the *Bhagavad-Gītā*, the core of which is the celebrated theophany in chapter xi: it is terrifying. So is the God of the Old Testament, the God of the Apocalypse, and the God of the Koran. The philosophical Absolute of India, Greece and China has no terrors because it is that unfathomable and changeless peace that transcends both the strife and the justice of Heraclitus; but the God of 'revelation', whenever and wherever he reveals himself, *is* terrible. As Jung saw, though it may be true that all opposites are reconciled in him, they are still there in all their uneasy tension. If you deny this, then you become a Zoroastrian dualist. If God is to be good and to be seen to be good, then you must posit a separate and *positive* principle of evil. But, as the history of religion seems to show, the human spirit seems to yearn for a single principle which harmonizes justice and strife into an Absolute which is beyond all change. If this Absolute is no more than the principle of eternity beyond space, time, causation, and discursive thought, then there would seem to be no metaphysical problem; but if it is also beyond good and evil and therefore indifferent to what men do here on earth, then literally all things are lawful, and it would be as foolish to blame Charles Manson for what he did as it would be to praise Mother Teresa for her sacrifice of self in the cause of the destitute.

But do we fare any better under the law of the Absolute turned 'Person' as he reveals himself as active in time? The second-century heretic, Marcion, doubted it, and many of us would agree with him. However, as Job found out, you cannot argue with *this* God; you can only submit. Hence I have entitled my last chapter 'Islam', which means 'submission with a good grace' to his terrors and gratitude for his occasional mercies.

In this book you will not find any answer to the perennial problems that all religions have tried to solve; for there is no answer. *Either* you will understand what the Hindi poet Kabīr means when he says: 'God is a Thug! . . . What of it? I'm pleased with the Thug as he is. For once I recognized the Thug, the Thuggery vanished away.' *Or*, if you are of a more reflective turn of mind, you may begin to understand how Aristotle came to see that 'it is contemplation that is supremely joyous and good'. And 'if it is thus that God possesses the good in eternity, even as we can so do on occasion, it is wonderful indeed: if even more so, then it is yet more marvellous. But this is just how it is . . . And so we roundly affirm that God is a living being, eternal and supremely good, and that in God there is life and coherent, eternal being. For that *is* God.'

Or again, you may accept neither, but prefer the perennial philosophy of Aldous Huxley in the light of which you will see that Charles Manson *is* Mother Teresa since all things are ever and eternally the *same*.

1

ROT IN THE CLOCKWORK ORANGE

The modern world is afraid of death. Modern youth is afraid of the modern world. The modern world is afraid of modern youth. The modern world is afraid . . .

'My parish is eaten up by boredom,' says the country priest whose diary the most famous work of that astonishing genius, Georges Bernanos, purports to be, 'that's the right word. Like so many other parishes. Boredom is eating them up under our eyes and there is nothing we can do about it. One day, maybe, the contagion will catch up with us too; we will discover this cancer within ourselves. You can live a long time like that. . . . Perhaps someone will say that the world has long got used to boredom, that boredom is man's real condition . . . But I wonder whether men have ever really known this contagion which is boredom – this leprosy: an aborted despair, a disgraceful form of despair which is, I suppose, like the fermentation of a Christianity in a state of decomposition.'[1]

Bernanos's parish might be seen as the microcosm of the modern world. The modern world is bored. It is bored because it has at last reached that material paradise which 'humanistic' materialism in all its forms has told us would bring us contentment and happiness. But let us not exaggerate, for by the 'modern world' we mean, of course, only that part of it which is fully developed, and by 'developed' we mean not, of course, spiritually enriched – an absurdly antiquated idea – but materially surfeited, jaded, and replete. The word 'humanistic', too, needs careful consideration, for only

1. Georges Bernanos, *Journal d'un curé de campagne*, in *Oeuvres romanesques* (Bibliothèque de la Pléiade, Gallimard, Paris, 1961, copyright Librairie Plon), pp. 1031–2.

recently was I asked to attend a conference at Los Angeles the subject of which was to be the 'humanization of man' at which, it was hoped, there would be present some three thousand American delegates plus some three hundred from Europe and elsewhere. The subject of the conference alone tells us volumes about our present condition as seen in the USA. Apparently man is not human: he is some sort of undefined biological species that must somehow be 'humanized', that is, made human, since he never was so before. It is, then, a little difficult to see why he was ever called a 'human' being. The logic of the conveners of the conference would seem to have been a trifle at fault. What they presumably meant and should have said is that man has become so dehumanized – so 'un-manned' – that he needs to be *re*humanized. Like Humpty-Dumpty he has had a great fall and needs to be put together again. Or, in the less clear language always preferred by American academics, the disintegrated pieces of what they once called man must be reintegrated and patched up into the semblance of a whole.

But isn't all this rather out-of-date? Hasn't science proved long ago that we, like the other animals, are simply the result of evolution, an admittedly surprising product of the two forces that control it, necessity and chance, possessing about as much freedom to choose our own destiny as a slug or a stone? We should indeed be happy that evolution has brought us to such a state of perfection that we have reached a point at which we have all but mastered our mother Nature and can simply carry on, in the natural order of things, getting richer and richer, accumulating more and more superfluities to administer to our wildest whims. Things may go wrong, of course: they often do, but we must *believe* that science and its handmaid technology will put all things right in the end. To doubt this would be to doubt the onward march of progress – from 'being' to 'more-being' as Teilhard de Chardin, the prophet of progress and a dynamic mysticism of progress, never tires of telling us. Never mind about the 'kill-count' in

Vietnam, never mind if your husband or son has been killed there, never mind about the mass rapes and murders perpetrated in Bangla Desh and elsewhere. This is all part and parcel of the grand forward sweep of evolution towards the final apotheosis when God will be 'all in all'.[2] As individuals, apparently, we do not count, and to think that we matter is the source of all our troubles (there is a grain of truth in this). We must see that 'the world . . . is an immense groping, an immense search, an immense attack; its progress can take place only at the expense of many failures, of many wounds. Sufferers of whatever species are the expression of this stern but noble condition. They are not useless and dwarfed. They are simply paying for the forward march and triumph of all. They are casualties, fallen on the field of honour.'[3]

It all sounds very grand and comforting (and they say it's 'scientific' too). Meanwhile we, the international bourgeoisie of the privileged third of the world, have 'never had it so good' (in Harold Macmillan's horrible phrase). Our bodies are content, we have plenty to eat, our homes are cosy and we can relax over the TV, we have washing-up machines and all the latest labour-saving devices, central heating and at least one family car, and, thanks to the astonishing advances of medical science in our modern age, we are more or less immunized against pain. As to our soul – well, the scientific establishment seems fairly confident about that: we haven't got one. Nothing much to worry about, then, on that account. The behaviourists too tell us that all talk of the soul is meaningless: 'Soul' and mind are simply functions of a complex physical structure called brain which, should we be unreasonable enough to feel depressed or unduly worried (that is to say, in Greek, should we show symptoms of neurosis), can be analysed out of existence (maybe – and at considerable expense) by our

2. 1 Corinthians 15:28.
3. Pierre Teilhard de Chardin, *Human Energy* (E.T., Collins, London, 1969, and Harcourt, Brace, Jovanovich, New York, 1970), p. 50.

psychoanalyst or manipulated for our own good by the psychiatrists as easily as can the rest of our bodies by the doctors, surgeons, and dentists. It is really all so simple, and it should be plain for even the most doltish of us to see if we will only perform the generally accepted modern trick of translating English words into Greek: in this case 'soul' into psyche. Since few people nowadays have any training in the classics they can scarcely fail to be impressed by the Anglo-Greek jargon by which the scientists and pseudo-scientists seek to bemuse us. The word 'psychiatrist', for them, has magical overtones; and the psychiatrists (and psychoanalysts) might well be described as the modern magicians. If they called themselves in plain English 'physicians of the soul', no one would believe them. How could they, since our humanist and pseudo-scientific *élites* have told them they have no soul? What the psychoanalysts and psychiatrists study, however, is not the 'psyche' of the man in the street, who cannot as yet afford their services, but the 'psyche' of the abnormal, the 'alienated' man, if we must use the fashionable jargon. And since, as we have been so often told (with a considerable measure of truth this time), you cannot understand another human being (if we are still allowed to designate ourselves as such) until you have entered into his very being by 'empathy' (Greek for 'feeling yourself in'), it follows that the psychiatrist must himself experience 'alienation'. Using the same linguistic trick we might point out that *aliéné* is one of the many French words for 'mad'. It is not for nothing that the French have the reputation for lucidity of mind. The mad misleading the mad.

The modern world is bored: and it is bored because it now has more leisure on its hands than it knows what to do with. Before the industrial revolution our forefathers used to take pride in their work, for work on the whole was still a craft involving individual skills as often as not passed on from father to son. It was possible for a man to take pride in his work and do his best to produce something precious by his work, which meant that he could recognize it as being genuinely his: it was not the product of an anonymous conglomeration of minds and hands in the finished product of which he could not recognize anything at all he could rightly call his own. Man has now ceased to be a human being in his own right, and in the new mechanical order any value he might have thought he had as an independent and self-reliant person has become a positive handicap since in a large industrial unit the individual has no value whatever in so far as he is a human being, he has only what Professor Monod calls in another context 'performance value'. Such is modern man at work.

What of modern man at play? Surely, if he is now for the first time favoured with so much leisure, he will be able to make good use of it. There is, after all, such a thing as adult education, the University of the Air, brains trusts on TV, and all that. Moreover, the student population of the country continues to expand (at the expense of the tax-payer), and so on and so on. Granted all this and without being as caustically critical of the common run of human beings as was Heraclitus (p. 29), the fact remains that not very many people want to be educated or are even capable of being educated, for *educare* in Latin means to 'draw out' – to draw out something that is already there, and, if Pascal's slightly misanthropic remark, 'How hollow is the heart of man, how full of filth',[4] is really true, then the process will be neither profitable nor palatable for either the 'drawer' or the 'drawn'. Moreover, it should be obvious to all except the most purblind egalitarian that the more rapidly we increase the quantity of our education the more surely we debase its quality. In the ancient world teaching was regarded as a vocation. The god of the modern academic is not teaching but research, which, in ninety-nine cases out of a hundred, means the production of unreadable theses about trivia which will as often as not remain for ever unread. And all this must be paid for by the tax-payer in the

4. Blaise Pascal, *Pensées*, in *Oeuvres complètes* (Bibliothèque de la Pléiade, Gallimard, Paris, 1957), p. 1145.

interests of what are supposed to be 'advanced' studies, whatever that may mean.

However, this would all be and is a perfectly legitimate way of keeping the not quite so young harmlessly employed if the older generations had the slightest idea of the values they thought worth offering them. They have not, and in the name of liberalism and freedom they leave it to the young to make their choices among the flood of opaque and incomprehensible drivel that comes flooding out of the USA. This is what Bernanos called, in another context, *'la grande peur des bienpensants'*, which we might paraphrase as 'the panic reaction of conforming fools'.

The trouble is not so much that we have totally lost touch with the little that is left of our Christian tradition but that we have lost or thrown overboard *all* our traditional values. As early as 1848 Marx could write: 'Constant revolutionizing of production, uninterrupted disturbance of all social conditions, everlasting uncertainty and agitation distinguish the bourgeois epoch from all earlier ones. All fixed, fast frozen relations, with their train of ancient and venerable prejudices and opinions, are swept away, all new-formed ones become antiquated before they can ossify. All that is solid melts into air, all that is holy is profaned, and man is at last compelled to face with sober senses his real conditions of life and his relations with his kind.'[5]

This description of the then state of affairs is even more true today than when it was originally written except that we do not face our 'real conditions of life' 'with sober senses'. We do not face them at all . . . because we are afraid: . . . and we are bored, and so we turn on the TV and forget about it all. All this intellectual laziness is being drummed into us all the time by the very machines we fall down and worship science for having invented, drummed in by that omnipresent monstrosity miscalled the 'media', and by the human machines who work the

5. *Manifesto of the Communist Party*, in Karl Marx: *Selected Works*, Volume 1 (E.T., Lawrence & Wishart, London, 1942), pp. 208-9.

machines which beguile us and the machines that assess the exact degree of our mental torpidity. Once again Bernanos understood this very well when he wrote:

'The machines distract [modern man], if we may use the word "distract" . . . not in its ordinary meaning but in its accurate, etymological sense: *distrahere* [to draw apart]. What he is asking them to do is brutally to break up the time-honoured, traditional, human rhythm of work. . . . We are not now speaking of simply utilitarian machines. No, the machines for which man has shown a particular predilection and on which he never stops lavishing all he has got in the way of inventive genius, and the perfecting of which, no doubt, takes up four fifths of his industrial effort, are those, and only those, which correspond and adjust themselves most exactly to the natural defence-mechanisms of a man in anguish – the intoxicating movement, the consoling light, the comforting voice.'[6]

So here we are back again at that old existentialist *Angst, angoisse*, 'anguish' which seems to prey on our comfortable, humdrum lives like the plague.

The modern world is bored; and because it is bored, it is in anguish; and because it is in anguish, it is mad. But the root of our madness is our boredom, and the root of our boredom is the fact that we have lost all sense of spiritual values. Everything must be reducible to quantitative terms and what is quantifiable is the subject-matter of science; and science alone, we are repeatedly told, is true because it is ruled and regulated, as Professor Monod has told us with all the weight of the scientific establishment behind him, by the sole criterion of truth, the 'principle of objectivity' but for which we might still be eking out a precarious living in a primeval swamp.

Worse still, not only are we creators of machines and fast becoming entirely dependent on them, we are ourselves

6. Georges Bernanos, *La liberté pour quoi faire?* (Gallimard, Paris, 1953), pp. 176–7.

machines built on microscopic machines which from bacteria to man are essentially the same and invariable: 'the entire [genetic] system is totally, intensely conservative, locked into itself, utterly impervious to any "hints" from the outside world. . . . the cell is indeed a *machine*.'[7] Being machines, then, it must be true that we have no volition of our own. But this is only half the story, for even common sense tells us that we are not identical machines mass-produced to resemble as nearly as possible an ideal blueprint. True, the basic structure is the same, and in this case Humpty-Dumpty was right when he told Alice that she was 'exactly like other people': 'Your face is the same as everybody has – the two eyes, so – . . . nose in the middle, mouth under. It's always the same. Now if you had the two eyes on the same side of the nose, for instance – or the mouth at the top – that would be *some* help.'[8] The variations from one human being to another are indeed, from this strictly scientific point of view where the 'principle of objectivity' rules supreme, purely incidental. But from the same point of view they are objectively undeniable. How, then, are they to be explained? The current scientific answer is scarcely encouraging: they are due to pure chance, what Professor Monod calls 'essential' chance. In a mechanical and 'dead' universe man then is a 'freak' produced by pure chance acting on a microscopic machine which nevertheless determines his whole development. So far from being the centre of the universe he must get used to the idea of seeing himself as the plaything of a mindless universe, 'alone in the unfeeling immensity of the universe, out of which he emerged only by chance'.[9] To claim freedom for such a phenomenon would, then, appear to make singularly little sense. This is the point that Professor Monod is making, and he is not prepared to let us off the hook: he is utterly uncompromising and proceeds to

7. Jacques Monod, *Chance and Necessity* (E.T., Collins, London, 1972), p. 108 (Monod's italics).

8. Lewis Carroll, *Alice through the Looking-glass*, ch. vi.

9. J. Monod, op. cit., p. 167.

reiterate his thesis in terms understandable even to the proverbial child of six:

'We say that these events are accidental, due to chance. And
since they constitute the *only* possible source of modifications
in the genetic text, itself the *sole* repository of the organism's
hereditary structures, it necessarily follows that chance *alone*
is at the source of every innovation, of all creation in the bio-
sphere. Pure chance, absolutely free but blind, at the very
root of the stupendous edifice of evolution: this central concept of modern biology is no longer one among other possible
or even conceivable hypotheses. It is today the *sole* conceivable hypothesis, the only one compatible with observed and
tested fact. And nothing warrants the supposition (or the
hope) that conceptions about this should, or ever could, be
revised.'[1]

A little arrogant perhaps; because science seems to have
proved time and time again that yesterday's certainties are
often forced to make way for what had hitherto seemed a sheer
impossibility owing to the emergence of new evidence which
forces the scientific establishment to accept the unacceptable.
But, however unjustified Professor Monod's rigid dogmatism
may be proved by further research into the structure of the
universe by younger men more widely open to the 'principle
of objectivity' itself, the layman is in no position to question
his view which seems to be accepted by the great majority of
scientists of repute. But he is bound to reject Monod's own
attempt to establish what he is pleased to call an 'ethic of
knowledge' based on the 'principle of objectivity' itself. The
arguments by which he attempts to effect this impossible con-
junction were discussed in my last book and found miserably
wanting. The simple fact remains that science is not and cannot
have anything to do with ethics of any kind. Even psychoanalysis, which studies the behaviour of human beings, can
do no more than analyse cases of behaviour that diverge from
the accepted norm and reintegrate them into that norm in the

1. Ibid., p. 110 (Monod's italics).

interests, it is to be supposed, of society and the individual himself. In so far as psychoanalysis investigates and interprets psychological facts (if, indeed, we can speak of facts at all in this context), we may grant it the status of a science, however grudgingly; but in so far as it seeks to manipulate those 'facts' into a current ethical and social norm, it will have abandoned the 'principle of objectivity' and thereby ruled itself out of the scientific establishment.

Science, of its very nature, must rule out subjectivity: its function is to observe, not to judge. It is not and must not be concerned with values. Once the scientist steps outside his role of constructive observer, he is simply one human machine among many, and his philosophical and ethical principles will be neither more nor less valid than those of anyone else. In other words they will have no value at all because value, if it has any meaning at all, is concerned with quality not quantity. It is concerned with what Aristotle called, in his lapidary and crystal-clear Greek, *to pōs* and *to poson*, 'the how?' and 'the how great?', and even with the *to poion*, 'the what sort of?' (usually misleadingly translated 'quality'): it is not and cannot be concerned with the *hou heneka*, 'the for [the sake of] what?' or 'the why?' That has hitherto been the province of religion and philosophy both of which are now in a state of manifest decay.

Philosophy, as traditionally understood, would seem to be dead: it no longer dares to concern itself with values. The *hou heneka*, 'the for the sake of what?', has been eliminated because, in a view of the world from which all idea of purpose has been banished, this is a question which philosophy refuses to ask because it is held to be meaningless, and to a meaningless question there can be no answer, not even a meaningless one. In a recent book Miss Iris Murdoch, Oxford philosopher turned best-selling novelist, has this to say about modern philosophy, on which she has, because she is both human and humane, turned her back in sorrow. Classifying 'together as existentialist both philosophers such as Sartre who claim the

28

title, and philosophers such as Hampshire, Hare, Ayer, who do not', she proceeds to say that 'characteristic of both is the identification of the true person with the empty choosing will, and the corresponding emphasis upon the idea of movement rather than vision. This emphasis will go with the anti-naturalistic bias of existentialism. There is no point in talking of "moral seeing" since there is nothing *morally* to see. There is no moral vision. There is only the ordinary world which is seen with ordinary vision, and there is the will that moves within it. What may be called the Kantian wing and the Surrealist wing of existentialism may be distinguished by the degree of their interest in *reasons* for action, which diminishes to nothing at the Surrealist end.'[2]

I am not at all clear what is meant by the 'empty choosing will', except that, as Miss Murdoch goes on to assure us, 'it does not in any way connect or tie the agent to the world or to special personal contexts within the world'. An 'empty choosing will', then, operating in an unrelated world. And 'this operation, it is argued, *is* the exercise of freedom'.[3] Man's 'freedom' would therefore seem to consist in the element of 'pure chance, absolutely free but blind', operating at the level of the human machine. If this is, indeed, a true picture of the central position of the British empirical philosophical establishment, then it is not surprising that its representatives should have reached the point at which the theologians arrived long ago where they hold endless dialogue with one another in calm disregard of the irrelevance of what they say to anyone except themselves. Like Heraclitus they are not interested in 'idiots who take fright at any sensible utterance'.[4]

On Miss Murdoch's reckoning the Kantian (British-empirical?) wing of existentialism takes *some* interest in 'reasons' for action, whereas the surrealist wing (the contin-

2. Iris Murdoch, *The Sovereignty of Good* (Routledge & Kegan Paul, London, and Schocken Books, New York, 1970), p. 35.   3. Ibid.
4. See Edward Hussey, *The Presocratics* (Duckworth, London, and Charles Scribner's Sons, New York, 1972), p. 38.

entals, mainly represented (for her) by Sartre) take none at all. *'Quand je délibère les jeux sont faits'* ('Once I decide, the die is cast'), she quotes Sartre as saying, and adds: 'If we are so strangely separate from the world at moments of choice are we really choosing at all, are we right indeed to identify *ourselves* with this giddy empty will? (Hampshire: "I identify myself with my will.")'[5]

Before discussing further the implications of this last memorable fancy, let us return to what Miss Murdoch has called 'moral vision'. 'There is no point in talking about "moral seeing" since there is nothing *morally* to see.' Thus does she sum up the views of the modern Oxford philosophers of whom she considers Professor Hampshire to be typical. This is, of course, exactly the reverse of Aristotle's whole philosophy, both 'naturalistic' (compare the 'antinaturalistic bias of existentialism' censured by Miss Murdoch) and ethical, the goal of both of which is precisely 'seeing, vision, contemplation' (*theōria*).

Everyone takes from Aristotle what suits him best, and it is perhaps for this reason that he never has been and probably never will be 'out-of-date'. Miss Murdoch, being a creative artist in her own right, has shaken the dry dust of Oxford philosophy off her feet. She found no truth there – scarcely surprising in itself since the quest for absolute Truth has been abandoned (and rightly so) ever since the unwieldy colossus of the Hegelian system, the ultimate in philosophy, as its originator thought, was brought crashing to the ground. Finding no truth in the degraded philosophy of her day which does nothing but 'corrupt' the consciences of 'the ordinary person',[6] she 'turned her eyes inward and saw the Self within'.[7] And this higher 'Self', though it may be the ultimate goal to which all traditional philosophy, whether Chinese, Indian, or European, has aspired, can never be

5. I. Murdoch, op. cit., p. 36, quoting Stuart Hampshire, *Thought and Action* (Chatto & Windus, London, 1959), p. 153.

6. Cf. I. Murdoch, op. cit., p. 97.   7. *Katha* Upanishad, 4.1.

satisfactorily formulated in words. Neither science nor any
philosophy which claims, usually fraudulently, to be based on
science can touch it, though the further it advances, the more
clearly does science come to see this Self as the unifying 'law'
or 'logos'[8] of the universe. However that may be, Miss
Murdoch became convinced that any understanding of the
'Good', the 'sovereignty' of which she now proclaims, can
more fruitfully be attained through the contemplation of art
than through philosophical argumentation. 'This is why', she
writes, 'it is and always will be more important to know about
Shakespeare than to know about any scientist: and if there is a
"Shakespeare of science" his name is Aristotle.'[9]

There seems to be no reason to suppose that Miss Murdoch
differs from the vast majority of her countrymen who take it
for granted that Shakespeare is unquestionably the supreme
genius of the English language, towering above all lesser
practitioners as Zeus came to tower over all the lesser godlings
in Greek religion. It is, then, a little surprising that she should
have turned not to him – her scientific and philosophical
Shakespeare – but to Plato as her justificatory model through
whose insights she would transvaluate the devaluators of all
values. She did this, no doubt, because in her fearless acclama-
tion of the 'sovereignty of the Good' she saw in Plato's un-
equivocal declaration of the Idea of the Good a more forthright ally than Aristotle, who reaches much the same ideal
by purely intellectual means: for Plato philosophy is disguised
as art or art disguised as philosophy (it depends on the way
you look at him), whereas Aristotle is rather philosophy for
philosophy's sake, which can be translated into English as the
'love of wisdom' for the sake of that same love. He is rather the
Balzac of philosophy; for Balzac, whose analysis of contemporary society and the infinitely complex individuals who
compose the raw material of society is probably unparalleled
in literature, is nevertheless the author of *Séraphîta* and *Jesus*

8. This key Greek concept will be examined later, pp. 86 ff.
9. I. Murdoch, op. cit., p. 34.

Christ in Flanders which show that he too, whose first pre-
occupation, like Aristotle's, was to analyse and describe, could
nonetheless pierce through the very real world of phenomena
('appearances') and catch a glimpse of that Unmoved Mover
who is at the same time the Thinking of Thought and the One
and supremely excellent living Being.[1]

Modern British philosophy has done little more than
elaborate and refine Aristotle's analytical method: it has completely rejected his goal, to reach which, presumably, the
method was devised. As to the atheist ('surrealist') existentialists, they are truly scientific in the sense that they accept the
universe as absurd and man as a freak within it. They are, it
seems to me, profoundly egotistical in that they are interested
only in themselves and their existential stance in an alien
world and their confrontation with (their own) death. Their
heroic posturings may impress some and disquieten more, but
most will prefer to pass by on the other side since they have
nothing to offer except *Angst* – anguish or anxiety – of which
most people have already quite enough and which they
certainly do not wish to be reminded of day in and day out.

As I said at the beginning of this chapter, modern man is
afraid of death. And for some inscrutable reason he is more
afraid of it now that he believes that death means no more than
simple annihilation in which all consciousness will be wiped
out. For what conceivable reason can a rational being be
frightened of that? Plato seems to have had much the same
idea, though he puts it rather differently.

'Most people', he says, 'are unlikely to be aware that those
who are seriously engaged in the pursuit of philosophy are
really studying nothing but dying and being dead. If, then,
this is true, it would be absurd to spend one's whole life in
devotion to this alone and then to be upset when it comes.'[2]

Plato believed in the immortality of the soul. He also believed
that the quality of the life one lived on earth largely conditioned
any future life there might be in store for us. If one believes

1. See below, p. 194. 2. Plato, *Phaedo*, 64A.

this and also believes in the reality of the 'Good', then the calmness of Plato's Socrates in the face of death is logical enough since as a virtuous man he saw that he had nothing to fear. For modern science and modern philosophy such speculations are unwarrantable hypotheses which should not be allowed to detain the hard-headed thinker. Science has but one principle – the principle of objectivity – and but one criterion – success, or what Professor Monod calls 'performance value'; and the performance value of the man-machine has in these last two centuries, been prodigious. It is by far the most efficient machine known to have been thrown up by evolution. But there is a price to pay, and Monod does not hesitate to say what it is. 'If', he says, 'he accepts this message [of science] in its full significance, man must at last wake out of his millenary dream and discover his total solitude, his fundamental isolation. He must realize that, like a gipsy, he lives on the boundary of an alien world; a world that is deaf to his music, and as indifferent to his hopes as it is to his suffering or his crimes. . . . It is at this point that modern man turns toward science, or rather against it, now seeing its terrible capacity to destroy not only bodies but the soul itself.'[3]

How odd that the apostle of the 'principle of objectivity' should be speaking of the destruction of the *soul* – an entity, if ever there was one, quite beyond the scope of that implacable 'principle of objectivity'. Monod talks like this because he instinctively sees himself as something more than a machine-man with exceptional performance value, and later in his little book he tries to 'prove' it by totally unscientific arguments. He invents an 'ethic of knowledge' out of nothing at all which is not far removed from the ethics of Aristotle but miles away from Professor Hampshire's 'I identify myself with my will'.

But Hampshire, who likes, it seems, to keep abreast of the views of the scientific establishment, is a far more logical adherent to Monod's principle of objectivity than is Monod himself. He does not and cannot believe that there can be an

3. J. Monod, op. cit., pp. 160–1.

33

'ethic of knowledge' because he separates the will, which is wholly subjective and must form an essential ingredient in any ethic, from knowledge, which, as for Monod, is governed by the 'principle of objectivity'. If this is a true picture of Hampshire's position,[4] then he would seem to be moving uncomfortably close to Aleister Crowley, the master magician whose fame or infamy amused or appalled the earlier generations of the twentieth century and whose rallying-cry was: 'Do what thou wilt shall be the whole of the law.'

Whether man is by nature good or evil has been debated all over the world, but nowhere with more precision than among the early Confucians in China where Mencius (390–305 BC) staunchly upheld the pristine goodness of human nature which his successor Hsün Tzŭ (about 312–238 BC) as vigorously denied. In support of his theory Mencius maintained that no *human* being could see a child about to fall into a well without feeling horror and distress. This feeling of distress was, therefore, natural to the human race, for 'not to have a sense of right and wrong is contrary to all human feelings'.[5]

Whether or not men were so obviously human in Mencius' time as he would have us believe is, to say the least, debatable; and the history of the development of religions would seem to show that though there may always have been ideas of right and wrong, good and evil, what was understood by these ideas was very different in primitive societies from what it was in the more developed ones. Ritual purity usually precedes moral purity, and the two need not and often do not coincide.

It was, perhaps, for this reason that the primacy of conscience was recently and unambiguously reaffirmed by the Second Vatican Council of the Roman Catholic Church. What our machine-world is ineluctably achieving is the suppression of conscience as being unacceptable to the principle of objectivity. Christians have always believed that conscience

4. See I. Murdoch, op. cit., pp. 4–9.
5. *The Book of Mencius*, 2A. 6 (6.1 in W.A.C.H. Dobson's translation (Oxford University Press, London, 1963), p. 132).

could be warped: it could indeed be totally destroyed and this is one of the things that 'damnation' means. If, however, 'I identify myself with my will', I am presumably free to make my will evil, to make it indeed as evil as I possibly can – and enjoy it. This is what Aleister Crowley did, and this is what Charles Manson did with his eyes wide open, and this is what Alex did in Anthony Burgess's amazing novel, *A Clockwork Orange*, turned by Stanley Kubrick into a film nobody liked but which few are likely to forget.

The three cases are interesting since they bring out in their different ways the 'rot in the Clockwork Orange', that is, the relentless cancer that feeds and thrives on our mechanistic civilization, from which all values have been banished and in which Charles Manson was able to found his happy Family on those very 'vices' which are condemned not only by all the 'higher' religions but by Aristotle himself, who did not even attempt to fit them into his ethical system, based, as it was, on the golden Mean, but who relegated them to an outer darkness of extremes which he thought were self-evidently evil and which he categorized as 'rejoicing in the evil done to others, shamelessness, envy, . . . adultery, theft, and murder'.[6] These self-evident evils were not at all self-evident either to the fictional Alex of the film or to the real-life Charlie Manson, who, on the contrary, found his own 'beatitude' (Aristotle's *eudaimonia*) and that of his Family in embracing and indulging these attitudes and practices to the utmost extremity. Neither he nor his accomplices felt the slightest remorse.

As to Kubrick's overpowering film, that too has roused much controversy, but few have denied its terrifying power. The hero-villain, Alex (played by the engaging Malcolm McDowell), has this in common with his prototype Charlie Manson that all distinction between (conventional) good and evil has been erased from his consciousness – apparently by drugs, not to mention Beethoven's Ninth Symphony, the terrific impact of which drives this impressionable boy to deeds

6. Aristotle, *Nicomachean Ethics*, 2.6.18 (1107a 10–12).

of truly heroic wickedness. The violence, rape, homicide, and the grotesque phallic uniforms affected by himself and his companions, are deliberately stylized so that on the whole the *voyeur* has little difficulty in taking them in his stride. It is all rather like a ballet – boisterous, no doubt, but a ballet none-theless – accompanied by cheerful classical music (Rossini, I think), but with that terrible Ninth Symphony always in the background. The essential Aristotelian ingredients are all there – rejoicing in the evil done to others, a shamelessness so frank that it has caused some eyebrows to be raised even in our permissive age, envy both of rich 'pigs' and more skilful and successful crooks, adultery committed on the wife of a crack-pot intellectual accompanied by the drum-beat supplied by the vicious kicking of the trussed-up husband, theft, and finally the murder of an eccentric and most unlikeable young lady who lives in solitary splendour surrounded by a mute chorus of decorous white cats, her sitting room embellished by the presence of an enormous white phallus which in the strong hands of the teenage Alex becomes the instrument of her murder. The whole macabre process takes place in the setting of a clockwork world – a machine-made world where man him-self is conditioned by his own inventions, 'the natural defence-mechanisms of a man in anguish – the intoxicating movement, the consoling light, the comforting voice'.[7]

Alex is spurred on to his feats of ultra-violence not only by the relentless rhythms of the Ninth Symphony but also, we are given to understand, by the use of a drug that makes violence seem sweet and which, it seems, is available for the asking. Basically, however, he seems to be a simple, dis-armingly likeable boy: for this seems to be the message con-veyed by the scene in which he returns home in the small hours of the morning, divests himself of his rudely phallic disguise, displays his body beautiful (which of course is *de rigueur* in any modern film), takes a small and amiable boa constrictor whose name is Basil out of an adjacent drawer, and

7. Above, p. 25.

proceeds to relax with him in innocent reflection on a night's work well done. Clearly any boy that can lavish his love on one of God's dumb creatures cannot be wholly bad, for 'love covers over many a sin'.[8]

Alex had been foolhardy enough to antagonize his associates by turning his violence against them. As a result of this and thanks to an almost insane disregard of elementary precautions which the use of the more potent drugs often produces, he is arrested and made to taste a little of the violence he has inflicted on others at the hands of the law. Beaten and spat upon like Christ, he is not crucified, since this form of punishment is unfashionable these days, but sent to prison on a murder charge. We are not shown very much of his prison life but we are shown the essentials. A model prisoner, he is befriended by the prison chaplain whose motives, we are given to surmise, are both evangelistic and pederastic. Like any good chaplain he interests his young charge in the Good Book. He loves it and for reasons that anyone not indoctrinated with the more mealy-mouthed interpreters of that terrifying document can understand and foresee. From beginning to end this book seems to be saturated with violence and a positive lust for revenge. This is the kind of God Alex can understand, and what ecstasy to identify himself with a Roman soldier lashing out at an already half-dead Christ as he carries his cross to Golgotha, the place of the skull! But the Old Testament – that was the real thing. Battles, violence, war – what a marvellous time those Yehoodies had! The boy sniffs up the fragrance of the Holy Book as Aleister Crowley might have sniffed his heroin. He leans back and his comely face is suffused with a look of wonderful beatitude. But, despite the Bible and the chaplain, prison life has its *longueurs*, and Alex comes to hear of the latest technological advance that will completely change the characters of maladjusted persons like himself who are not, of course, morally at fault but tend to upset the whole mechanics of the clockwork-orange society.

8. 1 Peter 4:8; cf. James 5:20; Proverbs 10:12.

He wants to be free and he wants to be 'good', or so he says.

Trundled off to the newly founded clinic, he is cared for by nurses whose mechanical compassion and care could not be faulted. He is injected with the latest wonder-drug which causes the human machine that happens to be addicted to ultra-violence and ultra-sex to veer to the opposite extreme of revulsion and disgust. He is made to sit alone in a clockwork cinema where his eyelids are prised open so that he can sit through scenes of ultra-violence and ultra-sex that even he had never imagined and the likes of which he had not come upon even in the Holy Book. He *has* to look since he cannot close his eyes. The drug begins to work and the boy is overpowered with nausea. A fortnight of this enlightened and compassionate treatment does the trick, and the monster emerges milder than a lamb. The mere sign of violence makes him sick, as do all the blandishments of sex. He has become so 'good' that even when violence is perpetrated on himself he cannot defend himself. He is no longer a machine programmed for the destruction of others, he is a machine programmed for the destruction of himself.

The moment he is set free to make his gentle way in the clockwork world, he is set upon and violently mishandled by his former associates, now turned cops, that is, administrators of the majesty of the law. Half dead, he crawls off to the nearest house, which happens to be the home of the crackpot intellectual whose wife he had raped and whom he had trussed up and viciously kicked out at in the good old days when evil was good and good was evil. He is too broken to recognize the old man or his plastic clockwork home, but the old man, whose wife has subsequently died, recognizes *him* and learns his secret. The boa constrictor's fangs have been excised: he can no longer rape or kill, nor can he even *desire* to do such things. He has been immunized against his former joys – *and against the Ninth Symphony of Ludwig van* (as he calls the great composer). 'Vengeance is mine', the Lord promises,[9] and the old

9. Romans 12:19.

gentleman takes him at his word. Not for him the wiser verse
that follows on this quotation from the Book: 'Resist evil and
conquer it with good.'[1]

The boy is tired and must be sent to bed. So to bed he goes,
and no sooner is he about to go to sleep than those dreadful
musical cascades with which the dreaded symphony opens
erupt from beneath the bedroom floor. In frenzied panic the
boy rushes to the door: it is locked. So here he is – locked in
with the blaring reminder of his erstwhile savage joys. There
is no escape but to 'snuff it', and 'snuff it' he does out of the
window. But he does not quite make it.

We see him next in plaster in yet another clockwork clinic,
tended by oh, such a jolly clockwork lady psychoanalyst. He
has already been brought from the extreme of excess to the
extreme of deficiency in the matter of his particular virtue
which is courage (I speak in the manner of our master Aristotle): he must now be brought back to his clockwork 'mean',
which, according to the clockwork manipulators, equals what
used to be called a human being. The cure is triumphantly
successful, and the progressive Minister who had given legal
authority to the new technique for turning monsters into useful members of the clockwork society appears in person to
bless the child of his clockwork brain. The boy is now as
happy as happy can be, tickled beyond words that he should
have become a figure as widely known as General de Gaulle
or the Beatles, and cosseted by the Minister himself. Here is
he, the erstwhile monster, 'cured' into helplessness by the
latest therapeutical techniques, and now, after attempted
suicide, restored to what, in the eyes of authority, he ought to
be – but not quite. For, after the laughter and the joy of health
'restored', the chin wobbles: he is going to be sick. He is still
sick with the sickness of a world out of which the soul has been
ripped, an 'aborted despair'.

'It is at this point that modern man turns toward science, or
rather against it, now seeing its terrible capacity to destroy not

1. Ibid., 12:21.

39

only bodies but the soul itself', as Professor Monod has warned us. Not surprisingly so since, just as the divine Logos (Reason) is said to have become man in Jesus Christ, so has human reason, refined and reduced to the 'principle of objectivity', become the only god we know. It has clothed itself in the prophetic garb of Jeremiah, and sees itself set up 'over nations and over kingdoms, to tear up and to knock down, to destroy and to overthrow, to build and to plant'.[2] It has been doing both the destroying and the building with an undreamt-of efficiency and speed which can only leave us spellbound by its loyalty to the only value it knows, the 'performance value', in which man is proud enough to think that he excels both the ants and the bees. Truly, the principle of objectivity is God: for does not Scripture say: 'Do not be afraid of those who kill the body but cannot kill the soul; fear him rather who can destroy both body and soul in hell'?[3] To whom do these terrible words refer? To God? or to Satan? or to a God who is both God and Satan? How can we be sure? For we cannot accept Professor Monod's improbable marriage of the principle of objectivity and the 'ethic of knowledge', because knowledge has no ethic, as Professor Hampshire has cogently pointed out. Classical Greek ethics was concerned in one way or another with the 'good', and the good was in some way connected with reason and due proportion (Logos).[4] The modern world, which has made science and its sacred principle of objectivity its god, is beginning to teach us that there may also be an ethics of evil – an ethics of discord and strife which is of 'the very nature of evil'.[5]

This surely is the ambiguous message of *A Clockwork Orange*; but the theory of it had already been worked out, though incoherently, by Aleister Crowley, who loved to be known as the 'Great Beast', but who saw himself as the founder of a new religion which would supersede Christianity,

2. Jeremiah 1:10.   3. Matthew 10:28.
4. See E. Hussey, *The Presocratics*, p. 39.
5. Aristotle, *Metaphysics*, 12(11).10.7. (1075b 8).

Buddhism and Islam, and the motto of which would be: 'Do what thou wilt shall be the whole of the law.' His first revelation came to him at the age of twenty-three. This is how he describes it:

'I was in the death struggle with self; God and Satan fought for my soul those three long hours. God conquered – now I have only one doubt left – which of the twain was God?'[6]

Crowley has been condemned as the arch-Satanist, but this is perhaps to do him less than justice, for he belonged to an age-old tradition which saw the Eternal as the ultimate unity in which all the opposites were reconciled, including good and evil. He had lived in the East and was familiar with the scriptures of both the Hindus and Buddhists for whom these ideas were a commonplace, but whereas the early Buddhists at least considered that training in the good life was a necessary prerequisite for the realization of the Eternal, there were occult sects among both religions who disputed this and practised what they preached. In Greece too we find the same insight in the 'darkling' Heraclitus for whom the ultimate transcendence was 'harmony' (*harmoniē*), for which Edward Hussey, after carefully weighing all the evidence as is his habit, suggests that the best translation is 'mutual adjustment'.[7] Perhaps it would not be too inaccurate to say that the 'harmony' or 'mutual adjustment' of Heraclitus was 'discordant concord' while for Crowley it was 'concordant discord'.

But there is another element of great importance in Crowley's first revelation which we have quoted above. Not only was the struggle between God and Satan ambiguous in that the distinction between the two became so blurred that he could later invoke 'our Lord God the Devil',[8] but the struggle was for his very soul, which meant that he had to identify his inmost self with one or other aspect of the God-Devil Absolute.

6. John Symonds, *The Great Beast* (Macdonald, London, 1971), p. 13.

7. E. Hussey, op. cit., pp. 43–4.   8. J. Symonds, op. cit., p. 64.

It may be assumed that in what John Symonds calls his 'Buddhist phase', when, in what is now Vietnam, he attained to one of the higher Buddhist trances ('Neroda-Samma-patti',[9] more correctly spelt *nirodha-samāpatti*), which corresponds to what we would call the annihilation of the ego, he was tempted to turn his back on the world which, for the Buddhists, is not only full of sorrow and anxiety but actually *is* sorrow and anxiety, thereby attaining to the unutterable peace of Nirvana. This, however, was not the way of his 'Holy Guardian Angel', Aiwass, who taught him that absolute bliss could only be attained by enjoying the good things of this world to the full – riches, power, and above all sex, the earthly counterpart of the transcendent union of the opposites.

To attempt to summarize the ideas of Aleister Crowley here would be impossible: they are too diffuse. He was a magician, and as the hierophant of the English branch of the *Ordo Templi Orientalis* ('Order of the Oriental Temple', or OTO for short), to which he had consented to attach himself in 1911, he developed elaborate rites of sexual 'magick', for magicians have their special rites like any other form of organized religion. OTO not only professed to descend from the medieval Knights Templar suppressed for alleged homosexuality in 1312 but also had connections with the left-hand Tantra in India, the adepts of which practised sexual magic, their purpose being to attain to the Absolute through the union of the opposites, that is, the male and female principles allegedly inherent in the one true God. Crowley's sexual tastes were catholic in the extreme, but the climax of the so-called 'First Working of the High Magick Art' first celebrated by two Cambridge graduates – Crowley himself (alias Frater Perdurabo, 'I shall last for ever') and one Victor Benjamin Neuburg (alias Omnia Vincam, 'I shall conquer all') – was an act of sodomy the significance of which, to judge by the two men's aliases, would seem to be the irruption of time into eternity, the logical sequel probably, according to Crowley's

9. Ibid., p. 94.

peculiar outlook, of the Incarnation in which, as orthodox Christians maintain, the Eternal entered into and sanctified the temporal.

Be that as it may, the fact remains that it was largely Crowley who was responsible for introducing Indian sexual magic into the West. That there is a link between the mysticism of love which culminates in what Christians call the 'spiritual espousals' and carnal sexual union has been known not only to the psychologists but also to the Christian mystics themselves from Origen (third century AD) on. Sexual magic, which may include sado-masochism, as it did in the cases of both Aleister Crowley and Charles Manson, is also a form of sexual *mysticism*, and is certainly so regarded by its adepts. It also shares with the more orthodox varieties of mysticism the following characteristics: (i) the transcendence of time and space and therefore of death, (ii) the disappearance of the everyday 'ego'-personality, including the mind, (iii) a sense of oneness with all things or more rarely of an absolute identity with the Absolute.

All this you will find in Crowley in rich abundance. We must, however, limit ourselves to a minimum of examples since, though Crowley considered himself to be the divine inaugurator of a new aeon which would put an end to Christianity, Charles Manson thought he was Jesus Christ himself; and, if, for the sake of argument, we take him at his word, then Crowley will be no more than his John the Baptist. This would in any case seem more logical since Manson carried Crowley's premises to their logical conclusion: if God and the Devil, good and evil, life and death, can really be transcended in an eternal Now, then sadism and sexual profligacy are not enough: you must transcend life and death itself either by killing or being killed. Charles Manson did not shrink from this ultimate 'truth'.

However, to return to the precursor. Let us quote from him more or less at random. For mystical category no. 1: 'I am living in eternity, and temporal things have become tedious and stupid symbols';[1] or, rather less succinctly: 'The world had stopped suddenly still. We were alone in the night and the silence of things. We belonged to eternity in some indefinable way; and that infinite silence blossoms inscrutably into embrace.'[2]

Mystical category no. 2: 'He was so far away from himself that he became some other, and strange, figure, to whom he referred in the third person. He had come to the point of conquering his mind. The mind had broken up . . . passing from this, he became as a little child, and on reaching the Unity behind the mind, found the purpose of his life.'[3] But does life have a purpose? Let us look at our next quotation which seems to combine our category 2 with –

Mystical category no. 3: 'Act, word, and thought were equally abolished. The elements of my consciousness did not represent me at all. They were sparks struck off from our Selves. Those Selves were one Self which was whole. Any positive expression of it was of necessity partial, incomplete, inadequate. . . . The idea of having a purpose at all is beneath contempt. It is the sort of thing a human being would have.

'How can a supreme being inhabiting eternity have a purpose? The absolute, the all, cannot change; how then could it wish to change? It acts in accordance with its nature; but all such action is without effect. It is essentially illusion; and the deeper one enters into one's self the less one is influenced by such illusions.'[4]

If this is so, then why do anything at all? Why proclaim the slogan of the new dispensation in the words: 'Do what thou wilt shall be the whole of the law'?

Well, in the idealized picture Crowley paints of his 'Sacred Abbey of Thelema' (Greek for 'will') which he founded in Sicily as the centre of his cult and where, according to him,

1. Aleister Crowley, *Diary of a Drug Fiend* (Sphere Books, London, 1972), p. 189.

2. Ibid., p. 79.   3. J. Symonds, op. cit., p. 92.

4. A. Crowley, op. cit., pp. 189–90.

the idyllic life of the community was directed towards gently 'unhooking' hard-drug addicts, he says:

'We had followed the devil through the dance of death, but there could be no doubt in our minds that the power of evil was permitted for a purpose. We obtained the ineffable assurance of the existence of a spiritual energy that worked its wondrous will in ways too strange for the heart of man to understand until the time should be ripe.

'The pestilence of the past had immunised us against its poison. The devil had defeated himself. We had attained a higher state of evolution. And this understanding of the past filled us with absolute faith in the future. . . .

'Not ours to speculate about the goal of our Going. Enough for us to Go. We knew our way, having found our will, and for the means, had we not love?

' "Love is the law, love under will." '[5]

This is, of course, a grotesque travesty of what the Sacred Abbey of Thelema was really like. Crowley was himself thoroughly 'hooked' on hard drugs and there is little doubt that these produced effects in him similar to those described by Aldous Huxley in *The Doors of Perception*. As to love, for him this could only mean the gratification of an apparently insatiate animal desire. The Abbey of Thelema was described as 'the Whore's Hell, a secret place of the quenchless fire of Lust and the eternal torment of Love', to which must be added an extensive use of hard drugs which apparently formed an integral part of the 'High Magick Art'.[6]

Crowley managed to survive the war, after which he founded, among other things, a 'thelemic' lodge called Agape Lodge in Pasadena, California.[7] Here his ideas took root and must have filtered through, via the 'Solar Lodge of OTO',[8]

5. Ibid., p. 381, but see also J. Symonds, op. cit., pp. 232–50.
6. A. Crowley, op. cit., pp. 12–13.
7. J. Symonds, op. cit., p. 391.
8. Ed Sanders, *The Family* (Rupert Hart-Davis, London, and E.P. Dutton, New York, 1972), p. 161.

to the impressionable mind of the young Messiah-to-be, Charles Manson, whose 'sandal-strap' the illustrious Crowley was surely 'not fit to undo'.[9]

Aleister Crowley seems to me to be repulsive by any standards. Educated at Malvern, Tonbridge, and Trinity College, Cambridge, opulent, an intrepid mountaineer who led the first known assault on the Himalayan giant Kanchenjunga, widely travelled, widely read in the religious classics of both India and China, he nevertheless chose to bury his very considerable talents and devote himself to a form of sexual 'magick' which managed to be both puerile and heartless, combining and exacerbating this 'high magick art' with heavy doses of hard drugs of which he was a connoisseur. If Aldous Huxley must be held responsible for initiating the psychedelic cult as a means to the higher forms of Eastern mysticism in the USA, then Aleister Crowley is far more responsible for purveying those forms of Eastern mysticism which are based on sex and drugs and are more open to abuse than any of the more orthodox 'yogas' which proliferate in the melting-pot of the new age that is in the process of being born in California today. It is possible, all too possible, particularly for the rootless bourgeois young, to sympathize with this fat, bourgeois rebel against a rigid, negative, and heartless morality, and to succumb to his radical denial of any and every accepted moral standard. For those half-baked intellectuals who had seen through the sheer hollowness and absurdity of the Christianity they had learnt at school, it must have seemed like a wonderful release to hear this intrepid Cambridge graduate proclaim: 'There is no good. Evil is good. Blessed be the Principle of Evil. All hail, Prince of the World, to whom even God Himself has given dominion.'[1]

Through OTO (of which, incidentally, that far more 'respectable' occultist Rudolf Steiner was also a member[2]), a *European* organization, Eastern 'wisdom' was to penetrate to

9. Cf. John 1:27.
1. J. Symonds, op. cit., p. 193.   2. Ibid., p. 154.

the USA long before the more innocuous version of it was to
be imported direct from India and Japan by such figures as
Suzuki and the Ramakrishna Mission.[3] Of the two the latter is
far the less radical or virulent (it all depends how you look at
it), but the former, as preached by Crowley and practised by
Manson, can also claim to represent an ancient undercurrent
that flows beneath the surface of official Hinduism.

One of the earliest scriptural texts that seems to justify
Manson's philosophy of killing and being killed is found in
the *Katha* Upanishad (2.19):

> Should the killer think: 'I kill',
> Or the killed: 'I have been killed',
> Both these have no [right] knowledge:
> He does not kill nor is he killed.

So too Charlie Manson draws his conclusions: 'There is no
good, there is no evil. . . . You can't kill kill' and 'If you're
willing to be killed, you should be willing to kill.'[4] In terms
of Indian religion this makes sense as we shall see: if all things
are ultimately One, as Heraclitus in our own tradition said,
then the individual as individual does not really exist. So,
according to his disciples, Charlie had transcended all desire:
qua Charlie, then, he was dead. 'It wasn't Charlie any more.
It was the Soul. They were all Charlie and Charlie was they.'[5]

It is, perhaps, not easy to sympathize with a man who was
responsible for and convicted of nine brutal and sadistic
murders and who was almost certainly responsible for many
more. It is, however, very possible to be fascinated by him,
for, unlike Aleister Crowley whose play-acting becomes rather
a bore, Charlie Manson is the symbol of a deep *malaise* in
American society. In his own slight person he represented
American youth's present revulsion against what Dr Leary has

---

3. It is true that Swami Vivekananda, the founder of the mission,
made his first impact on the USA in 1893, but it was not till much
later that it became fully organized.

4. E. Sanders, op. cit., p. 181.   5. Ibid., p. 212.

called the 'Protestant work ethic' which has become indistinguishable from the worship of Mammon, that is, the worship of money, the desire to have more and more, above all more than your neighbour, for that means 'status'.

American youth's revulsion against the capitalist establishment would appear to take three forms, two of them serious, one of them mindless. The serious two are the hippies and the so-called New Left. The hippies simply want to drop out of our mechanized clockwork civilization altogether. Some of them form communes in a natural 'orange' uncontaminated by any 'clockwork': they wish to live, to love, and to earn their own living in natural surroundings without seeking anything in excess of what they need. Others seek salvation by traipsing off to the East in search of Eastern wisdom at its source. Yet others group themselves into urban cliques, sequestered, as far as is possible, within the very society from which they seek to flee. All too often the two latter groups drop out into drugs, the effect of which may be either innocuous, stimulating, or disastrous. The first group, the communes, vary enormously: they may be genuinely dedicated to a natural way of life as far removed as possible from the mechanistic, cybernetic, polluted clockwork rottenness that the American way of life has become; or they may be simply a cover for such unpleasing sects as OTO, 'The Process', and similar fantasies. What all these groups have in common is that they want to have nothing to do with the money-making machine. They do not wish to change it because too many of them are dependent on it through the tolerance of parents or other well-wishers whom they despise.

About the New Left little need be said since everybody knows about them and their noisy antics through the Press and those odious 'media'. They *hate* the bloated, bourgeois, capitalist establishment which landed them in the seemingly never-ending tragedy and brutality of the Vietnam war, and they want to destroy it utterly. They have little or no idea of how this is to be done; they chatter about alienation, the early Marx now fashionable and refurbished, and, of course, the turgid hotch-potch of Germano-American 'ideas' churned out by the once fashionable Marcuse. As to the reconstruction of the mechanized society they propose to overthrow, their ideas are as vague as those of their hero, the early Marx.

As to the third form of protest that infected American youth and which we have called 'mindless', this is typified by what the Americans call 'bikers' (motorcycle gangs), the most harmless of which do little more than worship the idol-machine created by other men's brains and hands, while the more noxious varieties, though mindless, are infected at third hand by the pseudo-oriental ideas of our old friend Crowley. Two of them revel in those sinister initials SS (the Nazi élite corps committed heart and soul to Crowley's political avatar, Adolf Hitler[6]). For the one group the mystic letters stood for 'Satan Slaves', for the other for 'Straight Satans'. Both groups interested Charlie Manson who saw in them a possible military wing to further the ends of his Family.[7]

The protest of American youth against the established norms of American society takes many forms, but it is united in its condemnation of the monstrous thing the American way of life has come to be. What are the characteristics of this society? In a recent book the American neo-Freudian psychoanalyst, Erich Fromm, has summed the situation up as follows:

'As the chief traits of the bourgeois-capitalist spirit we have recognized: (1) restriction of the role of pleasure as an end in itself (particularly sexual pleasure); (2) retreat from love, with emphasis instead on collecting, possessing, and saving as ends in themselves; (3) fulfilment of one's duty as the highest value; (4) emphasis on "orderliness" and exclusion of compassion for one's fellowman.'[8]

6. J. Symonds, op. cit., p. 390: 'To her mind, the two leaders, one of a nation, the other of a mystic order, were working to the same end, that of establishing a new world order based on the true will.'

7. E. Sanders, op. cit., p. 150.

8. Erich Fromm, *The Crisis of Psychoanalysis* (Jonathan Cape, London, and Holt, Rinehart & Winston, New York, 1971), p. 186.

Or, as Bernanos has said, it is the triumph of the 'spirit of avarice' over the 'spirit of youth'.[9]

American capitalism is, quite literally, what Bernanos calls the 'spirit of avarice': it is the desire to 'have' and grab, at whatever cost to others. It exhibits itself on the individual, the family, the group, and the national planes: it is the 'habit' of 'having', as Aristotle might have put it, the necessary first-fruits of egoism, the root-sin, or as the Buddhists and Hindus would put it, the root-ignorance of mankind. 'These are the people who go to excess in getting ["go-getters" as we would say], grabbing everything they can from wherever they can as, for example, those who make their living out of ignominious occupations – pimps, brothel-keepers, and the like – money-lenders at a high rate of interest; for all these make money from improper sources and in quantities that are beyond all reason. What is common to them, it seems, is a sordid lust for profit. And the proof of it is that they will put up with any amount of obloquy so long as they make a profit, however small.'[1]

This is not some crackpot of the New Left denouncing modern American capitalism and capitalistic racketeering, but Aristotle calmly analysing the nature of man as he was in his time – 'ignominious' man: a more literal translation of the Greek (*aneleutherios*) would be 'illiberal', or more literally still, 'un-free'. Such men, he assures us, are more common than their opposites, the prodigal spendthrifts, and the evil they do is greater,[2] for you cannot really say that the spendthrift is ignoble, let alone evil, he is just silly.[3] The capitalist *qua* capitalist, on the other hand, is both ignominious and evil. If he were plain silly, he would scarcely have become the object of such bitter indignation.

Charles Manson is, perhaps, unique in that, in his bizarre

9. Georges Bernanos, *Les grands cimetières sous la lune* (Plon, Paris, 1938), p. 265.

1. Aristotle, *Nicomachean Ethics*, 4.1.40–2 (1121b 32–1122a 3).

2. Ibid., 4.1.44 (1122a 13–16).   3. Ibid., 4.1.31 (1121a 27).

way, he combines the seeming opposites of the drop-out hippies with the incoherent New Left. The victim of a rotten society, he collected a band of devoted disciples, withdrew into the desert, moulded his followers according to his will, and then descended once again into the unholy city of Los Angeles to strike terror in the fattened hearts of the overfed.

Unlike Aleister Crowley, Charles Manson did not have the advantage of being educated at those eminently bourgeois institutions, Tonbridge School and Trinity College, Cambridge. He was born 'underprivileged', as our nauseating, pharisaical modern jargon puts it. In other words he was destitute, despised and rejected. Son of a teenage prostitute and a casual client known only·by his pseudonym as 'Colonel Scott', he was from the start a being without a name – a being without personal identity, that is, for it is the name that identifies you as *you* as distinct from all other beings.

There is something highly symbolical in this as there is in everything about this extraordinary man. To be without a name means to be outside and beyond all that can be named.

> The Way that can be told is not an Unvarying Way;
> The names that can be named are not unvarying names.
> It was from the Nameless that Heaven and Earth sprang;
> The named is but the mother that rears the ten thousand
> creatures, each after its kind.[4]

These are the opening words of the famous Taoist classic, the *Tao Tê Ching* – mysterious words from a book as mysterious and as ambiguous as the character of Charles Manson himself. But though the Nameless may be the source of all that is, it is not good for a man to be without a name; and so this nameless boy, born of a teenage whore and a shadowy father whose name he never knew, received the name of Manson, a man his mother is believed to have married for a brief time to give him

4. *Tao Tê Ching* 1, tr. Arthur Waley, as *The Way and its Power* (Allen & Unwin, London, 1934, and reprints), p. 141.

a semblance of legitimacy. And so the nameless received a name – Manson – the Son of Man. Did he consciously realize that this was the name that Another chose for himself, and was this the reason why he came to regard himself as Jesus Christ? We are not told. Sometimes the name seemed to fit and sometimes it didn't. Sometimes he was the Son of Man, and sometimes he did not know who he was, the 'nameless' of which nothing positive can be said. Given these ambiguities, it should not be difficult to understand that he was speaking the truth when he said at his trial (or so it was reported at the time): 'I have killed no one and I have ordered no one to be killed. I don't place myself in the seat of judgment. I may have implied on several occasions that I may have been Jesus Christ, but I haven't decided yet who I am or what I am. I was given a name and a number and I was put in a cell, and I have lived in a cell with a name and a number.

'I don't know who I am.

'I am whoever you make me, but what you want is a fiend; you want a sadistic fiend because that is what you are.'

To my mind there is a real dignity and pathos in these words. Charles Manson knew his Bible and was inspired by it, though not after the manner of the scribes and Pharisees of the Christian establishment whose business it is to sweep under the carpet all that gory stuff that so delighted the heart of Alex, the hero of *A Clockwork Orange*. 'Judge not that ye be not judged', he must have remembered – remembered too that it was only at his trial that Jesus publicly confessed that he *was* 'the son of the Blessed One', for after Peter had acknowledged him as Christ he had given strict orders to his disciples that they should tell no one what they now knew. Again, had not Christ himself been accused by the Pharisees, the religious establishment of the time, of casting out devils through the prince of devils?[5] And was it not because they wanted him to be Satan that they accused him of working through Satan?[6]

5. Matthew 9:34.   6. Ibid., 12:26.

Rot in the Clockwork Orange

Again Charles Manson said: 'You want a sadistic fiend because that is what *you* are.' Was he pondering those scathing words of Jesus to those who rejected him:

> The devil is your father,
> and you prefer to do
> what your father wants.
> He was a murderer from the start;
> he was never grounded in the truth;
> there is no truth in him at all:
> when he lies
> he is drawing on his own store,
> because he is a liar, and the father of lies.[7]

Very little seems to be known of the early life of Charles Manson. Given his casual parentage, however, it is not unreasonable to suppose that he was unlikely to have been well-disposed towards the corrupt establishment which likes to think of itself as representing the forces of law and order. In any case he was sentenced at the age of sixteen for stealing a vehicle after 'doing time' in various correctional institutions and reformatories for boys. After a brief period and a move to Los Angeles from his native state of Utah, he was arrested and incarcerated once again on a charge of stealing a car. Until 1966 he had spent most of his life in jail with only brief periods of liberty. He was already what is known as a hardened criminal and a poor risk for probation. Stealing cars seems to have had a peculiar fascination for him, but he was also found guilty of possessing marijuana (a 'crime' of which few young citizens of the United States are innocent nowadays), of forging cheques and driving licences, and of rape. Prison life is not conducive to sexual purity and it is scarcely surprising that this slight and strangely attractive boy became the object of the sexual interest of the more virile young prisoners who, if we are to believe subsequent accounts, did not stop short

7. John 8:44.

of sodomy. Whether, even at this stage, he attached a mystical significance to what one of his 'Family' was to describe in court as a 'total experience', we do not know. So far as we *do* know, however, once he had left prison he confined his sexual activity entirely to girls. This seems odd, but, given Charlie's philosophy, there does seem to be a reasonable explanation. The 'total experience' means total submission to even the most violent onslaughts of your sexual partner in which the passive participant experiences the annihilation of his or her ego. The opposite of total submission is total domination, and Charlie's switch from the passive to the active role is his own form of sexual magic, which would explain, at least in part, his subsequent will to power and the absolute loyalty and devotion he inspired in his young female 'children', who did not hesitate to commit atrociously cruel murders at his behest.

His real hatred of the American establishment was nothing extraordinary. Indeed it was not only natural to a young criminal but also highly fashionable among the educated young, as we all know. This attitude comes out with all desirable clarity in the written statement he made at the trial. (Whether the statement is genuine or a forgery is immaterial: the contents seem so utterly typical of Manson's attitude to life.) Let him speak in his own words:

'I am not allowed to be a man in your society. I am considered inadequate and incompetant [*sic*] to speak or defend myself in your court. *You*[8] have created the monster. I am not of you, from you, nor do I condone your wars or your unjust attitudes towards things, animals and people that you won't try to understand. I haved [*sic*] Xed myself [sc. cut myself off] from your world. I stand in the opposite to what you do and what you have done in the past. You have never given me the constitution you speak of. The words you have used to trick the people are not mine. I do not accept what you call justice. The lie you live in is falling and I am not part of it. You use the word God to make money.

8. My italics.

'. . . You make fun of God and have murdered the world in the name of Jesus Christ. I stand with my X [cross? – during the trial his forehead was marked with a St Andrew's cross], with my love, with my god and by myself. My faith in me is stronger than all your armies, governments, gas chambers or anything you may want to do to me. . . . Love is my judge. I have my own constitution; its [*sic*] inside me.

'No man or lawyer is speaking for me. I speak for myself. I am not allowed to speak with words so I have spoken with the mark I will be wearing on my forehead [i.e. the cross]. Many US citizens are marked and don't know it. You won't let them come from under your foot. But God is moving. Moving, and I am a witness.'

The words are the words of Charles Manson but the tone of stern rebuke directed at a corrupt and self-satisfied *élite* we have heard before:

'Woe unto you, scribes and Pharisees, hypocrites! You who shut up the kingdom of heaven in men's faces, neither going in yourselves nor allowing others to go in who want to.'[9]

Charles Manson has been described as a paranoiac – a nice blanket word meaning more or less anything that is not mediocre and conformist. He was well aware of this but equated it with 'total awareness'. Describing the habits of the coyote, he says: 'He's always in a state of total paranoia and total paranoia is total awareness.'[1] Paranoiac or not, there is nothing feigned about his hatred of a violent, clockwork society. Many of the men he knew – and there were plenty of them among the Satan Slaves, Straight Satans, Gypsy Jokers and other 'bikers' of his acquaintance – had vivid memories of war in the raw in Vietnam. As someone closely connected with the trial is alleged to have put it (and, if so, he put it well):

'You take a boy from a middle class family, brought up to respect God and the flag, put him into the army and he's soon sighting down that barrel, pulling the trigger and murdering

9. Matthew 23:13.
1. E. Sanders, *The Family*, p. 129.

people *without any sense of guilt*.[2] A few of them never become
accustomed to it, but most do.' *This* is what the US establishment was responsible for, and Manson must have seen himself as the divinely appointed agent of the wrath of God. One
can imagine the familiar words running through his head:
'An eye for an eye, and a tooth for a tooth', and 'Vengeance is
mine; I will repay'. He did, and he did it ruthlessly and without
remorse: and he taught others how to do the same. *He made
them happy.* 'It was fun', said Tex Watson after the so-called
Tate murders in which five human beings were stabbed and
gunned to death, including the actress Sharon Tate, heavy
with child and pleading for the new life within her. What a
hope! They left her to the last so that she could see the
butchery of her friends and then sliced her up in her turn. 'It
was fun.' Or, in the words of Susan Atkins, the most savage
as well as the most devoted of Charlie's Family: 'It felt so good,
the first time I stabbed her.'[3] 'Charlie was happy.'[4] He had
done his duty, in however small a way, to avenge the crimes of
a rotten clockwork government that was daily guilty of mass
murder in the bombing of North Vietnam. During the trial
the President of the United States himself, 'Tricky Dick' as
he was once called, thought fit to prejudge the issue by himself
declaring that Charles Manson was guilty. Charlie's riposte
must have reflected the thoughts of thousands of young
Americans. 'Here is a man', he is reported to have said,
'who is accused of hundreds of thousands of murders, accusing
me.'[5]

One of the most shocking things about the Manson murders
was that they appeared to have been perpetrated at random.
So they were, but so too was the bombing of North Vietnam.
But the murders organized by Charlie were 'at random' only
within a given context, and the context was that of what he
called 'rich pigs', the spoiled, doped, bored, rich set that
infects Hollywood, perfectly happy to relish violence on the

2. My italics.
3. E. Sanders, op. cit., p. 289.   4. Ibid., p. 293.

screen but considerably less than happy when it is practised on themselves. Charlie did not like people rich enough to enjoy the fruitless luxury of having a daily appointment with their psychiatrist, as did Miss Abigail Folger, one of his victims,[5] nor did he like 'rich young ladies in search of truth'.[6] He is not alone in this respect.

Charles Manson saw himself as pitted against a ruthless mechanical society. What choice had he, then, but to mechanize – dehumanize – himself? A human being is the 'mean' between the extremes of the machine and the deity, I am sure Aristotle would have said, had he been alive today. But who can tell the difference? Do the whirling dervishes, for instance, gyrating around their sheikh, really taste divinity, or are they merely reducing themselves to the clockwork regularity of a machine? Whatever the explanation may be, one of the rituals of the Family was the 'chop-stab' dance in which they danced round in a circle flicking their knives or attacking 'trees, rocks and one another' with them.[7] According to the ancients, including Aristotle, circular motion is the most perfect form of motion – perhaps also the most perfectly mechanical one. Charlie danced. And 'when Charlie danced, everyone else left the floor'. He was 'like fire, a raw explosion, a *mechanical toy* that suddenly went crazy'.[8]

> I am a mechanical boy,
> I am my mother's boy.[9]

So went one of his songs. Did it mean anything? Almost certainly it did, for by deliberately dehumanizing himself he knew that he must become either a god or a machine, both of which have this in common – they are beyond good and evil.

There are many ways of passing beyond good and evil, and the 'mystic East' knows all about them at every level; but, to our Western way of thinking, the 'East' is singularly inept at

5. E. Sanders, op. cit., p. 264.   6. Ibid., p. 360.
7. Ibid., pp. 228, 233, 361.   8. Ibid., p. 188 (my italics).
9. Ibid., p. 198.

making distinctions between the levels – so much so that its modern representatives who operate in the West positively condemn the discursive intellect, reason, mind, thought, or whatever you want to call it, as being the worst enemy of 'enlightenment': they make a virtue of and revel in imprecision. The late Daisetz T. Suzuki and Krishnamurti are perhaps the most typical examples of this trend. Aldous Huxley, whose case we discussed in *Drugs, Mysticism and Make-believe*, was greatly influenced by this higher 'non-think'. He found enlightenment in psychedelic drugs – and this at least he had in common with Charlie Manson, except that Charlie, taking a leaf or two, maybe, out of Huxley's last novel, *Island*, went one better. To drugs he added 'ultra-sex', already adumbrated in *Island* (the island of the Blessed), and also ultra-violence. There was nothing half-hearted about Charlie.

The general verdict at the time was that the whole grisly business was due to drugs.

'This', a commentator said, 'will be remembered as the first of the acid murders; our changing social structure is making more people turn on and we're on the brink of a whole new concept of violence . . . violence perpetrated against society by people who have reached a *different plateau of reality*[1] through LSD.'

'You know,' he added earnestly, 'this acid thing has been around for a long time. I've taken acid, back when it was fashionable for so-called intellectuals to try it. It really works. It moves you on to *another level of awareness*.[2] . . . It really does turn you on.' In other words LSD, plus a burning indignation against an unjust and increasingly mechanized society, produces Manson, who is not just himself but a signpost to the future. His threats were not empty threats, nor was his vision of the world to come in any way absurd, as subsequent LSD-cum-Eastern-mysticism murders in the USA have shown.

'*You*[3] have created the monster', he roundly accused them,

1. My italics. 2. My italics. 3. My italics.

'I am not of you, from you, nor do I condone your wars or your unjust attitudes towards things, animals and people *that you won't try to understand.*'

So much for the condemnation. Now for the prophecy:

'You see, you can send me to the penitentiary; it's not a big thing. I've been there all my life anyway. What about *your* children, just a few, there is many, many more coming in the same direction; they are running in the streets and they are coming right at *you.*'

Here Charlie is speaking at the human level of awareness – for him the lowest; and it is at this level that he speaks towards the end of the trial: 'I am a human being. I am going to fight for my life one way or another.' And it is on the same level, presumably, that he adds, addressing the judge: 'In the name of Christian justice . . . someone should cut your head off.'

There is an Arabic proverb, attributed to the Prophet Muhammad, which says 'Die before you die', and there is a similar Zen Buddhist saying: 'Die while alive, and be completely dead.'[4] Charles Manson was, at this stage of the trial, obviously very much alive and not dead at all. This seems all wrong since his whole philosophy (which was derived from some very weird and sinister occult sects, influenced directly or indirectly by Aleister Crowley, which were then very active in Los Angeles) was that one had to kill one's ego in order to live the true ego-less life in which all things are seen as One. This is his second level of awareness. Charles Manson had claimed to be Jesus Christ, but he was also much influenced by Indian ideas which filtered through to him through such sects as OTO, 'The Process', and 'The Fountain of the World'. From these ultimately Indian sources he derived the theory of reincarnation and *karma*[5] (the inexorable law according to which, that

4. See R. C. Zaehner, *Drugs, Mysticism and Make-believe* (Collins, London, 1972), index, under 'death'.

5. E. Sanders, *The Family*, pp. 148, 157, 243 ('And so Charlie said . . . he couldn't be responsible for the karma that Gary was going to incur'), 256 ('[Charlie] told Bruce that Terry Melcher should be ready for death; it was his karma').

which you sow, that you shall reap) and the practice of vegetarianism and teetotalism (drugs, of course, were quite another thing). But none of these things were essential to the Indian religious tradition. They are the outward signs only: Charles Manson was more deeply involved with the inner core.

The end and goal of both Hinduism and Buddhism is to pass into a form of existence in which time and space and all the opposites that bedevil human existence are totally transcended and in which one is literally 'dead' to the world but alive in a timeless eternity. This ritual death Charlie had already experienced, and, as a result of the experience, he had taught his disciples that they must kill themselves in this way in order to kill others and be free from remorse. At the trial Linda Kasabian, who had witnessed the ecstatic massacre of Sharon Tate and her four fellow 'rich pigs' but had not yet managed to reach the state of complete egoless awareness that would have enabled her, if not to participate in the gory ritual, then at least to observe it with Stoic indifference, appeared as the chief witness for the prosecution and told the whole horrible truth as she had seen it with her own eyes. In other words she had 'snitched', the sin against the Holy Ghost and perhaps the only sin in the code of Charles Manson.[6] However, 'snitched' she had, and there she was in the witness-box accusing Charlie and his three egoless lady disciples of the most appalling atrocities. Susan Atkins, the most egoless of them all, mouthed the words, 'You're killing us.' To which Linda replied in a whisper quite audible to the jury, and, it may be added, in a language that made perfect sense to Charlie: 'I'm not killing you. You've killed yourselves.' She had heard it so often before. 'Yes,' she said again in that interminable cross-examination, 'he used to say "If you are willing to be killed, then you should be willing to kill."' Charles Manson *had* killed himself, but at the trial he had come to life again not as a superman or a god or even a machine but as the illegitimate

6. E. Sanders, op. cit., p. 335.

son of a teenage whore, despised and rejected by man if not by God.

It had all started when he was very young. Then, according to the Manson Family legend, he suddenly felt that he was as powerful and free as Superman. He acquired a makeshift cloak, climbed up to a roof, spread his arms and sailed through the air. It was a great feeling, they said, comparable to the orgasm, and one that he never forgot. When Sandy (Sandra Good, one of the Family) tells it there is the strong implication that Charlie really did fly. No matter. The point here is that the cloak and Superman and the *feeling* are part of the Family's Manson legend. The ability to fly at will, it may be noted in parenthesis, was one of the preternatural powers attributed to the Buddha, and indeed to all who had achieved 'enlightenment', by *his* followers. The disciples of C. G. Jung today would probably say that flying referred to the perfect freedom the enlightened person enjoys in his own 'inner space'. There is no reason to believe that Charlie did not have this experience. You do not have to be a saint to do that: LSD can do it for you, as I have explained elsewhere.[7]

Freedom of the spirit he had, then, already experienced, but not the complete extinction of the ego, the dying to self of which the mystics of all religions perpetually speak. Since he was thoroughly conversant with the Bible he realized that he must be crucified if he were to rise again reborn into eternal life. That crucifixion meant the death of the ego in order that the true Self or 'Soul' might be born, he probably learnt from an occult sect called 'The Fountain of the World' founded 'by a holy man named Krishna Venta', presumably an Indian or one who had assumed an Indian name, 'who died by violence'.[8]

For the crucifixion of Charles Manson my only evidence is Ed Sanders' gripping book, *The Family*. I leave it to him to describe it in his own words:

'Not far from the Spahn Ranch [the Family's headquarters]

7. See my *Drugs, Mysticism and Make-believe*, pp. 66–111.
8. E. Sanders, op. cit., p. 110.

the family discovered an almost secret clearing guarded by a natural surrounding wall of large boulders. On one side of the clearing was a hill, The Hill of Martyrdom. For upon this hilly boulder-shrouded secret clearing was performed perhaps the world's first outdoor LSD crucifixion ceremony.

'There they snuffed Charlie, in role as Jesus, strapping (not nailing) him to an actual rustic cross, while others, acting as tormentors and apostles, jeered and weeped. One chosen female was Mother Mary cloaked and weeping at the foot of the cross.

'Then they fucked, evidently after some form of resurrection service.'[9]

Clearly Mr Sanders has little sympathy for Charlie, but there seems to be no reason to doubt the veracity of his account. He worked for a year and a half to piece together his story, and the story is almost certainly true. And significant.

Manson's crucifixion symbolized for him the death of his ego. It was, however, still only a symbol. He had not experienced what the Zen Buddhists call the 'Great Death'. This 'total' experience, which, according to Mr Sanders, 'thousands have encountered, say, on psilocybin', a psychedelic drug which produces effects similar to those produced by LSD, Charlie went through while meditating in the desert.

' "Once", he is reported to have said, "I was walking in the desert and I had a revelation. I'd walked about forty-five miles and that is a lot of miles to walk in the desert. The sun was beating down on me and I was afraid because I wasn't willing to accept death. My tongue swoll up and I could hardly breathe. I collapsed in the sand.

' "I looked at the ground and saw this rock out of the corner of my eye. And I remember thinking in this insane way as I looked at it, 'Well this is as good a place as any to die.' "

'Then he started to laugh. "I began laughing like an insane man. I was so happy." Then he got up "with ease" and walked ten miles forthwith and reached safety.'[1]

9. Ibid., p. 111.   1. Ibid., p. 129.

Charles Manson had achieved what the Zen Buddhists call enlightenment, the supreme lightning flash of which shatters the time barrier, and through which one is reborn in eternity, where time does not exist and death is an almost laughable impossibility. All things are fused into one and one can sing, as the boy poet Rimbaud sang:

> Elle est retrouvée.
> Quoi? – L'Éternité.
> C'est la mer allée
> Avec le soleil.
>
> Ame sentinelle,
> Murmurons l'aveu
> De la nuit si nulle
> *Et du jour en feu.* . . .
>
> *Là pas d'espérance,*
> *Nul orietur.*
> Science avec patience,
> *Le supplice est sûr.*[2]
>
> Elle est retrouvée.
> Quoi? – L'Éternité.
> C'est la mer allée
> Avec le soleil.[3]

This is what the Zen Buddhists in Japan call *satori*, the intuitive flash that reveals that all things are really One – the coalescence of sun and sea – and this revelation brings a joy so great that the only natural response is apparently insane

2. My italics.

3. Arthur Rimbaud, *L'Éternité*, in *Oeuvres complètes* (Bibliothèque de la Pléiade, Gallimard, Paris, 1954), pp. 133–4 ('It is found again. What? – Eternity. It is the sea mingling with the sun./O sentinel soul, let us, murmuring, give testimony to the so empty night and the day ablaze. . . ./*There* there is no hope, no "he will rise again". Knowledge with patience. The punishment [and torture] is sure./It is found again. What? – Eternity. It is the sea mingling with the sun').

laughter. There are plenty of cases of *satori* which have been recorded. Here one example must suffice. It is the experience of a Japanese executive aged forty-seven (what Charlie Manson would call a 'rich pig'), and this is how he describes it.

'I was now lying on my back. Suddenly I sat up and struck the bed with all my might and beat the floor with my feet, as if trying to smash it, all the while laughing riotously. My wife and youngest son, sleeping near me, were now awake and frightened. Covering my mouth with her hand, my wife exclaimed: "What's the matter with you? What's the matter with you?" But I wasn't aware of this until told about it afterwards. My son told me later he thought I had gone mad.

' "I've come to enlightenment! Shakyamuni [the Buddha] and the Patriarchs haven't deceived me!" . . . I remember crying out. . . .

'That morning I went to see Yasutani-roshi [his guru] and tried to describe to him my experience of the sudden *disintegration*[4] of heaven and earth. "I am overjoyed, I am overjoyed!" I kept repeating. . . . Tears came which I couldn't stop. I tried to relate to him the experience of that night, but my mouth trembled and words wouldn't form themselves. In the end I just put my face in his lap. Patting me on the back, he said: "Well, well, it is rare indeed to experience to such a wonderful degree. It is termed 'Attainment of the emptiness of Mind.' You are to be congratulated!" '[5]

If this middle-aged Japanese executive is to be congratulated, so is Charlie Manson. To my mind there is absolutely no doubt at all that what he experienced is precisely and exactly what the Japanese executive experienced and the poet Rimbaud tried to figure forth in words. It is the experience of eternity in which all things dissolve and merge as in the sea, eternity suffused in a light far more effulgent than the sun, eternity which is *both* vacuous night *and* the blazing day,

4. My italics.

5. Philip Kapleau, *The Three Pillars of Zen* (Harper & Row, New York, 1966), p. 206.

eternity in which there is no hope because all hope is fulfilled, eternity which is supreme 'knowledge' and fortitude, eternity where the extreme of bliss *is* at the same time the quintessence of torture, agony, and pain. What Rimbaud described *is* what the Japanese executive and Charles Manson experienced. It is quite literally a 'total' spiritual orgasm. The secret of Charlie Manson is that he *knew* this, and he knew that this can at least be simulated by LSD and in a 'total' and brutal practice of the physical act. Lucidly he drew the obvious conclusion which our modern Zen Buddhists do all they can to hush up. Where he had been all things were One and there was 'no diversity at all':[6] he had passed beyond good and evil. At last he was *free*!

How that Japanese executive used his 'freedom' we are not told. Perhaps he too had a mind as consistently logical as Charlie's and, with his greater experience, he may even now be vicariously murdering the 'innocent' citizens of Tokyo. Like Charlie he too had done it the hard way, the way of 'just sitting' and sitting and sitting until that wicked discursive mind *disintegrates* and you *see* that right *is* wrong, and that good *is* evil. Charlie didn't sit: he walked forty-five miles until he reached the point of exhaustion: he collapsed and *saw*. He saw a rock: but it was no longer just an ordinary rock but the 'Uncarved Block' of the Taoists which 'is the symbol of the primal undifferentiated unity underlying the apparent complexity of the universe'.[7]

'The sun was beating down on' Charlie. The sun is hot, and one of the Sanskrit words for heat is *tapas*. But *tapas* also came to mean fierce ascetic practices resulting in the mortification – the making dead – of the mind. There is a *tapas* of sitting – Zen – and a *tapas* of walking – Charlie's *tapas*. The physical result of all forms of *tapas* is the same, it 'makes for vitamin and sugar deficiencies which act to lower the efficiency of what Huxley calls the cerebral reducing valve'. This too is

6. *Brihadāranyaka* Upanishad, 4.4.19.
7. Arthur Waley, *The Way and its Power*, p. 167.

the physical result of taking LSD and similar psychedelic drugs.

'For the sake of achieving this integral knowledge', those eminently sensible researchers in the sphere of psychedelic drugs, R. E. L. Masters and Jean Houston, write, 'men have willingly submitted themselves to elaborate ascetic procedures and have trained for years to laboriously master Yoga and meditation techniques. They have practised fasting, flagellation, and sensory deprivation, and, in so doing, may have attained to states of heightened mystical consciousness, but also have succeeded in altering their body chemistry. Recent physiological investigations of these practices in a laboratory setting tend to confirm the notion that provoked alterations in body chemistry and body rhythm are in no small way responsible for the dramatic changes in consciousness attendant upon these practices. The askesis and ascetic discipline of fasting, for example, makes for vitamin and sugar deficiencies which acts to lower the efficiency of what Huxley calls the cerebral reducing valve.'[8]

All very interesting no doubt. But Charles Manson instinctively knew that what he had experienced in the desert after walking forty-five miles in the blazing sun could also be experienced under LSD and ultra-sex. As he knew, so he acted.

The experience provided by Zen is sometimes called cosmic consciousness. This is the second level of consciousness from which Charles Manson acted. When under the influence of mescalin, Aldous Huxley had spoken of 'Is-ness'. By this he meant the experience of pure being in which 'time must have a stop', the title of the first novel he wrote after his conversion to Neo-Vedantism. Meister Eckhart, the medieval German mystic, and others have called this the 'eternal Now'. Charlie knew all about this too. 'No past – time burnt – books burnt –

8. R. E. L. Masters and Jean Houston, *The Varieties of Psychedelic Experience* (Anthony Blond, London, and Holt, Rinehart & Winston, New York, 1966), p. 248.

past burnt. All bridges melted with dope and fervor. All time factors in the now. The now of Charlie', as Mr Sanders puts it in his rather biased way.[9] The man who, like Charlie, has achieved cosmic consciousness, lives in and from the level of the Now, but the average mortal, who lives in, for, and from ego-consciousness only, can only find the Now in death. Hence it was only logical that Charlie should deal in death ('Death is Charlie's trip', as Tex Watson, the most devoted and savage of his murder-squad, laconically and truly observed). And so, if we are to believe an account attributed to local residents, when one of his minor associates, Shorty Shea, showed signs of 'snitching', 'they got Shorty in his car. . . . They hit him in the head with a big wrench. They took him with them. They let him sweat. When he would come to, they would cut him some more. He was begging for his life. They finally had to cut his head off. He got to NOW, and they killed him.' Logical enough, you will say, but Charlie was himself perfectly capable of making distinctions and could concede that there were occasions on which people were not ready physically to undergo the supreme experience: 'Her ego wasn't ready to die', he said of Linda Kasabian on one occasion, an imperfection on her part which was to prove fatal to him.

Once you have reached the stage of the eternal Now, all is One, as Parmenides taught in ancient Greece. 'After all', Manson said, 'we are all one.' Killing someone therefore is just like breaking off a piece of cooky. And did not the Manson adage say, 'If you're willing to be killed you should be willing to kill'?[1] He was perfectly sincere in this and sometimes would hand his knife to an adversary, bidding him kill him.[2] The offer was never accepted for the Family regarded Charlie as almost divine. This was his third level of awareness: the crucified ego merges into the Infinite, transcends Time and descends again, transfigured into a 'superego' or 'superman'.

9. E. Sanders, op. cit., p. 60.
1. Ibid., p. 195.   2. Ibid., pp. 208, 214, 341.

'We are all one'; this is the obverse of the eternal Now. This whole philosophy was long ago summed up in an ancient Hindu scripture: 'Whoso thus knows that he is the Absolute, becomes this whole universe. Even the gods have not the power to cause him to un-be, for he becomes their own self.'[3] Or, as country Sue, a member of the Family, puts it in her more rustic way: 'And like, I'm willing to die for anyone, anyone who's me, 'cause it's like one soul.'[4]

The 'Soul' plays an important part in the Manson ideology. As in Hinduism it is the Absolute both with and without attributes. Without attributes it is the Now of which nothing can be positively predicated: with attributes it is incarnate in Charlie Manson: 'I am Charlie and Charlie is me'[5] is a correct statement of the faith. More elaborately formulated, it could be put in this way: 'Charlie is above wants and desires – he is dead. It isn't Charlie any more. It is the Soul. They are Charlie and Charlie is they.'[6] And, of course, this total cohesion implies love: 'There were men there who were great lovers, lots of them, ready for love that was total.'[7] Not all, however, could reach this exalted state: they had to be brought there, so far as this is possible, by either LSD or ultra-sex, or both.

All adepts were indeed the soul in a sense, but Charlie was the Soul absolutely. For you can conceive of this total Soul either as the indwelling spirit that pervades all things or as the controlling genius of all things, what we would call God. As the same Hindu scripture we have just quoted puts it: 'The Soul (Self, *ātman*) is the Lord of all contingent beings, king of all beings. Just as the spokes of a wheel are fixed together on the hub and tyre, so are all contingent beings, all gods, all worlds, all vital breaths and all these selves fixed together in this Soul.'[8] This was precisely Charlie's relationship to the

3. *Brihadāranyaka* Upanishad, 1.4.10.
4. E. Sanders, op. cit., p. 200.   5. Ibid., p. 61.
6. Ibid., p. 212.   7. Ibid.
8. *Brihadāranyaka* Upanishad, 2.5.15.

Family: he was their essence and their Lord. Precisely the same idea occurred to Aristotle.

'We must consider', he said, 'in which sense the nature of the Whole is the "good" and the "supremely good"; whether it is something separate and existent in its own right or is [a principle of] order (*taxis*); or whether it is both, like an army. For the "good" (*eu*) of an army consists in its order, and yet it *is* the general, or rather it is chiefly the general.'[9]

You could scarcely have a more accurate description of the relationship between Charles Manson and his Family. Its 'good' consisted both in the order that reigned in its ranks and in the 'general' who gave it its orders. The difference is that Aristotle also believed in a moral order: he did not believe in that ancient Hindu assertion that, seen from the absolute point of view, good and evil, order and disorder, are reconciled in the One, as Heraclitus had done before him, and as Charles Manson was to believe long after him. Believing, Manson acted on his beliefs, and many a 'rich pig' was to meet a gruesome and untimely end because Charlie, so far from being mad, had a lucidly logical mind.

When acting on the purely relative plain, Charlie had developed his own techniques for destroying that wicked little ego with its absurd pretensions to independence. The sufficient formula on which these techniques were based was simply 'ultra-sex', performed either with or without the help of LSD. There was nothing half-hearted about Charlie's 'sexual magic': 'It could be called an exhaustion grope. . . . [He] felt that it was only after the first three or four hours that the sex really got good – when the woman "gave up", lost her ego entirely, then the act was of the Soul. *And it was true*.'[1]

Take the case of Linda Kasabian.

'That night Linda Kasabian encountered her first mystic experience at the ranch. She and Tex Watson made love in a dark shed and it was, as she later testified, unlike anything

9. Aristotle, *Metaphysics*, 12(11). 10.1 (1075a 12–15).
1. E. Sanders, op. cit., p. 62 (my italics).

she'd ever experienced. It was total, but eerie, as if she were being possessed by some force from without. Her hands were clenched at her side at the culmination of the sex and her arms were paralysed.

'Later she asked Gypsy about the meaning of such paralysis. Gypsy reportedly told her that such things occurred when you don't give in completely to a man: her ego was dying.'[2] Alas, it was not quite dead, and Linda 'snitched'. But even after she had become the principal witness for the prosecution, and had decided that perhaps Charlie was not really Jesus Christ but the Devil, she continued to love him as she loved everyone. Whatever Charlie's defects may have been, he certainly inspired love and absolute devotion. As 'God' he could be both the Christ of St John who is love and the Christ of the Book of Revelation who wreaks terrible vengeance on the unrepentant wicked or, in Charlie's peculiar mythology, 'rich pigs'.

There is no need to go into Charlie Manson's eschatology, which was extremely bizarre. It must, however, be said that his power over women was based on a masochism that seems to be innate though usually dormant in the female sex. To be violently raped can result in a real dissolution of the ego, and Charlie knew it. Being sexually totally possessed was, he thought, what every woman really wanted: *ergo* woman is naturally a slave and a whore. Once this truth is brought home to her she must rejoice in her own annihilation and degradation. Hence she must be prostituted to real one-hundred-percent he-men – the bikers (Satan Slaves and the Straight Satans whose device was 'love-hate'[3]), who 'loved it'.[4] This was the role of women in the bringing about of the new era.

And then there were the negroes. Charlie had little respect for their intelligence, but they were much nearer to the Oneness of the Soul. He used to say, we are told, that blackie was much more aware than whitey and super together, and whitey

2. Ibid., p. 213.
3. Ibid., p. 180.   4. Ibid., p. 150.

was just totally untogether, just would not get together; they were off on these side trips, and blackie was really together. This was his strength, as it was that of Charlie's Family. Hence 'blackie', through his sense of togetherness and Oneness, would be God's instrument in destroying the fragmented clockwork rot that was whitey. Meanwhile, the Family would retire to a strange underground paradise biding their time. When all was over, blackie, realizing his total incompetence to organize himself, could appeal to the hidden Messiah who would emerge to take charge of the New Jerusalem which would also be Aristotle's orderly army in which the general and his ordered ranks were in some sense one. His vision of the new era may have been slightly mad, but it was certainly no madder than Teilhard de Chardin's vision of a world converging on itself in joy. This vision apart, which did *not* derive from his own enlightenment but from the mystico-occult sects that proliferated in the Los Angeles of his time, Charles Manson was absolutely sane: he had been *there*, where there is neither good nor evil, and he had read and reread the Book of Revelation. These two facts explain his crimes.

'This is not I: this is not mine: this is not the self: this has nothing to do with a self.' This refrain runs throughout the whole Buddhist tradition in all its multifarious forms. Your ego does not exist in any shape or form that you could possibly identify with yourself. This is indeed the essence of the gospel according to Charles Manson too. But he did not know that the Buddha, like the God of the Old Testament, had, though perhaps for less obvious reasons, commanded his disciples not to kill, not to fornicate, and not to steal. For Charlie, who, after that forty-five-mile walk, had surmounted death and tasted of 'enlightenment', no such commands and prohibitions had any relevance. He was not mean. Generous to a fault, he stole, since he believed that all private property was stolen goods anyhow, and in his Family all things were held in common: but what he stole he was always happy to give away again. 'This is not mine.'

'This is not I.' This dawned on him with marvellous clarity as he collapsed as if dead in the desert. It was no longer he that was alive but the Soul that lived in him. He *was* the Soul, and the Soul is all things, present in all things, just as Christ, according to Catholic belief, is wholly present in every single consecrated Host throughout the world. In eternity – the eternal Now – there was no Charles Manson, only the Soul. And yet, as in the case of his precursor, Crowley, once he emerged from the Now, he emerged not as himself nor yet as the Great Beast whose number is 666, as did Crowley, but as the avenging Christ of the Apocalypse himself. This, he seems to have thought, was his role on earth, just as it had been the role of Jesus to suffer and die at his first coming. The two roles are the two faces of the same coin. In the Now and the One Soul all the opposites are united:

> Should the killer think: 'I kill',
> Or the killed: 'I have been killed',
> Both of these have no [right] knowledge:
> He does not kill nor is he killed.

So spake the ancient Hindu text; and it spoke rightly, for in eternity there can be no action, but in time each man seems to have his own particular part to play: everyone has his own *karma*, as Charlie knew, and, for better or for worse, 'death was Charlie's trip'.

This is a great mystery – and the eternal paradox with which the Eastern religions perpetually wrestle. If the ultimate truth, or the 'perennial philosophy' as Aldous Huxley called it, is that 'All is One' and 'One is All', and that in this One all the opposites, including good and evil, are eternally reconciled, then have we any right to blame Charles Manson? For seen from the point of view of the eternal Now, he *did* nothing at all.

If this indeed is the perennial philosophy which lies at the very heart of all mysticism, then perhaps we should try to bring a little more precision into it. Can we do so without discrediting the mystical vision of unity as such? Well, with the aid of both the ancient Greeks and Hindus, we can but try since the moderns have only succeeded in making confusion more confounded.

2

THE GHOST OF HERACLITUS

Both Charles Manson and Aldous Huxley, in their very different ways, turned to the East for enlightenment. One wonders why. Aldous Huxley was a typical product of his time. He had not only seen through but violently reacted against the sombre 'Christian' tradition in which he was brought up – that lapidary morality based on the Ten Commandments, the dominant tone of which is 'positively' negative: 'Thou shalt not.' True, Christianity had always advertised itself as being a religion of love, and the great Augustine had himself said: 'Love, and do what you will.' He did not specify very precisely, however, exactly what it was that you should love. Jesus, indeed, had put it in a nutshell and Augustine must have had what Jesus said in his mind. Jesus had said: 'You must love the Lord your God with all your heart, with all your soul, and with all your mind. This is the greatest and the first commandment. The second resembles it: You must love your neighbour as yourself. On these two commandments hang the whole Law, and the Prophets also.'[1] In pronouncing these words he brought together what he considered to be the quintessence of the Mosaic Law.[2] It sounds all very plain and easy, and it does indeed make sense in a Jewish context where God was *the* accepted Reality, the supreme Lord who hated all evil and sin, at least as these were committed by his human creatures. To love God meant to hate evil, for 'Yahweh loves those who repudiate evil'.[3] That love and evil were, in the human sphere at least, irreconcilable opposites was an

1. Matthew 22:37–40.
2. Cf. Deuteronomy 6:5 and Leviticus 19:18.
3. Psalm 97:10.

axiom to the Jews. You cannot, for example, love God and money.[4]

Judaism, however, was unique among the ancient religions in that the Jews became convinced that they were a people uniquely chosen by God in that it was their unique privilege to proclaim not only that God is One (for this had occurred to most other nations in some shape or form) but that he was an austere Father as ready to chastise the wicked as to reward the just. In strictly human affairs he made it clearer and clearer that he demanded not only justice but mercy. What he came to demand with increasing insistence was love and mercy rather than sacrifice, knowledge of God, not holocausts.[5] This could never be easy since though it may be not too difficult to feel well-disposed towards your fellow-men, whom you have at least seen, it is exceedingly difficult to love God since you can only do so in faith and hope because you have never seen him.[6] As to loving your neighbour as yourself, the problem immediately arises of what self you are to love. What, indeed, *is* your self? Charles Manson saw his 'self' as the universal Soul, free from all attachment and desire, and as such, presumably the supremely lovable: 'Charlie is above all wants and desires – he is dead. It isn't Charlie any more. It is the Soul: They are Charlie and Charlie is they.'[7] Once this truth is realized, love of self means a 'love' that is total because, since each and everyone is the All, to love oneself is to love the All – total love – 'love-hate' as the bikers preferred to call it. This identification is endemic in Hinduism: since it must transcend all the opposites, it must therefore transcend good and evil. It is true that the same case is arguable against the Lord God Yahweh of the Old Testament, as Jung showed in his little classic, *Answer to Job*. Of this we shall have much to say later. For the present I should like to consider what the early Greek philosophers and their Hindu counterparts thought of God. There are close parallels between the two,

4. Cf. Luke 16:13. 5. Cf. Hosea 6:6.
6. Cf. 1 Peter 1:8. 7. Above, p. 68.

except that the Greeks try to analyse before they synthetize, whereas the Hindus simply present us with oracles held together by some kind of unity but never clearly differentiated. This is why we find them strange, for our civilization is substantially based on Greek thought rather than on Judaeo-Christian prophecy. We are or were the heirs of Greek rationality and our intellectual father is Aristotle, our spiritual stepfather Jesus Christ. We have rejected both.

From the earliest documents we know that the Greeks, like the Hindus, were no monotheists. The pantheon of gods was a pretty disorderly affair and it was not long before both races found this arbitrary mythological situation unsatisfactory. In both traditions philosophy started with a search for a unity that would underpin and give some coherence to the apparent incoherence of a universe in flux. How they tackled the problem in their different ways will be the subject-matter of this and the following chapters.

The origins of Greek philosophy, as indeed of Hindu philosophy, may be traced to the time when a purely mythological way of thinking was succeeded by a deeper reflection on what it was that was primary in our universe of multiplicity and change. It is the contrast between two apparently contradictory remarks attributed to Thales, generally considered to be the first of the Presocratics (the 'natural philosophers' who preceded Socrates) and therefore the founder of Greek philosophy: these are 'All things are full of gods' – a typical 'animist' view of life prevalent in both ancient and Modern Japan and India – and 'Water is [the origin of all things]'[8] – a statement which may not appear particularly profound to us but which was almost revolutionary in his

8. See E. Hussey, *The Presocratics*, p. 19. I am heavily indebted to Hussey for the Greek material quoted in this and the following chapter. He has compressed all that most of us need know about the Presocratics into his very concise book. When I quote from their fragments, I use his translation and give the page references from his book rather than the original sources which he in any case invariably quotes.

time. Man was no longer content with an erratic galaxy of irresponsible immortals who did nothing very much except intrigue against each other and make war against each other while plaguing and occasionally showing favour to mortal men, a pastime which seemed to afford them much pleasure.

It was, it seems, some time towards the end of the sixth century BC that this momentous change in their thinking about the Divine took place in both Greece and India, the very time when the great prophets were to appear in Israel, the Prophet Zarathushtra or Zoroaster in Iran, and the great sages Confucius and Gautama Buddha in China and India respectively. It was the great creative age of religion. The Jewish experience was, as the Jews have always claimed with that consistency which is so peculiarly theirs, that their own experience was unique in that the One True God who had first spoken to them through Moses was now speaking to them again in terms at once more urgently imperative and severe, and at the same time more pleadingly tender, about himself, the kind of God he was and how he expected this uniquely chosen and uniquely stubborn nation to behave. If we are to take the Old Testament on its own terms, it is unmistakably the history of God's self-revelation to man. You will find nothing like this either among the Greeks, the Indians, or the Chinese. There we will find rather man's reverent search for a true, because consistent, picture of the Divine which could replace the chaotic fancies of a divine assembly of capricious beings handed down to him by his forefathers.

In Greece it was Xenophanes of Colophon, a city in what is now Asia Minor, who first proclaimed the unity in God:

One God there is, greatest among gods and men [in Iran the Great King Darius was to inscribe much the same faith in stone as a testimony to posterity], in no way like mortal creatures either in bodily form or in the thought of his mind.

77

The whole of him sees, the whole of him thinks, the whole of him hears.

He stays always motionless in the same place; it is not fitting that he should move about now this way, now that.

But, effortlessly, he wields all things by the thought of his mind.[9]

The key word in this passage would seem to be 'fitting'. If there is to be a 'God' at all, then he must utterly transcend the human. He must not in any way resemble the ancient gods of Homer and Hesiod who were simply men on a larger scale though often morally inferior. 'If', as the same Xenophanes caustically remarked, 'oxen or horses or lions had hands to draw with . . . as men do, then horses would draw the forms of gods like horses, oxen like oxen', and so on. As to the great national poets, Homer and Hesiod, *their* concept of Deity was beneath contempt: they had 'attributed to the gods everything which brings shame and reproach among men: theft, adultery, and fraud'.[1]

Such gods are not 'fitting', for the universe, it seemed to these ancient Greeks as it did also to their contemporaries in India and China, was an orderly whole which behaved according to some preordained 'law'. It must then, they thought, be directed by some wise power who in some sense saw and heard and thought, himself changeless though the author of change, 'wielding all things by the thought of his mind'. This God is also the Truth, always the same yet motionless behind all the transient appearances (Greek 'phenomena') that go to make up our world. He is a mysterious God – so mysterious indeed that he cannot be known. And 'even if a man should chance to speak the most complete truth, yet he himself does not know it; all things are wrapped in appearances'.[2]

Pessimistic, you may think. Yet the ancient Hindus were even more persuaded of the essential unknowability of this 'One':

9. E. Hussey, op. cit., p. 13.   1. Ibid.   2. Ibid., p. 35.

Then neither Being nor Not-being was,
Nor atmosphere, nor firmament, nor what is beyond.
What did it encompass? Where? In whose protection?
What was water, the deep, unfathomable?

Neither death nor immortality was there then,
    No sign of night or day.
The One breathed, windless, by its own energy:
    Nought else existed then. . . .

Who knows truly? Who can here declare it?
Whence it was born, whence is this emanation.
By the emanation of this the gods
    Only later [came to be].
Who then knows whence it has arisen?

Whence this emanation has arisen,
Whether [God] disposed it, or whether he did not –
Only he who is its overseer in highest heaven knows.
    Or perhaps he does not know![3]

    Philosophical and religious doubt must precede philosophical conviction and religious faith. In our modern world the wheel has turned full circle. Starting with doubt we came to accept philosophical conviction (whether Plato or Aristotle, or the Neo-Platonists who combine the two) and religious faith (Christianity). Rejecting both, we sought to return to first 'self-evident' truths (Descartes), building on these metaphysical systems, the later perfecting (or abolishing) the earlier. Now once again we have rejected both traditional metaphysics and the Christian religion and we are left with Professor Monod's bleak 'principle of objectivity' on the one hand and a seemingly empty form of Buddhism on the other which asks us to be content with 'Suchness', that is, accepting things as they really are. The Taoist classic, the *Tao Tê Ching*, puts the whole thing in a nutshell:

3. *Rigveda*, 10.129.

Quietness is called submission to Fate;
What has submitted to Fate has become part of the always-
      so.
To know the always-so is to be Illumined;
Not to know it, means to go blindly to disaster.[4]

This kind of thing has a certain insidious attraction to the modern mind. You cannot rightly call it either metaphysics or religion: it has a certain modern respectability: it is hauntingly beautiful and commits you to nothing. You might describe it as the philosophy of 'As it is, so be it': and that is, in fact, just the way that Charles Manson saw it.[5] Having seen the 'always-so', he must have been illumined, but he fell from this level of illumination and 'went blindly to disaster'. He is not the only one to whom this has happened, for it is always dangerous to take the plunge into that indeterminate sphere where 'neither Being nor Not-being was'. If it is possible that 'its overseer in highest heaven' knows it, it is equally possible that he does not. How much more the case with mortal man who disregards the sceptical Xenophanes who warned us so wisely that even if a man 'should chance to speak the whole truth, yet he himself does not know it'.

All philosophy can be no more than a groping for an ultimate truth which, even if we could know it, we could never adequately describe. Xenophanes knew this, as did the early Indian sages. For they too could at first see no further than their Greek counterpart. What, indeed, can you say of the Imperishable except what it is *not*?

'It is not coarse', we read, 'nor fine; not short nor long; not red (like fire) nor adhesive (like water). It casts no shadow, is not darkness. It is not wind, nor is it space. It is not attached to anything. It is not taste or smell; it is not eye or ear; it is not voice or mind; it is not light or life; it has no face or

4. *Tao Tê Ching*, 16 (tr. Arthur Waley).
5. E. Sanders, *The Family*, p. 150.

measure; it has no "within", no "without". Nothing does it consume, nor it is consumed by anyone at all.'[6]

This is even more negative than the Presocratics, since, if 'it' is not life (literally 'the *breath*' (*prāna*) of life) or mind, it is difficult to see how it can 'wield all things by the thought of its mind'. But it can: for no Hindu has ever shrunk from paradox any more than did Heraclitus himself. However indescribable the 'Imperishable' may be, it is yet the first cause that sets all things in motion and assigns them their individual roles which are fitting to each. Hence we read in the very next paragraph:

'At the behest of this Imperishable . . . sun and moon are held apart and so abide. At the behest of this Imperishable . . . sky and earth are held apart and so abide, . . . seconds and minutes, days and nights, . . . seasons and years are held apart and so abide, . . . rivers flow from the snow-white mountains to the east, others to the west, each pursuing its appointed course.'

Whatever this Imperishable is, it too, like the God of Xenophanes, does only what is 'fitting' in a well-ordered world. Again, like the God of Xenophanes and most of the Presocratics, the Imperishable is the unchanging reality 'concealed from men by an impenetrable veil of "seeming" '[7] (what the Hindus were later to call *māyā*). If God is the 'Truth', then the world we know which is wielded into its 'fitting' shape by the divine mind must reflect God's changeless thought: the relative unity of the universe must reflect the absolute unity of God. As Mr Edward Hussey aptly says: 'If God is all things, then appearances are certainly deceptive; and, though observation of the *kosmos* may yield generalisations and speculations about God's plans, true knowledge of them could only be had by a direct contact with God's mind.'[8] This point of view was at least as prevalent in India as it was in Greece, and the solutions offered were not dis-

6. *Brihadāranyaka* Upanishad, 3.8.8.
7. E. Hussey, op. cit., p. 35.   8. Ibid.

similar. If 'justice' or 'order' is the law of the universe, how are we to account for injustice and disorder so strikingly obvious in our world of 'appearances'? In other words, how are the 'opposites' which both the Greek and the Indian traditions regarded as being the principal (and to them obvious) constituents of our universe to be reconciled in one harmonious whole? This did not matter so much on the purely physical level where the most obvious opposites appeared to be 'the hot' and 'the cold', 'the wet' and 'the dry', but things became much more uncomfortable when these opposites obtruded themselves into the moral order.

One of Xenophanes' immediate predecessors, Anaximander, saw the interaction of the opposites as a perpetual struggle of the one against the other. 'The destruction of things that are', he is quoted as saying, 'takes place by their turning back into those things from which they had their origin, *according to necessity*; for they *make requital and recompense* to one another for their injustice, according to the *assessment of Time*.'[9]

This may sound obscure, but what it seems to mean, as Mr Hussey lucidly points out, is this: 'It is clear that "injustice" consists in the encroachment by one "opposite" on the other, and that the "requital" is the restitution of the unjust gains and a corresponding loss as well. There is an overall regulation of the fight; however it may go in small areas of space and time, it is evened up in the long run over the whole *kosmos*, the cycles of day and night, and of the seasons, being the most obvious evidence for the existence of such a law. . . . The law-like behaviour occurs "by necessity" . . ., which implies a power imposing the necessity, and "according to the assessment of Time." '[1] Time, according to Mr Hussey, is quite possibly another name for Anaximander's 'God', the 'Unbounded', which, being God and therefore eternal Life, must also, one supposes, reabsorb our *kosmos* into itself when its time has run out. Hence Anaximander's Time means both the eternal life of the whole and the death of the individual parts

9. Ibid., p. 23.   1. Ibid., p. 24.

that had originally proceeded from it. It is, then, not un-natural that in India Kāla, the god of Time, finally became a synonym for death; death, you will remember, was Charlie's 'trip'.

The point I would stress here, however, is that though 'injustice' may encroach upon its opposite, 'justice', from time to time, the total picture must be one of total equilibrium. This makes sense in the physical world. Does it make quite so much sense in the moral one which we shall shortly have to consider? And this brings us to the hero of this chapter, Heraclitus of Ephesus.

One thing about Heraclitus seems sure, and that is his obscurity. He speaks not so much as a philosopher, as that word has come to be understood in the West, but rather as a prophet or an oracle. It was not he who spoke, but the Logos who spoke through him, and the message of the Logos was that All is One – the 'perennial philosophy' of Aldous Huxley, which some would prefer to call the ineradicable over-simplification that the human mind in all its natural sluggish-ness makes when faced with the mystery of the Divine. So too, Heraclitus, speaking with an authority not his own, pro-nounced: 'Having heard not me, but the *logos*, it is wise to concur that all is one.'[2]

Man, however, as the Buddha too realized, is rarely fit to receive, let alone understand, the divine Word (Logos). The mass of mankind is compared by Heraclitus to 'sleepers in private worlds of their own; to children who believe what their parents tell them; to dogs who bark at strangers; to deaf men, "as good as not there"; to idiots who take fright at any sensible utterance'. As to their opinions, they 'are toys with which they childishly amuse themselves'.[3] They are not interested in truth, the quest of which is the function of philosophy and science, but only in 'appearances'.[4] It *is*, however, possible for an inspired man to become 'like God' – that very aspiration which, according to Genesis (3:5), was to bring about the 'Fall'

2. Ibid., p. 39.   3. Ibid., p. 38.   4. Ibid.

of man – but between the average man and God there is a gulf fixed.

'It is characteristic of God, but not of man, to have discernment', Heraclitus says. And again: 'A man is considered silly by God . . . as a child is by a man.' Wisdom consists in discerning God through the plan he establishes for the universe, 'to be skilled in the plan upon which all things are controlled throughout the universe'.[5] Wisdom, he seems to suggest, is 'the only attribute of what is the only truly living thing'.[6] Wisdom in God may be said to be absolute, for it is this alone that makes him absolutely alive, but man can participate in the wisdom of God and thereby become like him if he uses his own understanding (*nous*) to penetrate the mystery by making right use of his senses, for God too, according to Xenophanes, not only thinks but *sees* and *hears* totally.[7] But man's senses can only be of service to him if he uses them in accordance with his intuitive understanding. Hence 'all that can be learnt of by seeing and hearing, this I value highest'. But the converse is equally true: 'Bad witnesses to men are eyes and ears, when they belong to men whose souls cannot understand their language.'[8] There is nothing wrong with the senses as such, it all depends on how you use them. They can lead you away from the vision of the Logos or God, or they can enable you, under the direction of true understanding, to see how God who is living Wisdom itself works and to understand how he orders the universe through the Logos. The ancient Greeks, with the possible exception of Parmenides, never condemn sense-perception as such as being an impediment to what is nowadays so often called 'God-realization'. Before they generalize, they first distinguish, and they are quite right to do so. It was no part of Greek philosophy to disintegrate the thinking mind as it was in the classical Hindu Yoga, Taoism, and Zen Buddhism. It was their business to create, or rather discover, order in chaos, not to return to a state of no-mind

5. Ibid., p. 36.   7. Ibid., p. 13.
6. Ibid.   8. Ibid., p. 37.

which itself *is* chaos. Though Heraclitus might have agreed
with the Taoist sage, Chuang Tzŭ, that we must 'join in great
unity with the deep and boundless', he could never have
agreed with the context in which those words occur. This is
what, in fact, Chuang Tzŭ says:

'You have only to rest in inaction and things will transform
themselves. Smash your form and body, spit out hearing and
eyesight, forget you are a thing among other things, and you
may join in great unity with the deep and boundless. *Undo the
mind, slough off spirit, be blank* and soulless, and the ten thous-
and things one by one will return to the root – *return to the
root and not know why.* Dark and undifferentiated chaos – *to
the end of life none will depart from it.* But if you try to know it,
you have already departed from it. Do not ask what its name is,
do not try to observe its form. Things will live naturally and of
themselves.'[9]

This is pure Taoism – and pure Zen. And it is just the kind
of thing that Charles Manson understood. 'Tear down the
mind'[1] was essential to his 'way of enlightenment', as it so
often is in Eastern religions and their religious offshoots.
It was not the way of Heraclitus, though there are ambiguities enough in the system of the Grecian prophet, as we shall
very soon discover.

Heraclitus, as we have seen, seemed to have had a visionary's
'prophetic' view of the universe in which he was taught by the
Logos itself that 'All is One'. This was also the principal insight of the Upanishads, but they rarely went on to consider
in what way this apparent paradox could be true. They did,
however, try, and perhaps the nearest parallel to Heraclitus is
this verse from the *Katha* Upanishad (5.9):

As the one fire esconced within the house
Takes on the forms of all that's in it,

9. *Chuang Tzŭ*, ch. 11, in *The Complete Works of Chuang Tzŭ*, tr.
Burton Watson (Columbia University Press, London and New York,
1968), p. 122.
1. E. Sanders, *The Family*, p. 162.

So the One Inmost Self of every being
Takes on their several forms, [remaining] without [the while].

The Self, then, or God is the 'fire' that not only illumines everything but also 'takes on their forms': in the language of theology he is both wholly immanent and wholly transcendent. So too, for Heraclitus, God was not only Wisdom,[2] but also fire – a divine fire, present everywhere, sustaining and consuming the universe at the same time. The significance of this we shall have to discuss later.

Central to the philosophy of Heraclitus is the concept of Logos, the very word that is applied to Christ in the prologue of the Gospel according to St John and almost invariably translated as the 'Word', to the utter confusion not only of generations of schoolboys but also of the adults they have grown up to be. 'In the beginning was the Word, and the Word was with God, and the Word was God', we used to learn parrot-like at school, and, of course, we hadn't a clue as to what the apparent gibberish was supposed to mean.

Mr Edward Hussey, on the other hand, being a trained philosopher and not a theologian, applies his razor-sharp mind to what precisely Heraclitus can have meant by the word *logos*, which even in his time had a variety of meanings as it later had for Plato and Aristotle, Philo, and St John himself. ' "Word", "story", "reckoning", "proportion" are all possible renderings in different contexts', he says, 'and all are relevant to its use by Heraclitus.'[3] He then goes on to quote three fragments in which, he thinks, the word is used in a technical sense. These are:

' "Of this *logos* which is so always [one may compare the 'always-so' of the Taoists] men prove to have no understanding both before they have heard it and immediately on hearing it; though everything comes to be according to this *logos*, they are like persons who have no experience of it. . . .";

2. E. Hussey, op. cit., pp. 36, 47.   3. Ibid., p. 39.

' "Though the *logos* is common . . ., most men live as if they had a private source of understanding";

' "Having heard not me, but the *logos*, it is wise to concur that all is one."

'The last of these fragments', Hussey goes on to say, 'shows that the *logos* is independent of what Heraclitus himself may have to say. The first suggests that it is the expression of the cosmic law; and this is borne out by a further fragment, which also sheds further light on what is meant by calling the *logos* "common":

' "Those who speak with understanding (*xun noōi*) must make themselves strong with what is common (*xunōi*) to all, as a city does with its law, and far more strongly than that. For all human laws are nourished by the one divine law. . . ." '[4]

From this Mr Hussey concludes that 'the minimal sense that can well be given to the word *logos* here is . . . something like: "the true account of the law of the universe".' But there is more to it than this since 'in the first half of the fifth century the sense of "reason" or "reasoning" appears to be well established. This sense is presumably a development from the meaning "proportion", which is already attested in Heraclitus. . . . What is reasonable or unreasonable is in or out of proportion in some sense.' If this is so, then 'his thought is that the *logos* expresses a proportion or analogy in the universe; and, therefore, that the *logos* is reasonable and the law it expresses, in virtue of this proportion'.[5]

Hussey's argumentation seems to be wholly convincing, but it still does not explain the paradoxes for which Heraclitus is famous and which invite comparison with the thought of the Indian Upanishads, so apparently scornful of anything that smacks of logical thinking. Leaving Hussey's subsequent arguments aside for the moment, let us return to the third of his quotations cited immediately above: 'Those who speak with understanding must make themselves strong with what is common to all, as a city does with its law, and far more

4. Ibid., pp. 39–40.   5. Ibid., p. 40.

strongly than that. For all human laws are nourished by the one divine law.'

This has a strangely Hindu ring, and the comparison with the Hindu scriptures almost forces itself on us. The idea that immediately invites comparison is that which 'is common to all' and which gives strength to 'those who speak with under-standing', 'as a city does with its law'.

'Common to all' would most easily be rendered into San-skrit by the adjective *sama* (etymologically connected with English 'same') and the corresponding noun *sāmya* or *samatva*, often translated as 'identity'.

Our principal source for the use of these words in the Hindu texts is the *Bhagavad-Gītā*. Here they are applied either to what is common to all among men, to 'Brahman', which is the eternal element in both God and man, and to God himself. Strangely enough the word *sama-tva*, 'sameness', is also used to define Yoga[6] – a word which has come to be associated in English with all sorts of occult ideas. In the *Bhagavad-Gītā*, however, things are very different. The word imperceptibly changes its meaning throughout the book, but in chapter 2, when it is used for the first time, it means simply 'practice' as opposed to 'theory': more specifically, in the context it means the performance of one's caste-duty – in this case the duty of a warrior whose business it is to kill or be killed in battle. To do this without remorse or compunction, however, is not easy for most people and would indeed be considered most reprehensible in members of castes other than the warrior caste since according to Hindu 'law' (*dharma*) each caste has its own specific duties which it alone may perform. It is better to do one's own caste-duty, *though devoid of merit*, than to do another's, however well. This duty is prescribed by your own nature, and by doing it you cannot be defiled.[7] As we have seen, the same scripture says: 'Should the killer think, "I kill", or the killed, "I have been killed", both of these have no right

6. *Bhagavad-Gītā*, 2.48.   7. Ibid., 18.47.

knowledge, he does not kill nor is he killed.'[8] This is precisely the doctrine that motivated Charles Manson: 'If you are willing to be killed, then you should be willing to kill.'[9] But willingness to kill as well as to be killed implies a literally god-like detachment from all worldly concerns: you must behave as if you were already dead. As Charles Manson's principal henchman laconically said: 'Death is Charlie's trip.'[1] For 'trip' substitute either the Sanskrit word *dharma* ('duty', 'religion', 'justice' or 'law') or the Greek *nomos* (translated as 'law' by Mr Hussey in the passage from Heraclitus quoted above, but also meaning 'custom'), and you will find that the message is almost identical.

Charles Manson taught his 'children' to kill without having to endure the qualms of conscience that lesser mortals feel. This is precisely the message which the incarnate God, Krishna, passes on to his beloved disciple, Arjuna, in the *Bhagavad-Gītā*. Leaving aside for the moment the purely theoretical arguments he uses to convince his protégé – the essentially non-temporal nature of the innermost soul and the heavenly bliss that awaits the warrior who has manfully performed his caste-duty of killing or being killed – let us pass on to his more practical advice. The 'yoga' (practice) of killing is not enough in itself even if prescribed by caste-law. It must be done in a spirit of complete 'sameness', that is, indifference and detachment. 'Hold pleasure and pain, profit and loss, victory and defeat *to be the same* (*sama*): then brace yourself [*yuj-yasva* – *yuj-* is the root from which the word *yoga* derives] for the fight. So will you bring no evil on yourself.'[2] So spake the incarnate God to the Pāndava prince.

Arjuna must do his duty as a warrior: he must fight to the death, but in a frame of mind that is wholly indifferent to the outcome. So, Krishna says: 'Stand fast in Yoga [that is, get on

8. *Katha* Upanishad, 2.19; repeated with slight variations in *Bhagavad-Gītā*, 2.19.
9. Above, p. 47.
1. Above, p. 67.   2. *Bhagavad-Gītā*, 2.38.

with the job proper to you], surrendering attachment; in success and failure be *the same* and then get busy with your works. Yoga means "sameness" [and indifference].'[3]

The Sanskrit word *sama*, 'the same', corresponds almost exactly to the Greek *xunos*, translated by Hussey either as 'common [to all]' or 'universal'.[4] What is the 'same' or 'universal' in the two systems would appear to be what we would call 'equilibrium', in a cosmic, a political, and a personal sense, and this is a characteristic both of the universe and God, who, both in Heraclitus and the Hindu scriptures, is sometimes regarded as coterminous with the universe, sometimes as transcending it. This is perhaps only another way of putting Hussey's 'mutual adjustment' (*harmoniē*). Thus, just as on the Hindu side Arjuna is told that the 'practice' (*yogà*) of his caste-duty is really 'sameness' – indifference and equilibrium – so too Heraclitus can tell us that 'one must know that war is universal (*xunon*), and that justice *is* strife, and that all things happen according to strife and necessity', and that 'the Sun will not overstep his measure; for the Erinyes [the representatives of strife (*eris*)], *the assistants of Justice*, will find him out'.[5]

Much the same is true in the *Gītā*: there must be war against an overweening enemy if justice – a just equilibrium – is to be restored. This is the whole point of the supreme God Vishnu's successive incarnations on earth. 'For', he says, 'whenever the law of righteousness (*dharma*) withers away and lawlessness arises, then do I generate myself [on earth].'[6] There must be war if 'justice' is to be preserved. Strife and war are quite as much part of the true earthly equilibrium and 'justice' as are tranquillity and peace. The divine 'justice' in this case reached what must have been an all-time record in

3. Ibid., 2.48. For the development and variations in the meaning of the word 'Yoga', see my *The Bhagavad-Gītā* (Clarendon Press, Oxford, 1968), index, under 'Yoga', where all important passages are given in bold type.

4. E. Hussey, op. cit., p. 48.

5. Ibid., pp. 48–9.   6. *Bhagavad-Gītā*, 4.7.

terms of 'kill-count' – 1,660,020,000 dead, as against 24,165 survivors.[7] This is a lot of people to kill compared to Manson's paltry nine: and it gives one pause for thought.

'Justice is strife', Heraclitus tells us, or, put in another way, 'justice and strife' are 'the same'. 'Sameness' is a virtue in man, and this is because it is a reflection of the 'sameness' of God which is his very essence. This 'sameness', the 'one divine law' of Heraclitus, pervades the entire universe in equal measure; for, as the *Gītā* tells us: 'The wise see *the same* thing in a Brahmin, wise and courteous, as in a cow or an elephant or even in a dog or an outcaste. While yet in the world they will have overcome [the process of] emanation [and decay], for their minds are stilled in [that very] *sameness*: for devoid of imperfection and [ever] the same is Brahman: therefore in Brahman [stilled] they stand.'[8]

In the *Gītā* Brahman is rather the principle of eternity than the personal God who transcends eternity itself and who claims to be 'the base supporting Brahman – immortal Brahman who knows no change'.[9] Vishnu himself, however, of whom Krishna is an incarnation, the 'One God' who is 'the greatest among gods and men', as Xenophanes put it, claims to be '*the same* in all contingent beings, abiding [without change], the Highest Lord [who], when all things fall to ruin, himself is not destroyed'.[1]

The 'sameness' of the *Bhagavad-Gītā*, which recurs with monotonous regularity in the later Hindu and Mahayana Buddhist texts, seems to be identical with the 'what is common to all' of Heraclitus. The wise are admonished to make themselves strong with it 'as a city does with its law [*nomos*, also "usage"], and far more strongly than that. For all human laws are nourished by the one divine law.'

As a city makes itself strong with its own laws, so presum-

7. See R. C. Zaehner, *Concordant Discord* (Clarendon Press, Oxford, 1970), p. 183.
8. *Bhagavad-Gītā*, 5.18–19: cf. 6.29, 32.
9. Ibid., 14.27.   1. Ibid., 13.27.

ably must the 'city of God' be 'made strong' by the divine law
which is 'mutual adjustment', equilibrium, and the identity of
opposites.[2] The 'city of God', which we find not only in St
Augustine but in the Upanishads, is not indeed mentioned in
so many words in the surviving fragments of Heraclitus, but
there is something very like it. This is 'the unity of the
universe', which, according to Edward Hussey, 'will consist,
essentially, in the fact that all the large-scale cosmic processes
are oscillations in the state of God'.[3] This surely is the same
as the 'city of Brahman' we read about in *Mundaka* Upanishad,
2.2.7:

> To him, the omniscient, all-knowing,
> Belongs [all] this magnificence on earth;
> And he it is, the Self, who is established
> In Brahman's heavenly city, the firmament.

The law, custom, or 'habit' of the divine city would appear
to be, in Heraclitus, the unity of the opposites. The Upanishadic 'city of God' is not identical with God any more than is
Heraclitus' 'cosmos' or universe fully identical with him. In
neither system does God 'make' the world out of nothing as in
the Judaeo-Christian tradition. Rather the world derives from
or actually is a divine 'fire' which is at the same time the
divine mind – 'what is common to all'.[4] This common factor,
it would appear, is war or strife, for 'one must know that war
is universal (*xunon*), and that justice *is* strife', and 'war is the
father of all, and king of all'.[5] But if this were entirely true, it
would make nonsense of the unity of opposites roundly
asserted in such fragments as these:

'Conjunctions: wholes and not wholes, the converging, the
diverging, the consonant, the dissonant, from all things one,

---

2. E. Hussey, op. cit., p. 42.   3. Ibid., p. 47.

4. Ibid., pp. 48 and 39, where the philosophical pun *xun noōi –
xunōi* ('with understanding' and 'common [to all]') is well brought out.
These popular etymologies are also common in the Upanishads.

5. Ibid., pp. 48–9.

and from one all things.'[6] And again: 'God is day night, winter summer, war peace, surfeit famine; but he *is modified*[7] . . ., just as fire, when incense is added to it, takes its name from the particular scent of each different spice.'[8]

God and the 'city of God' are thus in a state of perpetual oscillation between two 'opposites' which are, however, ultimately identical. This paradox we meet with all over the world. In China the opposites are the *yang* and the *yin*, literally the 'sunny side' and the 'dark side', roughly corresponding to the 'day' and 'night' of Heraclitus: between them they include all the opposites – light and dark, male and female, strong and weak, rough and smooth, and so on. In India, always more metaphysically minded, the essential pair of opposites is the eternal and the temporal, the static and the moving, Being and Not-being, the compounded and the uncompounded. Together they are fused into the One Absolute who may or may not be identified with a personal God. Of this Absolute you can say quite simply and without any consciousness of contradiction:

> It moves. It does not move.
> It is far, yet it is near.
> It is within this whole universe,
> And yet it is without it.[9]

Our world of change and 'appearance', the 'compounded', is equated with cosmic 'ignorance'; the transcendent and unchanging world, the 'uncompounded', with 'wisdom' or 'knowledge'. So we have these parallel stanzas:

> Blind darkness enter they
> Who revere the uncompounded:
> Into a darkness blinder yet
> Go they who delight in the compounded.[1]

And the corollary:

6. Ibid., p. 45.   7. My italics.   8. E. Hussey, op. cit., p. 46.
9. *Ishā* Upanishad, 5.   1. Ibid., 9.

> Blind darkness enter they
> Who reverence unwisdom:
> Into a darkness blinder yet
> Go they who delight in wisdom.[2]

The two – the compounded and unwisdom on the one hand, and the uncompounded and wisdom on the other – are of course opposites, but 'mutually adjusted' in One who is Other than they.[3] This idea is more clearly expressed in the *Shvetāshvatara* Upanishad (5.1), which appears to be an almost exact replica of what seems to be one of Heraclitus' key ideas:

> In the imperishable, infinite city of Brahman
>   Two things there are –
> Wisdom and unwisdom, hidden, established there:
> Perishable is unwisdom, but wisdom is immortal:
> Who over wisdom and unwisdom rules, He is Another.

The 'city of Brahman', however, is not only our compounded universe conditioned by space and time, plus the eternal universe beyond time. It is also the human being who has a similar dual nature and is therefore a reproduction in miniature of the great city of Brahman which is the entire universe animated by the spirit of God. At the heart of the human city of Brahman dwells the indestructible human 'self' or 'soul', the 'divine spark' of the medieval mystics.

'Now, in this city of Brahman there is a dwelling-place, a tiny lotus-flower; within that there is a tiny space. What is within that is what you should seek: that is what you should really want to understand.'

What manner of thing can this be? the aspiring pupil wonders. To which his master replies:

'As wide as is this space [around us], so wide is this space within the heart. In it both sky and earth are concentrated, both fire and wind, both sun and moon, lightning and the

2. Ibid., 12.   3. Ibid., 13.

stars, what a man possesses here on earth and what he does not possess: everything is concentrated in this [tiny space within the heart].

'*This* is the real city of Brahman; in it are concentrated all desires. *This* is the Self, exempt from evil, untouched by age or death or sorrow, untouched by hunger or thirst: [this is the Self] whose desire is the real, whose idea is the real.'[4]

So, too, for Heraclitus, true wisdom, the perfection of which belongs to God alone, makes man godlike, or, one might almost say, part of God.[5] In the *Chāndogya* Upanishad final death (and we have to say 'final' since in both Hinduism and Buddhism death is only the necessary prelude to yet another life) – final death, then, means the release of the eternal centre and ruler of the human 'city of Brahman' into the same eternal mode of being that is natural to the divine city. All that is not true Being but subject to change, to coming-to-be and passing away, is dissolved into the elements from which it arose. So too for Heraclitus, Mr Hussey suggests, 'a good and wise soul, being fiery, would at departure ascend to the upper regions, whether it was absorbed into the divine fire or . . . became a star'.[6]

Heraclitus was what is usually called a 'natural philosopher', not a moral one, but for him, as for most of the Greek philosophers, 'good' and 'wise' were almost interchangeable terms. It is true that in Heraclitus' God all the opposites, of which the chief were strife and rest or war and peace, coalesced and became One; and it is also true that Aristotle was later to equate strife with evil,[7] but he does not say or imply that evil as such (which he does not in any case define) has any place in God. In the Upanishads this is much less clear. Brahman itself, the 'real of the Real' or the 'truth of Truth'[8] (for the Sanskrit word *sat(i)ya* means both 'real' and 'true'), is infected

---

4. *Chāndogya* Upanishad, 8.1.5.   5. E. Hussey, op. cit., p. 39.
6. Ibid., p. 57.   7. Aristotle, *Metaphysics*, 12(11).10.7(1075b 7).
8. *Brihadāranyaka* Upanishad, 2.1.20.

with 'unreality', 'untruth', or simply what is 'wrong' (*anrita*), that is, evil. And so we are told:

'Brahman is the Truth (the Real). . . . The word *satiyam* has three syllables: *sa, ti, yam*. . . . The first and last syllables are Truth. In the middle is falsehood. This falsehood is surrounded on both sides by Truth. Indeed it becomes Truth once again. Falsehood does not injure anyone who knows in this way.'[9]

This very early Hindu text lies behind much later Hindu thought, and its essential ambivalence authenticates the excesses not only of the so-called left-hand Tantra, on which Aleister Crowley based much of his sexual 'magick', but also Aleister Crowley himself, not to mention Charles Manson.

You may regard the Absolute as beyond good and evil or as comprising good and evil since it must include within itself *all* the opposites. Your ultimate goal is to become one with the One Absolute in some sense; but, whichever view of the Absolute you take, your good actions will perish along with your evil ones, for where all is absolutely One and therefore absolutely static and still, neither good nor evil can be in any way relevant, since both imply activity either in deed, word or thought. 'Those who speak with *understanding* must make themselves strong in what is *common to all*', Heraclitus had said, and Mr Hussey has demonstrated what he meant. So too we read in the *Mundaka* Upanishad (3.1.3.):

When the seer beholds the Maker, Lord,
The Person golden-hued, whose womb is Brahman,
Then does he understand: immaculate,
He shakes off good and evil and reaches *sameness* supreme.

'Men can make progress in wisdom just in so far as they make themselves divine', says Edward Hussey, summing up his carefully assessed judgment of Heraclitus' views on God and man. 'They can do this because their souls are potentially divine and can realize their potentiality.'[1] This is precisely

9. Ibid., 5.5.1.   1. E. Hussey, op. cit., pp. 57–8.

what the ancient wisdom of the Hindus taught about man's relationship to the divine. Man is not God, but what is eternal in him *is* God in very truth. And just as the God of Heraclitus must make room for war as well as peace or, in Hebraic terms, for wrath as well as tenderness, so do the Hindus postulate wrong at the very heart of Truth.

Man, however, as he traverses the causeway that links this world of action to the eternal Absolute where 'time must have a stop', must shed all his good and evil deeds, his virtues quite as much as his vices. 'Shaking off evil as a horse shakes off its hairs, shaking off the body as the moon delivers herself from the eclipse, with self perfected, I merge into the unmade Brahman-world – I merge into the Brahman world.'[2] So speaks the Upanishad. And Heraclitus would, no doubt, have taken its point. But the Hindu sages would go further than this, for it is not only evil that the soul shakes off on his age-old pilgrimage that will at last bring him to Brahman, it is also all the good he may have done, now seen as useless luggage burdening him on his weary way.

'As a man riding in a chariot might look down on the two chariot-wheels on either side, so does he on either side look down on day and night, on deeds well done and deeds ill done, and *all the opposites*.[3] Delivered from both good and evil deeds, and knowing Brahman, to Brahman he draws near.'[4]

But this is not yet the end, for just as the Absolute is both hub and tyre of the great wheel which is the universe and whose spokes are individual souls,[5] so is the individual 'self' or soul the hub and tyre of the human personality. The spokes must disappear if the unity of hub and tyre is to be seen to be real. Using the same simile of the chariot the same Upanishad goes on to describe the journey's end of his pilgrim from time to eternity.

'Just as the tyre of a chariot-wheel is fixed on to the spokes, and the spokes on to the hub, so too are these objective

2. *Chāndogya* Upanishad, 8.13. 4. *Kaushītaki* Upanishad, 1.4.
3. Lit. 'dualities' (my italics). 5. See above, p. 68.

elements fixed on to the elements of consciousness, and the elements of consciousness on to the Breath of Life. And this same Breath of Life is nothing less than the Self which consists of consciousness – joy, unageing and immortal. He does not increase by good works, nor is he diminished by evil ones. For it is He who makes him whom he would raise up from these worlds perform good works, and it is He again who makes him whom he would drag down perform evil works. He is the guardian of the worlds, sovereign of the worlds, He the universal Lord. Let a man know: "He is my Self." Let a man know: "He is my Self." '6

This is a dangerous doctrine, implicit in Heraclitus, explicit in the Upanishads – and the *Bhagavad-Gītā*. In God there is both good and evil, and, this being so, he *makes* men do good and evil deeds. Can we, then, be surprised if the sage, fully liberated from the bonds of space and time and therefore from the whole world of 'appearance' in which alone the opposites of good and evil have any validity, should act out his life in accordance with either the good or the evil aspect of God since, when all is said and done, they are the *same*? If this philosophy means what it says, then Manson too is right: there is no distinction at all between Jesus Christ and Charles Miles Manson. And so it must follow that 'the man who knows in this way will be at peace, tamed, quietly contented, long-suffering, recollected, for he will see the Self [that is, God] in himself: he will see all things as the Self. Evil does not touch him: all evil he shrugs off. Evil does not torment him: all evil he burns out. Free from evil, free from doubt, immaculate, he becomes a Brahmin [in very truth, for he is at one with Brahman, the Absolute Spirit of Being, Awareness, Joy].'7

'At peace, tamed, quietly contented, long-suffering, recollected': these, no doubt, are the signs of a holy man, but they were also the outward and visible signs displayed by

6. *Kaushītakī* Upanishad, 3.9.
7. *Brihadāranyaka* Upanishad, 4.4.23.

many of Charles Manson's 'children' which astonished and outraged a still fundamentally Aristotelian Western world.

Of course, it is true that the man who is not yet liberated from our human condition, governed as it is by time, space, and conventional morality, must abide by the laws of his 'city'; but these laws, unfortunately, vary from city to city, and in the Hindu 'city' the laws governing the warrior class are very different from those governing the other classes. The Incarnate God Krishna makes this very clear indeed. Not only is the duty of killing and being killed laid down in the Law books, but, theologically, the reasons for so doing are, from the Hindu point of view, self-evident. 'If you are slain', Krishna assures his friend, 'paradise is yours, and if you are victorious, you will enjoy the earth. Stand up, then, resolute for the fight!'[8] If, however, you manage to achieve perfect detachment, all things will be the 'same' to you in that 'sameness' which is God. There you will finally have killed that nasty little ego as Manson did, and you will legitimately do so, for 'a man who has reached a state where there is no sense of "I", whose soul is undefiled – were he to slaughter all these worlds, slays nothing. He is not bound.'[9]

God is the sole agent: and if there is any responsibility for good or evil, it is his. All man has to do is to obey his will or whim. 'Cast all your works on me',[1] says Krishna, since whatever Arjuna does has already been fore-ordained by God. 'And so stand up, win glory, conquer your enemies and win a prosperous kingdom! Long since have these men in truth been slain by me: yours is it to be the mere occasion.'[2]

In all religions God's purpose is inscrutable. It could scarcely be otherwise, given the manifest imperfection of our world. But most religions assume he *has* a purpose, and the *Gītā* is no exception in this respect. A more popular theory, however, was to develop later, and that was that God was simply playing with the world, though what sort of game and

8. *Bhagavad-Gītā*, 2.37.   1. Ibid., 3.30.
9. Ibid., 18.17.   2. Ibid., 11.33.

according to what rules we are rarely told. Heraclitus, however, is more precise.

'Time', he says, 'is a child at play, playing draughts; a child's is the kingdom.'[3] On which Edward Hussey, with his usual sensitivity, comments: 'Here, as probably in Anaximander, "Time" is a name for God, with an etymological suggestion of his eternity. The infinitely old divinity is a child playing a board game as he moves the cosmic pieces in combat according to rule.'

The 'infinitely old' and the 'infinitely young' are death and life, and the game that God is playing is a game in which one of the opposites must win, only to be defeated by the other in its turn. Only so can the 'mutual adjustment' be maintained. You cannot win and you cannot lose, and, conversely, you must both win and lose. For 'the same thing is in us as the living and the dead, the awake and the sleeping, the young and the old; these change to become those, and those change back again to become these'.[4] The game God plays is quite literally the game of life and death: 'Heads I win, tails you lose', Heraclitus' God seems to be saying to us. And he is right, for what we lose is our fleeting ego and what God wins is that perfect equilibrium which the unjust encroachments of foolish individual men seek to disturb and which only 'justice' and 'necessity' can restore. In eternity life *is* death, and death *is* life – life-in-death counterbalancing death-in-life. The game of Heraclitus' God has its dark and its sunny side. Charles Manson chose the darker aspect and he taught us that the ghost of Heraclitus still stalks the world today.

But the game of life and death is not the only game. There is also a lovelier game – the game of love itself. And this is the game that Krishna played and plays, with his devotees in India as with the 'Hare Krishna' enthusiasts now thriving in our midst.

The game of love is the game of life, for it is only too true that 'it is love that makes the world go round'. If God is love,

3. E. Hussey, op. cit., p. 49.   4. Ibid., p. 42.

as St John says, then there must be a lover and a beloved whom he can love. Yet another pair of opposites, and perhaps the most fundamental of them all – lover and beloved, which, in human terms, usually means male and female, positive and negative, *yang* and *yin*. These two, though opposites and *as* opposites, must be present in the Godhead too. They are: and so we read in the *Shvetāshvatara* Upanishad (4.3):

> Thou art woman. Thou art man.
> Thou art the lad and the maiden too.
> Thou art the old man tottering on his staff:
> Once born thou comest to be, thy face turned every way!

God is male and female – and hermaphrodite. But he is also none of these: 'He is not male, not female, nor yet hermaphrodite', the same Upanishad (5.10) says of the great God Shiva, generally supposed to be the celestial rival of Vishnu, the supreme God who became incarnate in Krishna. All this, however, is on a lower level of understanding or awareness; for in eternity all things are one, and Shiva (Hara) is Vishnu (Hari) and the two are One, and as One they receive the name that does honour to them both – Harihara.

But Vishnu too has his male and female aspects through which he fertilizes himself in order to create the world. 'Great Brahman is to me a womb', he declares. 'In it I plant the seed: from this derives the origin of all contingent beings.' He is the giver of the seed, the seed, and what receives it.[5] As Walt Whitman may have said and constantly implies: God is sex.

The union of the male and female principles was, therefore, ritually enacted by the devotees of the so-called left-hand Tantra in order to experience here on earth the Unity-in-duality which is God. In their sexual rituals everything was permitted, for all the opposites melted into the One. In the 'total experience', as Charles Manson would say, there was

5. *Bhagavad-Gītā*, 14.3. See the note ad loc. in my *The Bhagavad-Gītā*, p. 352.

neither right nor wrong. Whatever one does is supremely good.

And so, 'when the heroic adepts have entered [the circle of their female counterparts], there is neither right nor wrong. Desire alone is Holy Scripture. . . . In that stage of bliss whatever actions of whatever sort are performed are lawful. But he who takes thought of right and wrong is a sinner. . . . Spontaneously they give free vent to their desires. Slowly they enquire of those at their side, forgetting what they want to say. Putting the wine-cup to their lips, they abide in bliss. One frenzied woman embraces another's man, thinking him her husband. . . . In his madness one man embraces a man instead of a girl. A crazy woman asks her husband: "Who are you? Who am I? and who are these? What have we come here to do? Why are we assembled here? What is this garden, and what is this house, and what is this courtyard?" . . . The female adepts of the "Family" dance with stumbling footsteps, singing songs in which the syllables fall indistinct – with hypnotizing rhythm. The Yogis, mad with liquor, fall upon the women's breasts: the Yoginis [female Yogis], confused with wine, fall upon the men. Together they enjoy the full pleasure of their desires. . . . But when the Bliss holds sway, turning their minds, those bulls among Yogis participate in the Divine.'[6]

There is much nobility and probably much truth in the theory of the 'union of opposites' proclaimed by Heraclitus and the Upanishads alike, and Aldous Huxley is not far wrong in calling it the 'perennial philosophy' since it crops up everywhere, in every form, and at all times. But it needs to be rigorously checked by the rational mind which it would destroy. If not, then 'all things are lawful'. And is it a coincidence that this particular sect called itself the 'Family' as Charlie Manson called his own devoted band? Or is there a

6. *Kulārnava* Tantra, VIII, 57–75, Arthur Avalon, *Tantrik Texts* (Luzac, London, 1916), Vol. V. This text was brought to my notice by my friend, Mr Alexis Sanderson, whose translation I largely follow.

mysterious but real solidarity in what Manson called the 'total experience', which for this Tantric family was 'Bliss' and 'participation in the Divine'?

For Manson's children there seems to have been a strange connection between the 'total experience', murder, and adoration of their leader. So too, in another Tantra we read: 'Let a man murder a hundred Brahmins if by so doing he honours his spiritual master's command.'[7]

It is all very frightening. But there is logic in it; for if you take the words of Heraclitus' 'Justice *is* strife' literally and out of their context, or if you accept the precept that falsehood and wrong lie at the heart of truth without balancing it with other 'truths' found in the Hindu scriptures, the result may well be the realization not of a Good that is beyond good and evil but of an Evil that degrades us to a level far below that of brute beasts because we have chosen it of our own free will. Modern philosophers have told us that we must identify ourselves with our will since they have left us with nothing else with which we might identify ourselves. What they have asked for is Charles Manson, and Charles Manson is what they have got – a living testimony to and a satanic blasphemy against the ghost of Heraclitus and the wisdom of the Upanishads.

7. *Bhuktimuktiprada* Tantra, XII, 104. Reference kindly supplied by Mr Sanderson.

3

THE PHANTOM OF PARMENIDES

To the traditional Western mind, which looks to science as its infallible guide and god, the theories of Heraclitus must seem decidedly queer. To the once submerged and now aggressive minority who have at last come to realize 'the terrible capacity' of science 'to destroy not only bodies but the soul itself', it may come as a rather pleasant surprise to find that not only in our own more modern tradition but also in the cradle of our civilization – in supposedly rational Greece – the 'wisdom' of the East, as understood by Aldous Huxley and his multi-farious epigones, appears in all its ambiguous paradoxicality in the person of Heraclitus. The West, it would appear, has not always and everywhere submitted without protest to the dis-cursive mind: the element of intuitive insight, irrationality, the welling up of the creative unconscious into the creative conscious, 'enthusiasm' in short, that is, 'possession by the divine', has never for long remained beneath the surface.

There is indeed so striking a resemblance between the thought of Heraclitus and many of the other Presocratics and that of the Upanishads, which must have been developing in India at much the same time, that many thoughtful people have been driven to the conclusion that somehow or other Indian thought *must* have penetrated into Greece during the seventh and sixth centuries BC. The question is how and through what channels.

That Greek thought, as is only natural, was influenced not only by its Lydian and Phoenician neighbours but also by the great civilizations of Egypt and Mesopotamia, has long been known. But how is it that what would seem to be specifically *Indian* ideas should reappear in the Grecian world at much the same time that they were being formulated in India itself? How is it that the correspondences between the two are so often so disconcertingly exact? Does this mean that there was direct influence at work or that there is indeed a fixed pattern in what C. G. Jung calls the 'collective unconscious' of mankind? In a recent book Dr M. L. West has tried to prove that such direct influence did indeed exist. His case is not convincing. The reason is simple. India was separated from the Mediterranean Grecian world by the vast and sparsely populated land-mass that succumbed *in toto* to the power of the Persian Empire; and despite the fact that the 'laws of the Medes and Persians' have become proverbial in the West for their inalterability, there is no evidence that the Persian Empire was ever a melting-pot of ideas in which a cross-fertilization between the Indian and Greek civilizations could take place. Of course it *might* have been, though not by any exchange and translation of written documents but by personal contact of like-minded men. We must be content to say we do not know and leave it at that.

To me it seems unlikely that Heraclitus was so influenced. His whole system is so characteristically his own, he is so conscious of playing a prophetic role in which not he but the Logos proclaims the 'truth' that 'All is One', that it would seem most unlikely that he was repeating at second hand the message of some Indian and therefore 'barbarian' guru he might have run into somewhere. Again, though the correspondence between many of his sayings and the leading ideas of the Upanishads is surprisingly exact, the words he uses to express the ideas are often totally different in any of their meanings from the corresponding words expressing the same ideas in Sanskrit. For instance, the ideas expressed by the word *logos* in Greek, which Mr Hussey has so cogently analysed, all converge quite naturally on to the technical meaning that Heraclitus was to give it, namely, the 'divine law', whereas it is not an obvious translation of any of the Sanskrit words that convey the same meaning. It seems, then, to me that Heraclitus at least is a genuine representative within the Greek tradition itself of Huxley's 'perennial philosophy', which has erupted, is erupting, and will, no doubt, continue to erupt in the United States and Northern Europe for a very long time to come. 'Earnest seekers' after 'truth' might well put him on their reading list: they will find all they need between pages 32 and 59 of Hussey's lucid little book.

Whether or not, then, there was any direct intellectual communication between India and Greece in the sixth century BC must remain an open question. But that other 'barbarian' influences did make themselves felt in the Greek world now seems to be as certain as that, for instance, the Gospel according to St Mark is the earliest of the four Gospels: that is to say, it is very probable indeed in the light of all the evidence at present available. Primary among these influences would appear to be the irruption of Central Asian shamanism into Greece via Scythia and Thrace. The evidence for this will be found concisely summarized and meticulously documented in Professor E. R. Dodds's now classic *The Greeks and the Irrational*,[1] particularly in his chapter, 'The Greek Shamans and the Origin of Puritanism' (the title alone gives us plenty of food for thought).

In the strict sense of the word shamanism is a term applied to a form of religious ecstatic experience in Siberia and Central Asia. Shamanism Professor Mircea Eliade defines primarily as a 'technique of ecstasy', and the Shaman as 'the great master of ecstasy'.[2] He specializes in a trance during which his soul is believed to leave his body and ascend to the sky or descend to the underworld.[3] The soul indeed is his speciality and it is separable from the body both in dream and trance and presumably most of all at death. The Shaman may be a hereditary

1. University of California Press, Berkeley and Los Angeles, and Cambridge University Press, London, 1951.
2. Mircea Eliade, *Shamanism* (E.T., Pantheon Books, New York, 1964), p. 4   3. Ibid., p. 5.

functionary, or he may have a special 'vocation' from a higher power. If the power of the Shaman is passed on from father to son, this does not mean that the recipient of the power is necessarily the eldest son, for not everyone has the natural ability to perform the feats expected of a Shaman. The Shaman-to-be must display abnormal symptoms from an early age. He will show signs of acute nervous tension or, better still, be subject to epileptic fits: he will see visions and walk in his sleep: he will seek solitude. He may become frenzied and then lose consciousness: he will retire to the forest, live off the bark of trees, fling himself into water or fire, or wound himself with knives. A certain amount of mental derangement is in any case *de rigueur*.

When all or most of these symptoms have manifested themselves with sufficient regularity, the postulant will be considered ripe for instruction. This can be effected by a full-fledged Shaman either living or dead. In either case the initiate's soul leaves his body, carried off by the spirits of the dead. 'Received in the palace of the gods, the neophyte's soul is instructed by the ancestral Shamans in the secrets of the profession, the gods' forms and names, the cult, and names of the spirits, and so on. It is only after this first initiation that the soul returns to the body.'[4]

It is not surprising that many modern researchers have equated the ecstasies of Shamans and Shamans-to-be simply with hysteria or psychic disorder. This is, no doubt, true, but it is also true of some mystics, though not, of course, of all, and Professor Eliade is quite right to class shamanism among the 'mysticisms',[5] the variety of which I have been at pains to distinguish in a series of books starting with *Mysticism Sacred and Profane* (1957) and culminating in *Drugs, Mysticism and Make-believe* (1972). The difference between the Shaman and the ordinary lunatic, however, is that for the Shaman the lunacy is a phase through which he must pass – not to remain there, but to transcend it in order to control it, cure it, and

4. Ibid., pp. 19–20.   5. Ibid., p. 8.

know how to cure it in others. 'For the Yakut,' Professor Eliade assures us, 'the perfect Shaman "must be serious, possess tact, be able to convince his neighbours; above all, he must not be presumptuous, proud, ill-tempered. One must feel an inner force in him that does not offend yet is conscious of its power." '[6] Such Shamans, however, appear to be comparatively rare.

One further point, perhaps, needs stressing; and this is that 'the central theme of an initiation ceremony [is the] dismemberment of the neophyte's body and renewal of his organs: ritual death followed by resurrection'.[7] This must be a ritual enactment of the 'disintegration' of the mind which is the necessary psychic 'death' that must precede rebirth – that same 'tearing down the mind through pain, persuasion, drugs and repetitive weirdness . . . and rebuilding the mind *according to the desires of the cult*'.[8] This, as we have seen, was practised by Manson's 'Family' and similar Californian cults. It corresponds too to the classical definition of Yoga as the 'bringing to an end of discursive thought'.[9] But there is a difference – and it is important. The Shaman aims at 'ec-stasy', that is, at the separation of his soul from its bodily envelope, whereas the Yogi's goal is 'en-stasy' – the delving into the depths of his soul, 'whether in the body or out of the body, I do not know', as St Paul said,[1] there to find the timeless 'self' which is his true being. This, indeed, is the classical Yoga of Patanjali. That other very different forms of Yoga existed has already been indicated in the last chapter, and it is these Yogas that in one form or another have found their way into California and its occult dependencies in the West. In any case the present writer has not as yet heard of any accredited Shaman setting up shop in the United States – which, on reflection, is hardly surprising since the true Shamans are a product of Siberia and Central Asia and would doubtless en-

6. Ibid., p. 29.   7. Ibid., p. 38.
8. E. Sanders, *The Family*, p. 162 (my italics).
9. Patanjali, *Yogasutras*, 1.1.   1. 2 Corinthians 12:3.

counter considerable difficulty in getting an exit visa from
that almost perfect clockwork bureaucratic machine without
a name which likes to be known only by four impersonal
letters – USSR.

If, however, the Central Asian Shamans must be held
guiltless of infecting the already polluted air of California, they
are not quite so innocent of having besmogged the clear
Mediterranean air of ancient Greece. They came from the
north, from Thrace and Scythia on the Black Sea coast, and
their ideas seem to have travelled with them. It was, in all
probability, they who decisively influenced Pythagoras and
certainly his school, who introduced into Greek philosophy
ideas that had found no place there before. The most promin-
ent of these is reincarnation. This, of course, is not quite the
same as the personality of a living Shaman being replaced by
that of a dead one, but, as Professor Dodds says (and he is
little given to speculation unless it is very strongly supported
by the evidence): 'In view of [Pythagoras's] enormous prestige
we must surely credit him with some power of creative thinking.'[2]

What we do know, moreover (and when Professor Dodds
says we 'know', we can be pretty sure he is very certain of his
ground), is 'that Pythagoras founded a kind of religious order
of men and women whose rule was determined by the expectation of lives to come'. This seems certain, but it is
equally certain that reincarnation, as it is understood and
indeed taken for granted in India, never took firm root in
Greek soil. It certainly found a home in Plato's philosophy, as
did almost everything in that all too capacious mind, and
through Plato in the mainstream of his followers who were to
come to be known as the 'Neo-Platonists', and thence into the
intellectual and religious underground of medieval and
Renaissance Europe.

Apart from Pythagoras, whose theory of reincarnation
necessarily implied the separation of body from soul and the

2. E. R. Dodds, *The Greeks and the Irrational*, p. 144.

absolute necessity for the soul to shake off this impure body, there were, of course, the Orphics, of whom so much has been written, so much more assumed, and so little definitely known.

Orphism takes its name from Orpheus, best known in later literature as being the divine minstrel who sought to bring back his beloved Eurydice from the underworld. That Orpheus was, in fact, a reasonably ordinary human being, seems fairly certain, but it would be more fitting, in this marshy field which has never been my own, to let Professor Dodds speak for himself:

'About Orpheus himself', he says, 'I can make a guess, at the risk of being called a panshamanist. Orpheus' home is in Thrace, and in Thrace he is the worshipper or companion of a god whom the Greeks identified with Apollo. He combines the professions of poet, magician, religious teacher, and oracle-giver. Like certain legendary shamans in Siberia, he can by his music summon birds and beasts to listen to him. Like shamans everywhere, he pays a visit to the underworld, and his motive is one very common among shamans – to recover a stolen soul. Finally, his magical self lives on as a singing head, which continues to give oracles for many years after his death.'[3]

So much for Orpheus. What about Orphism? Professor Dodds warns us again. 'I must confess', he says, 'that I know very little about early Orphism, and the more I read about it the more my knowledge diminishes.' What little he knew in 1951 about the Orphism of the fifth and fourth centuries BC amounts to this: 'Three things were taught in some at least of [the religious poems ascribed to a mythical, not the real, Orpheus], namely, that the body is the prisonhouse of the soul; that vegetarianism is an essential rule of life; and that the unpleasant consequences of sin, both in this world and in the next, can be washed away by ritual means.'[4]

Thus, if we are to believe Professor Dodds (as I do, since in this he agrees with Professor Eliade whose approach to the

3. Ibid., p. 147.   4. Ibid., p. 149.

subject is totally different), it was from the shamanism of
Scythia and Thrace that Greece derived the twin ideas of reincarnation and the absolute dichotomy of soul and body. This
latter concept of human nature as being composed of a 'pure'
soul imprisoned in an 'impure' body was to become so much
part and parcel of the Platonic tradition, which, rather than
the Aristotelian, dominated Hellenistic thought for centuries,
that New Testament scholars habitually ascribe it to the
Greeks in general. This is quite natural since in the early
Christian centuries this *was* the dominant trend in Greek
thought: but it had not always been so. The original Greek
view of our human condition was identical with that of the
Hebrews: man lived but once and, after death, if anything
survived at all, it was something like those horrible bird-like
creatures squatting in the darkness whose food is dust and
whose meat is clay – a quite gratuitously gruesome idea which
both nations inherited from the profoundly pessimistic
civilizations of Mesopotamia.

Hitherto it had been the aim of Greek philosophy to dis-
entangle philosophy proper from religion. It was an anticipa-
tion in ancient Greece of what came to be called the Enlightenment in eighteenth-century Europe. In this it stands in sharp
contrast to the Indian experience where philosophizing starts
not as a rejection of current religious ideas, but as a reassess-
ment of traditional mythical thinking and ritual along esoteric
lines – so much so that it is the proud boast of almost all
modern Hindu writers that in their country philosophy has
never become divorced from religion, but has always been its
handmaid in that it points the way to the final release of the
soul from the body which is its prison and from the whole
process of reincarnation, which, in India, was seen as a burden
almost too ghastly to be borne.

Another sharp difference between India and Greece was
that India possessed an authoritative body of scripture which
all Hindu philosophers accepted as sacred and to which they
ceaselessly appealed in support of their own views, just as

Christian philosophers were to do until the 'modern' age began with Descartes. Both had an infallible authority which, throughout all their philosophizing, they could not neglect even if they had wanted to do so. Only the Buddhists (and some lesser sects that had broken with the mainstream Hindu tradition) were free to treat philosophy as an objective search for 'truth', but even the Buddhists were more interested in explaining and further developing the insights of the Buddha as they understood them.

With the Pythagoreans the principle of 'authority' crept into Greek philosophy too: 'The words of the master had absolute authority.'[5] This was something new, for though Heraclitus might have seen himself as a divinely inspired sage, he appears to have considered his fellow-men with such contempt that he did not even try to found a 'school' of philosophy, let alone a religious sect under his guidance and inspiration. The Pythagoreans, on the other hand, became not only a religious sect but a political force in Southern Italy, where Pythagoras, a native of Samos in the eastern Aegean, had finally settled down. They must have been regarded with the same kind of suspicion as were the Freemasons on the continent in the nineteenth century or the Gnostics in the first three Christian centuries: and for the same reason. They were a secret society holding esoteric views which were expressed in the exercise of magic, Pythagoras himself being dubbed by Heraclitus – never a man to mince his words – as 'the pioneer of swindles'.[6] Despite all this, the Pythagorean view of the absolute duality between soul and body, in which the soul was imprisoned, and their prescribing the means by which the soul might attain to liberation, left an indelible mark on Plato and most of the later Platonists. This absolute dualism is indeed paralleled in India, but only in one current of the mainstream – the Sānkhya-Yoga. The word *Sānkhya* in the *Bhagavad-Gītā* meant simply 'theory', as opposed to *yoga* which then meant practice. The 'theory', as it later developed,

5. E. Hussey, *The Presocratics*, p. 64. 6. Ibid., p. 63.

presupposed an infinite number of souls or rather timeless spiritual monads which somehow got mixed up in matter and were beguiled by it. This, however, is an unnatural state of affairs, and salvation consists in returning to one's own natural 'splendid isolation' in which one contemplates oneself for ever in timeless bliss. This is almost exactly the Pythagorean position, and particularly that of Empedocles who may have been converted to Pythagoreanism at some time during his life.[7] Just as the Indian Sānkhya (as well as the non-Hindu Jains) see man not as a harmonious whole but as an unnatural union of a timeless spirit with an ever-changing bundle of ever-changing matter, so does Empedocles see man as a divine being fallen from a heavenly state into a corrupt body. 'One of these I now am,' he laments, 'an exile and a wanderer from the gods, for that I put my trust in insensate strife.'[8] 'I wept and wailed when I saw the unfamiliar land.'[9] And well he might: 'For I have been ere now a boy and a girl, a bush and a bird and a dumb fish in the sea.'[1]

In Hinduism the Sānkhya system distinguishes itself from the whole Upanishadic tradition in that it admits of no God or Absolute that either includes all things spiritual and material or transcends them. The individual spiritual monads, then, not being mutually adjusted to and compensated by a universal 'justice-strife', as Heraclitus puts it, are, in some sense, responsible for their actions once they have mysteriously and, apparently, through no fault of their own, become immersed in this world of flux. By being united with the element of 'purity' or 'goodness' (*sattva*), which is one of the three strands that pervade all matter, they can win through to final release. This they can do by the practice of Yoga (the 'practical' side of 'theoretical' Sānkhya), which, in the first instance,

7. Or it may have been the other way round. See E. Hussey, op. cit., p. 70.

8. Fragment 115. See John Burnet, *Early Greek Philosophy*, 4th ed. and reprints (A. & C. Black, London, 1930), p. 222.

9. Ibid., p. 223.   1. Ibid.

means the practice of what Aristotle would call the 'natural' virtues which happen to be those commended, if not commanded by all religions: 'Do no hurt to anyone, tell the truth, do not steal, do not fornicate, do not covet.'[2]

This was true of Empedocles too. The fallen god *is* responsible for his own fall: he has yielded to Strife, which in his system is and must be at variance with its opposite Love, and it is therefore only through total renunciation of this strife-ridden world that he can hope to regain his divine beatitude. This seems to be a very long way indeed from shamanism as usually described by the anthropologists; and it is not perhaps too much to suppose that he was himself responsible for the 'moralizing' of his Pythagoreanism rather than for the mildly absurd dietary regulations attributed to him such as this strange admonition: 'Wretches, utter wretches, keep your hands from beans'![3]

Once again we have another extraordinary resemblance between an early Greek philosopher and early Indian thought. But whereas the thought of Heraclitus and of the hero of this chapter, Parmenides, has been transmitted to Europe and the United States not in their own version but in that of a people of whom they probably knew nothing, the thought of both Empedocles and his Indian equivalents has left the modern West unmoved because it stands in defiant contradiction to the 'perennial philosophy' of 'One is All' and 'Good is evil'. The ghost of Empedocles, for whom 'the soul was a unitary, free and responsible agent',[4] has been effectively laid, and we must now turn to the far more menacing and perplexing phantom of Parmenides.

The interest of Parmenides lies in the fact that his thought is even more strikingly similar to that of the Upanishads, or rather the Upanishads as classically developed by Gaudapāda and Shankara along more purely monistic lines, than is any-

2. Patanjali, *Yogasutras*, 2.30.
3. Fragment 141. J. Burnet, op. cit., p. 226.
4. E. Hussey, op. cit., pp. 69–70.

thing we find in Heraclitus. Even more than Heraclitus he regarded himself as a prophet, and the introduction to his poem is reminiscent of the visions of the Hebrew prophets and even more so of some of the passages we quoted from the Upanishads in the last chapter, for, just as the soul of the dead in the *Kaushītakī* Upanishad is mounted on a chariot and 'looks down on night and day, deeds good and evil, and all dualities',[5] so does Parmenides see himself transported in a heavenly chariot, 'escorted into the Light [by] the daughters of the sun, leaving the halls of Night, and thrusting aside with their hands the veils from their heads. There is the gate of the paths of Night and Day.'[6]

The allegory seems plain enough. The 'daughters of the sun' are 'the element of illumination and intuition' without which the discursive reason cannot begin to operate validly. Night and Day represent a false and a true line of reasoning, as Hussey puts it, or, as the Hindus would say, the 'path of action' and the 'path of knowledge', while the gate is the causeway that separates 'good and evil' from what is beyond, the 'compounded' from the 'uncompounded',[7] time from eternity, space from spacelessness, 'unwisdom' from 'wisdom',[8] the unreal from the real; for, as Mr Hussey justly remarks, 'in [Parmenides'] opinion the ordinary world was totally unreal',[9] as, for the Upanishad, are the good and evil that characterize it.

The goddess welcomes Parmenides on the far side of the gate with these words: 'Young man, . . . no bad destiny is it that sent you out to come this way – it is indeed a way remote from the paths of men – but that which is right and just. You are to learn everything: both the immovable heart of well-rounded truth, and the opinions of mortal men (in which there is no truly convincing force) – still, that too you shall learn, how these opinions are to cover everything in acceptable fashion.'

5. Above, p. 97.
6. E. Hussey, op. cit., p. 79.
7. *Ishā* Upanishad, 9.
8. Ibid., 12.
9. E. Hussey, op. cit., p. 81.

There are, then, two ways, either of which Parmenides may choose: 'The immovable heart of well-rounded truth' or 'the opinions of mortal men'.

As we have seen, Truth and falsehood are not always clearly distinguished in the Upanishads, but they are nonetheless two levels of truth (or 'knowledge' as they prefer to call it), the greater of which negates the lesser. As the *Mundaka* Upanishad (1.1.4-5) puts it: 'There are two modes of knowledge that must be known, . . . a higher and a lower. Of these the lower consists of Holy Scripture and the secular branches of learning.[1] The higher is that by which the Imperishable can be understood.' The one way, then, is that of discursive reason – book learning, including the study of Scripture: the other is the intuitive apperception of what Scripture really means.

The *Katha* Upanishad, perhaps the most poetic and haunting of all those extraordinary texts, puts the following words into the mouth of Yama, the god of Death, who is prevailed upon by the young ascetic Naciketas to reveal to him very much what the goddess of Justice had revealed to Parmenides. He does it much against his will, for the Hindu gods, like the Hebrew Yahweh, are jealous gods, and 'are not at all pleased that men should know this'.[2] However, Death speaks: and what he is to divulge is the secret of immortality:

> The better part is one thing, the agreeable another;
> Though different their goals, both restrict a man:
> For him who takes the better of the two all's well,
> But he who chooses the agreeable fails to attain the goal.

> Better and agreeable present themselves to man:
> Considering them carefully the wise man discriminates,
> Preferring the better to what only pleasure brings:
> Dull men prefer the agreeable –
> For the getting and keeping [of the things they crave].

1. Free rendering of the detailed list of sacred and profane learning given in the text. 2. *Brihadāranyaka* Upanishad, 1.4.10.

Thou, Naciketas, hast well considered [all objects of] desire,
[All] that's agreeable in form: thou hast rejected them.
Thou wouldst not accept this garland of wealth compacted
In which how many a man has been dragged down, sub-
    merged!

Different, opposed, wide separated these –
Unwisdom and what men as wisdom know:
Wisdom it is that Naciketas seeks, I see;
Not thou to be distracted by manifold desire!

Self-wise, puffed up with learning, some
Turn round and round imprisoned in unwisdom's realm;
Hither and thither rushing, round they go, the fools,
Like blind men guided by the blind!

No glimmering have such of man's last destiny –
Unheeding, childish fools, by wealth deluded:
'This world alone exists, there is no other', so think they;
Again and ever again they fall into my hands.

Many there are who never came to hear of him,
Many, though hearing of him, do not know him:
Blessed the man who, skilled therein, proclaims him, grasps
    him;
Blessed the man who learns from one so skilled and knows
    him![3]

Who or what is it, then, that must be known? Let us first
hear what the goddess of Justice revealed to Parmenides:

'Come then,' she says, 'I will tell (and do you take in the
story you hear) the ways of inquiry which alone are to be
thought of: the first, that says that (it) is and it cannot be that
(it) is not – this is the path of true persuasion, for it follows the
truth; the second, that says that (it) is not and that it must be
that (it) is not – *this* track, I tell you, is quite undiscover-
able . . .'[4]

3. *Katha* Upanishad, 2.1–7.   4. E.Hussey, op. cit., p. 81.

Mr Hussey, who here seems to be carrying accuracy to a fault, finds difficulties here where to me, who have read and re-read and translated the principal Upanishads, there seems to be no difficulty at all. When Parmenides says '([he, she, or] it) is', he can surely only mean that 'nothing *is* but Being', which may be a tautology, but which effectively precludes not only 'Not-being' (however that may be interpreted) from any claim to existence but also every form of becoming, movement, or change, all of which are simply the 'opinions of mortal men', for whom Parmenides has every bit as much contempt as Heraclitus – and, for that matter, as the author of the *Katha* Upanishad. Ordinary men, 'the two-headed creatures' (who are stupid enough to believe two contradictory things at the same time (?)), know nothing. 'Helplessness it is that steers the wandering minds in their breasts, and they drift along, deaf and blind, in confused throngs, like men amazed.'[5] 'Men amazed': this might equally be translated as 'deluded' or 'bemused' – a condition to which both the Hindus and the Buddhists ascribe man's congenital inability to see what they claim to be the Truth.

Thus 'Truth' is, for the *Katha* Upanishad, the same as what it is for Parmenides: and it is summed up in the same word, 'is' – *esti* in Greek, *asti* in Sanskrit, both from the same Indo-European root. But the Upanishad does at least tell us *what* it thinks *it* 'is': it is the 'Self' or 'Person' or 'Brahman', but even these are only names that can only point to what is essentially inexpressible. And so, in a passage that is exactly parallel to the extreme position of Parmenides, we read:

Not thus can it be apprehended
    By voice or mind or eye:
How then can it be understood,
    Unless we say: '[It] is.'

'[It] is'; so must we understand it,
And as the true essence of the two:

5. Ibid., p. 86.

118

'[It] is': when once we understand it thus,
   The nature of its essence is limpidly shown forth.[6]

The first of these stanzas corresponds exactly to the uncompromising monism of Parmenides' original proclamation of
'the immovable heart of well-rounded truth': 'Is'. The second,
however, makes room for the 'opposites' of Heraclitus, for it
is 'the true essence of the *two*' – that is, the opposites. We shall
later briefly sketch out how Parmenides gets round this apparent inconsistency. For to do more would be incompatible
with the sort of book this is supposed to be.

The second path 'that says that (it) is not and that it must be
that (it) is not', Parmenides makes short work of. This 'path'
is literally a non-starter since you cannot start from any point
that is totally non-existent: indeed, you cannot even think of
such a thing. As Mr Hussey says, after having brought out the
full subtlety of Parmenides' thought, 'it is meaningless'. And
even the layman will instinctively agree that he must be right.

The ancient Indians, however, were for ever oscillating
between the two poles of what they call Being and Not-being,
and the words, as used by them, are highly ambivalent. This
was already clear in the Vedic hymn we quoted above (p. 79):
'Then neither Being nor Not-being was.' In the Upanishads,
however, the priority is sometimes given to Not-being, sometimes to Being. Thus in the *Taittirīya* Upanishad (2.7) we
read:

In the beginning this universe was Not-being only,
   Therefrom was Being born.

The *Chāndogya* Upanishad (3.9.1), however, tries to have it
both ways, rather as Heraclitus had done in Greece:
   'In the beginning this universe was Not-being: [yet] it was
Being [too]. It developed. It turned into an egg' – the 'cosmic
egg' we find in the Orphic poems in Greece.
   The same Upanishad (6.2.1-2), however, then proceeds
   6. *Katha* Upanishad, 6.12–13.

flatly to contradict both positions, proclaiming, with Parmenides, the absolute primacy of Being:

'In the beginning . . . this universe was Being only – one only – without a second. True, some say that in the beginning this universe was Not-being only – one only – without a second; and that from Not-being Being was generated.

'But . . . whence could this be? . . . How could Being be born from Not-being? No, it was Being alone that was this universe in the beginning – one only – without a second.'

In all three accounts, however, the original One (whether it is Being or Not-being) develops into what is more than one: and in Hinduism this is a 'fall'. The One represents perfection (Plato called it the 'Good'), the many, since each member of it is imperfect and dependent in itself, is a lapse from perfection and, in this sense, evil. This is how things seem from the point of view of the 'lower mode of knowledge'.[7] The many proceed from the One as sparks proceed from fire[8] or a spider's web is generated from the spider.[9] From the point of view of the higher mode of knowledge, however, all is absolutely One, and there is no diversity at all because there is no space in which one thing could be separated from another:

> What is here is also there beyond;
> What there, that too is here:
> Death beyond death does he incur
> Who sees in this what seems to be diverse.
>
> Grasp this with your mind:
> Herein there's no diversity at all.
> Death beyond death is all the lot
> Of him who sees in this what seems to be diverse.[1]

In the Upanishads, and in the Vedanta philosophy which is based on them, this oscillation between pure monism ('One' – 'is') on the one hand and pure pantheism ('All is One and One

7. Above, p. 116.
8. *Mundaka* Upanishad, 2.1.1.

9. Ibid., 1.1.7.
1. *Katha* Upanishad, 4.10–11.

is All') on the other is always present. Monism (or 'non-dual-ism' as most people nowadays prefer to call it, adhering to the literal translation of the Sanskrit word) represents the 'higher knowledge' considered to be the 'absolute Truth', while the pantheist solution is regarded by the more strict adherents of the Vedantin school as belonging essentially to the 'lower knowledge'. It is most clearly expressed in the *Bhagavad-Gītā* (13.16):

'Undivided it abides, seeming divided: this is That which should be known – the one who sustains, devours, and generates all beings.'

Is there any trace of this two-tier theory of knowledge in Parmenides, whom I have hitherto regarded, along with the great Hindu Vedantin thinker, Shankara, as being the prince of monists? After reading Hussey's very careful analysis of his poem I am inclined to think there is. At the risk of boring the reader, who may be wondering what the finer points of the philosophy of Parmenides have to do with Charlie Manson and his happy Family, I must stress one or two points which do seem to have a bearing on that interesting case.

Parmenides states his thesis thus:

'Only one story of a path is now left; namely that (it) *is*. On this path there are very many signs, showing that what *is* is un-created [or "ungenerated"] and indestructible, whole, unique, unmoved and perfect; nor was it, nor will it ever be, since it *is*, *all together*, *now*, *one* and *coherent*.'[2]

This seems to be monism with a vengeance. The One is necessarily 'ungenerated and indestructible, whole, unique, unmoved and perfect', for this means it is utterly beyond space or, in other words, it is the omnipresent 'Here'. 'It was not, nor will it ever be, since it *is*, all together, now, one and coherent.' This too seems plain enough: because it is 'now', it can never have existed in the past nor can it ever exist in the future since it wholly transcends time in an eternal Now (a

2. E. Hussey, op. cit., p. 88 (my italics: I have also added two commas).

term particularly dear to the medieval German mystic, Meister Eckhart, accepted too by Charles Manson and his Family who 'did not believe in time and months and days, [since] it was all Now',[3] and applied with literally ruthless logic to Shorty Shea. Justifying their gruesome butchery of the wretched boy, they said, paying homage to the phantom of Parmenides, unknowing though they were: 'He got to NOW, and they killed him'[4]).

The 'Now', of course, cannot beget, nor can it be begotten like the Allah of the Koran. The point does not need stressing.

'Nor is it divided.' That too seems obvious enough to any self-respecting monist. But, Parmenides explains, it is not divided, 'since it is all alike, and it is not any more or any less in any way, so as to prevent itself from being coherent, but it is all full of that which is. Therefore it is all coherent, for what *is* sticks close to what *is*.'

That 'it is not any more or any less in any way' seems perfectly respectable since one of the Upanishads says much the same thing and adds: 'He neither increases by good works nor does he diminish by evil ones.'[5] But the statement that it is 'all full of that which is' and that 'what *is* sticks close to what *is*' surely implies some kind of duality. Mr Hussey's explanation of this passage is both ingenious and convincing but rather too complex to be discussed in this context. And here again I think a Hindu parallel might help.

In the *Bhagavad-Gītā* (6.20–32) the ascent of the soul from time to eternity and from 'pure' eternity to an eternity shared with God is described. The essential verses, from our present point of view, are 27–28, for they seem to contain the key to the mystery of Parmenides. This is what they say:

'Upon this Yogi whose mind is stilled the highest joy descends: all passion laid to rest, free from all stain, *Brahman he becomes*. And thus, all flaws transcending, the Yogi, con-

3. E. Sanders, *The Family*, p. 191.
4. Above, p. 67.
5. *Brihadāranyaka* Upanishad, 4.4.22.

stant in integrating himself, with ease attains unbounded joy, *Brahman's [saving] touch.*'

Brahman, in the *Gītā*, corresponds more or less exactly to the 'One' and 'Is' of Parmenides: it is the stuff of eternity, indivisible and undivided. And yet the individual self can be described as a 'part' of God (15.7), who *is* both the eternal Brahman as well as our whole world of appearance, which issues from it, *and* transcends them both. From the point of view of the 'lower' mode of knowledge this makes sense since the 'many' are really distinct but unified in the One. How do matters stand on the 'higher' plane of knowledge? Here, it has been said, 'there is no diversity at all': therefore, no division. But there is coherence, for the One is also a continuum (*suneches*), as Parmenides says. Thus, even on the higher plane of knowledge we can speak of 'becoming Brahman' and 'attaining contact (for this is the literal meaning of the Sanskrit word *samsparsha*) with Brahman'. This is, I think, what Parmenides means by 'what *is* sticks close to what *is*'. Whatever *is*, is *both* identical with Being *and* an individual modification of it. In the words of the *Chāndogya* Upanishad (6.1.4): 'Just as all that is made up of clay can be known by one lump of clay – its modifications are verbalizations, mere names – the reality is just "clay-ness".' So too the One of Parmenides is both undivided and indivisible *and* a coherent whole.

But, as we have seen, Parmenides makes an absolute separation between Being – 'the immovable heart of well-rounded truth' – and 'becoming', a mere appearance thought up by idiotic mortals. Yet there is a 'path' from the sphere of opinion to that of Truth, and this must pass through the 'gate' which separates the 'Night' of opinion from the 'Day' of Truth. This is the path trodden, immemorially, by the Yogis in India – the path described in the *Bhagavad-Gītā*. Plotinus, the prince of the Neo-Platonists, described it as the 'flight of the alone to the Alone'.[6] The meaning of all this is that at the higher level of knowledge there are no distinctions

6. Plotinus, *Enneads*, 6.9.11.

because there the 'opposites' simply do not exist: there is neither white nor black, male nor female, good nor evil. Hence what we do on earth can from the absolute point of view have no significance whatsoever, and Crowley's 'Do what thou wilt shall be the whole of the law' is precisely as meaningful (and meaningless) as Augustine's 'Love, and do what thou wilt'. Whatever foolish mortals may say and however they may try to express the inexpressible, 'everything will be mere name – all that mortal men, believing to be true, have established by convention as coming into being, being destroyed, being and not being, changing its place and altering its bright colour'.[7] This is Parmenides speaking, not the Hindu scriptures: for even in these exalted realms of esoteric thought Europe can hold its own with the wisdom of the mystic East.

In the Indian tradition there are passages in the Upanishads (though they are rare) which make as clear a break between spirit and matter as does the Sānkhya system – and Empedocles in Greece, not to mention 'the deep-sea swell raked by wicked Thracian winds'[8] which broke upon Greece out of the Black Sea and beyond. This distinction, however, was rarely fully maintained, and an attempt was made to bridge the gulf through the concept of *māyā*, too often rendered into English simply as 'illusion', but better translated as 'appearance' or (if you prefer it in Greek) 'phenomenon'.

To deal fully with this concept would mean both to extend the length of this book unbearably and to exacerbate the probably already exacerbated general reader. We will be as brief as possible.

The word *māyā* appears to be derived from the root *mā*, 'to measure', and is therefore a natural term to apply to all that can be measured, what we call 'matter', that sphere of existence which alone is proper to science. The first time we meet the word in a technical sense is in the relatively late

7. E. Hussey, op. cit., p. 89.
8. Sophocles, *Antigone*, 586–9; tr. E. R. Dodds, op. cit., p. 49.

Shvetāshvatara Upanishad (4.10), where we are laconically told that '*māyā* is *prakriti*', which can best be translated as '[God's] power to allot everything its proper measure is Nature' or 'matter', since for the Hindus matter included everything that changes including the mind and what we would call the contemplative intellect or soul. There is nothing outside Māyā-matter in this sense except pure, changeless spirit.

In the *Bhagavad-Gītā* 7.14–15, however, Māyā has already assumed a highly ambivalent role: from one point of view it is 'divine', from another 'devilish':

'[The whole of Nature which is basically identical with matter] is Māyā, . . . divine, hard to transcend. Whoso shall put his trust in Me alone [that is, Krishna as incarnate God], shall pass beyond this Māyā. Doers of evil, deluded, base, do *not* put their trust in me; their wisdom swept away by this Māyā, they cleave to a devilish mode of existence.'

Māyā, then, is both 'divine' and 'devilish'. It all depends on the way you look at it. If you are 'open' and desire enlightenment and release from Māyā, then Māyā itself is no more than a tenuous curtain that reveals the eternal partially – a curtain so flimsy that it can easily be drawn aside. If, on the other hand, you shut yourself obstinately up in your ego, the flimsy curtain becomes an impenetrable screen which shuts out completely the clear light of eternity. You are like the men in Plato's celebrated allegory of the cave, perfectly happy to live by artificial light in semi-darkness because you know nothing of the sunlight outside.

The first systematic treatment of the concept of Māyā, as of Vedantin monism in general, seems to be that of Gaudapāda who probably lived in the eighth century AD. To a short consideration of this we must now turn.

The best known work of Gaudapāda is his commentary on the late, short, and consistently monist *Māndūkya* Upanishad. This Upanishad is primarily concerned with the nature of sleep, a subject that had obsessed the Upanishadic thinkers from the earliest times. In the West it has always been assumed that man is at his creative best when he is wide awake and intensely alert: it is then that he is most 'himself' and most conscious of himself. In this he is most 'godlike' since the Greek gods, as later rationalized, were no more subject to sleep than is the Hebrew Yahweh. And so Aristotle can quite naturally say of them that 'they have always been conceived of as being alive and active and not always asleep as was the case of Endymion'.[9] But, he concedes, being divine and therefore free from matter of any kind, they cannot act upon others, let alone make things as a craftsman might; so there is nothing left to them but contemplation. This is their constant joy, and man's final bliss must, then, consist in contemplation, for it is in this, and in this only, that he shares in the divine nature.

According to the Upanishads, however, despite the fact that the ultimate principle is described in one of them[1] as consciousness and in another as consciousness and the Breath of Life,[2] the ultimate unity in which the individual self realizes that it is really nothing less than the One in its total simplicity is most nearly realized in dreamless sleep. The subject fascinated them and they returned to it time and again. The waking state, so far from being the most 'godlike', is the most matter-bound of all: matter appears to be 'given' and there is nothing you can do about it. In dream, however, you reach a higher level of reality since you make your own matter. In deep, dreamless sleep you enter into a yet deeper mode of reality where all appears to be one – and that for the Hindu is ultimate Truth.

Man is a microcosm – a reproduction in miniature – of the macrocosm which is the universe; and his three states of consciousness correspond to three states of the three principal components of the natural universe – gross matter, subtle matter, and, of all things, God. God, therefore, equals deep,

9. Aristotle, *Nicomachean Ethics*, 10.8.7 (1178b 19).
1. *Aitareya* Upanishad, 5.3.   2. *Kaushītakī* Upanishad, 3.9.

dreamless sleep: he *is* Endymion. Given the Hindu premises, however, this (to us) extraordinary identification is not really unnatural, for neither the Greeks nor anyone else that I know of, except the Jews and the two great religions that derive from them, ever supposed that God created the universe out of nothing, whatever that may mean (for Parmenides, as we have seen, it was a contradiction in terms). Rather, the universe emanates from God as a spider's web does from a spider. Hence it is quite natural that subtle matter, the stuff of dreams, should emanate from a sleeping God, and gross matter, our everyday reality, from the divine dream. After all, this was the whole theory that lay behind the practice of shamanism too; and, as we have seen, there is a close affinity between Central Asian shamanism and Yoga techniques. Dreamless sleep, moreover, is the nearest thing we know to death, and the Upanishads were well aware of this too. To die means to become one; and to become one means to become *the* One.

' "He is becoming one, he does not see", they say. "He is becoming one, he does not smell", they say. "He is becoming one, he does not taste", they say. "He is becoming one, he does not speak", they say. "He is becoming one, he does not hear", they say. "He is becoming one, he does not think", they say. "He is becoming one, he does not feel", they say. "He is becoming one, he does not understand", they say.'[3] 'After death there is no consciousness: this is what I say.'[4] There is no *individual* consciousness, that is to say, but this does not mean annihilation, but that one has, through death, entered into the universal life, the universal thought, and the universal understanding of him who lives and thinks and understands all things, but whom not even the dead can fully understand; for 'with what should one understand him by whom one understands this whole universe?'[5] This is the 'fourth' state beyond dreamless sleep and it is death – what the

3. *Brihadāranyaka* Upanishad, 4.4.2.
4. Ibid, 2.4.12 and 4.5.13.   5. Ibid., 2.4.14＝4.5.15.

Zen Buddhists call the 'Great Death' which is yet the awakening to eternal life.

'Conscious of neither within nor without, nor of both together, not a mass of wisdom, neither wise nor unwise, unseen, one with whom there is no commerce, impalpable, devoid of distinguishing mark, unthinkable, indescribable, its essence the firm conviction of the oneness of itself, bringing all development to an end, tranquil and mild, devoid of duality, such do they deem this fourth to be. That is the Self: that is what should be known.'[6]

This is indeed 'the immovable heart of well-rounded truth' of Parmenides. How, then, if at all, is it to be connected with the three other states of being – God=dreamless sleep, subtle matter=dream, and gross matter=being awake? The eighth-century philosopher Gaudapāda tries to give the answer in his verse commentary on this most uncompromising of the Upanishads.

Gaudapāda adopts the double standard of truth originally proclaimed in the *Mundaka* Upanishad (p. 116). This process of what some might be inclined to call 'double-think' was in his day common practice among the Buddhists too and had been unequivocally laid down by one of the earliest and greatest of the Mahayana Buddhist philosophers, Nāgārjuna, during the first or second century AD.

'The teaching of the doctrine laid down by [all] the Buddhas', he wrote, 'is based on two truths, namely, worldly (empirical) truth and the absolute Truth. Those who do not recognize the distinction between these two truths, do not understand the profound quintessence of the Buddha's teaching.'[7]

This is precisely the view of Gaudapāda, whose dependence on earlier Mahayana Buddhist philosophy is obvious. The worship of God or the gods is a 'pitiful' affair suitable enough,

6. *Māndūkya* Upanishad, 7.
7. Nāgārjuna, *Mūlamādhyamakakārikā*, 24.8–9. Text and translation in Kenneth K. Inada, *Nāgārjuna* (Hokuseido Press, Tokyo, 1970), p. 146.

no doubt, to the common run of deluded mortals but wholly inadequate to the 'true' philosopher who has seen the 'truth'.[8] The 'truth' is that God, who is from the absolute point of view identical with the Self (the One of Parmenides), nevertheless himself 'imagines' both himself as God and the whole world of appearance through his own Māyā on the empirical level of knowledge.[9] The absolute Truth, however, which is 'not pitiful', is the purest Parmenides; '(It is) unborn and the *same* throughout';[1] and 'the ungenerated is knowledge which is inseparable from the knowable, devoid of any kind of imagination: the ungenerated is eternal and to be known as Brahman. Only the ungenerated knows the ungenerated.'[2]

Basically Gaudapāda's problem is the same as that of Parmenides: it is simply this: 'How can we account for change once we have understood by intuition that there is an absolute One which is by definition changeless?' The answer is that from the absolute point of view there is only the One, which may be referred to as Brahman or the 'Self', which is changeless and 'coherent' in the sense that it is always 'the same'; but, from the empirical point of view, though we may have some instinctive knowledge of an underlying unity behind what appears to us to be a world in a perpetual state of flux, for ever coming to be and for ever passing away, what is real to *us* is this world of change, conditioned by time, space, and causation, the world from which Aristotle started and which led him to conclude that the whole causal process must go back to an ultimate cause which is not caused and which he called the 'Unmoved Mover'. In Gaudapāda's system this is God who is the source of Māyā and who imagines both himself and our world into an imaginary existence. None of this, Gaudapāda maintains, can make sense unless you accept the two levels of knowledge.

Gaudapāda, however, was a Hindu, not a Buddhist, and he had to accept the authority of the Veda and particularly the

8. Gaudapāda, *Kārikā* on the *Māndukya* Upanishad, 3.1.
9. Ibid., 2.12: 3.19, etc.   1. Ibid., 3.2.   2. Ibid., 3.33.

Upanishads as being divinely given and 'heard' by the ancient sages who had faithfully passed the divine message on in Scripture. The Upanishads, however, as often as not contradict each other. How can you, then, decide between the validity of one text as against that of another? To this he replies that only such scriptural passages as agree with reason can be regarded as authoritative, which, in practice, means only such passages as agree with his absolute monism. All that does not falls within the province of the lower-empirical knowledge which, from the higher standpoint, is simply false. All this seems to be pure Parmenides. But there is a difference.

For the Hindu, transcendental knowledge is never an end in itself: it must be experienced. In other words the human being must realize that contrary to all the appearances of body and mind he *is* in fact Being itself, 'One without a second'. This intuitive realization is called *samādhi*, which can best be translated as 'concentration' and which corresponds almost exactly to the Greek *suneches* which Edward Hussey translates as 'coherent'. This identity of the state of *samādhi* with the changeless One is best brought out in the following passage:

'*Samādhi* is beyond all expression by words and transcends any kind of thought: it is wonderfully at peace, effulgent with a once-for-all effulgence, motionless, and without fear. Then there is neither giving nor receiving, since thought does not exist there. Then [*samādhi*] is seen to be knowledge consistent with itself (*ātmasamstha*), ungenerated, and the same throughout.'[3]

This is called the Yoga 'in which there is no contact' (*asparsha*), as opposed, presumably, to the Yoga of the *Bhagavad-Gītā* (6.28) which mentions 'Brahman's [saving] touch' or more literally 'contact' (*samsparsha*).[4] This is because 'it' '*is* all together, now, one, and coherent', as Parmenides said. It is beyond the 'merging into the all' experienced by most nature mystics, because this is equivalent

3. Ibid., 3.37–8.   4. But see above, p. 123.

to disintegration. Admittedly this must precede the awakening of 'thought' (*citta*), that is, the contemplative intellect, to a totally new form of existence which is eternal and *the same* throughout.[5] Here there is only the higher 'knowledge' which is now identical with all objects of thought. On this plane everything shines with an identical effulgence: there is no I, no you, no time, no space, no cause, no effect, no God, no devil, no good, no evil. If you must say anything at all, say *esti* with Parmenides in Greek, *asti* with the *Katha* Upanishad in Sanskrit, *est* with St Thomas Aquinas in Latin, or in plain English 'is'. If you happen to speak a language, like Arabic, which has no verb 'to be', you will find it very difficult indeed to say anything at all that conveys the same sense of absolute Being, as the Arabic translators of the Greek philosophers very soon found out. In this state to say you are a god or even God is hopelessly to understate the case, for you will be talking the language of 'ignorant mortals, those two-headed creatures', as Parmenides described them. Such a one was Empedocles, who proclaimed to the citizens of 'the great city on the honey-coloured hill of Acragas': 'I go about among you all, an immortal god, no longer a mortal man, receiving due honours, crowned with triumphal headbands and heaped with green garlands.'[6]

But to be a god is not enough, for you will only have exchanged an earthly body for a spiritual one, the 'appearance' of evil for the 'appearance' of good. To break down the discursive mind and dissolve the ego is not enough if you are only to build it up again in a more godlike form. It doesn't matter very much whether you call yourself a god, as Empedocles did, or Jesus Christ, as Charles Manson did: you are still in the realm of Heraclitus where 'justice *is* strife' and God *is* the Devil. You have not yet reached 'the immovable heart of well-rounded truth' of Parmenides, which no ordinary mortal can begin to understand, and, so far as the ordinary man is

5. Gaudapāda, op. cit., 3.44.
6. E. Hussey, op. cit., p. 72.

concerned, he will think you no better than a 'dolt' or a 'thing inanimate',[7] or maybe he will take you for a bloodless phantom descended from on high – the phantom of Parmenides, perhaps, or even that phantom man called Jesus Christ, whose 'appearance' appeared to be crucified in this world of 'appearance' as the Christian Gnostics thought. Have done with all these silly fantasies, for Parmenides has told you once and for all: 'From this path . . . I block you.'[8] Repeat, rather, the words of the *Katha* Upanishad:

> It cannot be apprehended
> By voice or mind or eye:
> How then can it be understood
> Unless we utter 'IS'.[9]

7. Gaudapāda, op. cit., 2.36.   8. E. Hussey, op. cit., p. 83.
9. *Katha* Upanishad, 6.12. Cf. above, p. 118.

4

THE PERILS OF PLATO

The last two chapters will have proved heavy going for many a reader. This, unfortunately, cannot be helped: for what Heraclitus and Parmenides were trying to do in ancient Greece and what the authors of the Upanishads were trying to do in ancient India, what others have been doing there ever since, and are doing now in modern America and to a lesser extent in Northern Europe, is to find some way of expressing the inexpressible.

Ever since the Hindus turned their backs on polytheism and acknowledged that one power, and one power only, both indwelt and ruled the universe, they have sought to identify it, and, having identified it, to commune with it. The earliest Greek philosophers, rejecting the old theogonies, were also concerned with finding some more logical explanation of the working of the universe and with discovering a single principle that bound it together. One of them, Thales, saw such a principle in water, Anaximenes in air, the 'Breath of Life' which keeps the universe *alive*, Anaximander in the 'Boundless' which rules 'according to the assessment of Time', Heraclitus in fire.[1] So, too, the early Hindu speculators identified the 'ground' of the universe with water,[2] with *prāna* (again the 'Breath of Life'), with Time, and, of course, with fire, which had almost certainly been a god in its own right long before the Aryans invaded India some time during the second millennium BC, since, by 'devouring' the oblation, it acted as an intermediary between men and the powers above.

1. See E. Hussey, *The Presocratics*, pp. 16ff.
2. *Rigveda*, 10.129.3.

In the Upanishads the old gods have been dethroned though they appear from time to time either in a quite subordinate role or as a personal 'appearance' of the supreme principle. Like the Presocratics in Greece the Upanishads think of this principle as alive (the perennial 'vitalist' heresy now condemned for ever by modern science, as Professor Monod would have us believe). Sometimes they identify it with food, sometimes with the breath of life, sometimes with space – or with the sky, the sun, the wind, water, the earth, or, on the purely human scale, with each or all of the organs of sense, the mind, the understanding, semen – indeed with almost anything. It is true that the resemblances between *some* passages in the Upanishads and *some* of the Presocratics – notably Heraclitus and Parmenides – are striking, but the *ways* in which these two quite distinct traditions arrived at the same results were as strikingly different. In the Greek case, as we have seen, the ancient gods were rejected by the first rational thinkers in that they could supply no coherent picture of the universe. What Heraclitus and Parmenides were trying to do was to provide such a picture, a system, that is, which was consistent with itself. They were as consciously breaking with their own religious tradition, probably, as was Xenophanes when he directly attacked the gods as they were traditionally depicted in the epic poetry of Homer and Hesiod.

In India the process was much less simple. Even in the *Rigveda*, the oldest part of the Hindu religious scriptures, there are not only the late cosmological hymns which show that the Indians too were already beginning to reflect on the nature of the universe, but also hymns so obscure that we can only guess that they must have had some *magical* significance now lost to us. This magical element becomes only too apparent in the *Atharva Veda*, which is certainly a later compilation and describes purely magical processes which are quite foreign to the general spirit of the earlier work. Much of this magic is what we now call 'sympathetic' magic, meaning that, by identifying yourself with someone or something else, you obtain power over it. Thus, in the extreme case, when you identify yourself with everything and can say: 'Whoso thus knows that he is Brahman, becomes this whole universe', it must follow that 'even the gods have not the power to cause him to un-Be, for he becomes their own self'.[3] Franklin Edgerton, it seems to me, was basically right when he wrote:

'The real underlying motive and rationale of all this "monism", this seeking for a single principle in the universe, cannot be understood without reference to the principle of *identification* as it appears in Vedic texts; . . . A very striking feature of these works is their passion for identification of one thing with another, on the slenderest possible basis; indeed, often on no basis at all that we can discover. The purpose was strictly practical; more specifically, magical. It was to get results by setting cosmic forces in motion. To this end a cosmic force was said to "be" this or that other thing, which other thing we can control. "By grasping and controlling one of the two identified entities, the possessor of the mystic knowledge as to their identity has power over the other, which is in fact not other" but really the same. For instance, "the cow is breath"; I control a cow, therefore I control breath, my own life-breath, or someone else's. That is the only reason for the fantastic identification. We want to control, let us say, the breath of life, in ourselves or someone else (perhaps an enemy); so we earnestly and insistently identify it with something that we *can* control, and the trick is turned.'[4]

'Turned' perhaps, but not fully turned. These magical identifications are surely *also* gropings in the dark towards that 'perennial philosophy' of which Aldous Huxley speaks, the two characteristic formulations of which we find in ancient Greece in Heraclitus (the unity of opposites) and Parmenides ('It *is*, all together, now, one and coherent'). That there was a real difference between these two solutions of the problem of

3. *Brihadāranyaka* Upanishad, 1.4.10.
4. Franklin Edgerton, *The Beginnings of Indian Philosophy* (Allen & Unwin, London, and Harvard University Press, 1965), pp. 21-2.

how a universe which is composed of an infinite number of compounded units which are for ever changing, coming to be only to pass away in a never-ending ebb and flow of strife and love, as Empedocles saw it, can be coherently related to an eternal, timeless, uncompounded, and static One, was obvious to the Greek mind which was already concerning itself with making distinctions. It was not at all clear to the Indian mind, and such passages as deny that it makes any sense to say that Being arises from Not-being, which we quoted in the last chapter (p. 120), are very rare indeed. Attempts, however, *are* made to distinguish *degrees* of reality. Sometimes they seem to be wholly inconsequential,[5] at other times the sequence seems perfectly logical. Take, for example, this passage from the *Taittirīya* Upanishad (2.1–6).

In the physical order man is derived from the Absolute (the Self which is Brahman) in the following chain of being: 'From the Self space came to be, from space the air, from air fire, from fire water, from water earth, from earth plants, from plants food, from food [transformed into semen] man.' In other words man, as a purely physical phenomenon, is simply a food-eating and excreting organism: seen thus he is 'Brahman-as-food'. But a living organism needs not only food but also breath in order to keep alive: in this capacity, then, he is 'Brahman-as-breath or life'. But man is also a 'rational animal', as Aristotle told us. As such he is 'Brahman-as-mind', and again 'Brahman-as-understanding'. But man is potentially still more than this: he is also 'Brahman-as-joy'. This is the

5. e.g. *Chāndogya* Upanishad, 7.1–15, where you have the following' entities, each of which is said to be higher than the one that precedes it: name, speech, mind, will (or imagination), thought, meditation, understanding. So far, so good: each entity is more intellectual than the last. But the series does not stop here, but goes on to strength, food, water, heat, and space, that is, material entities each regarded as greater than the last. Then we revert to the intellect (and will) again – memory and hope. Finally we come to the 'breath of life' which ends the series. I have never understood this passage and probably never will.

real Brahman, the real Self, the sweet 'taste' that pervades the whole universe: and 'once a man has tasted this, he is suffused with joy. For who could breathe, who could live, were this joy not suffused throughout space? For this alone brings joy.'

This *is* coherent: and it has a rough logic of its own. 'Our father' Aristotle himself would have understood and approved it, since he said very much the same himself, as we shall very soon see. Whether he would have approved the final identification must remain a matter for dispute. He certainly would not have approved of it absolutely, but, to my way of thinking, he would have admitted its essential correctness, though certainly not without qualification. What, then, is this final identification? It is this:

'This one that is here in a man, and that one there in the sun – He is One.'

And the corollary and summing-up of the whole process:

'The man who knows this, on departing from this world, draws near to the self that consists of food, . . . to the self that consists of the breath of life, . . . to the self that consists of mind, . . . to the self that consists of understanding, . . . to the self that consists of joy.'

> That from which all words recoil together with the mind,
> Unable to attain it –
> That is the bliss of Brahman: knowing it,
> A man has naught to fear from anywhere.

But then comes that sinister refrain: 'Such a man is not worried [by the thought]: "Why did I not do good? Why did I do evil?" Knowing both [good and evil] in this way, he saves [him]self; for whoever knows them both as such, saves [him]self. Such is the secret teaching (*upanishad*).'[6]

Over this secret teaching comes the parting of the ways between Greece and India. To say that it was a parting of the ways between East and West would be an absurd over-

6. *Taittirīya* Upanishad, 2.8–9.

simplification, for, despite tireless propaganda on behalf of the 'spiritual' East as against the 'material' West emanating from India, the Indian subcontinent has about as much right to speak for the 'East' as has France or England (or Germany or Italy or Spain for that matter) to speak for the 'West'. In the East China's altogether more refined and equally varied contribution to Eastern religion cannot be so easily set aside, as Rabindranath Tagore learnt to his consternation when he visited China and Japan.

With the advent of the Sophists on the intellectual scene in Greece during the second half of the fifth century BC two changes took place. First Parmenides' denial of any reality to this world of ours and the powerful arguments used by himself and his pupil Zeno on their behalf induced a mood of scepticism typified by Democritus' 'in truth we know nothing about anything'. Further, there was a new interest in that rational, political, and social animal, man himself, as being the proper field of study for a human being. As Mr Hussey aptly says: '[Protagoras'] famous slogan, "Man is the measure of all things", combined beautifully, as a good slogan should, the different components of his position: relativism or pragmatism in questions of truth, but also humanistic optimism about the problems of human conduct and society.'[7]

This is the atmosphere into which Socrates was born. Socrates, presumably, needs no introduction since he has come to be known as the father of 'dialectics' – not, of course, in the sense of 'dialectical materialism', but in the sense of probing argument in which all established philosophical positions are questioned, overthrown, only to lead to further and more far-reaching problems. As such, it might be thought, Socrates has more right to be called the 'father of the West', in so far as the West is allegedly preoccupied with making distinctions – the essential basis for any scientific enquiry, the principle of objectivity of Professor Monod – than has Aristotle, the disciple of Socrates' disciple Plato. For our purpose, however,

7. E. Hussey, op. cit., p. 109.

this would be incorrect, for Socrates seems to have possessed a dual personality: he was both the super-dialectician *and* a deeply religious man. It is true that it is at least as difficult to reconstruct the historical Socrates as it is the historical Jesus, since he left nothing in writing. The fact, however, remains that, when condemned on the charge of corrupting the young, he chose death rather than exile, which was the alternative offered by his judges. He did this, according to Plato, because he firmly believed in the immortality of the soul, and the only way that he could convince his still incredulous disciples was by practical demonstration. He drank the deadly hemlock to prove to them that he did really believe that the soul existed as a separate entity apart from the body and prior to the body, and that, because he was not conscious of having done any grievous wrong, he could be quite certain that his soul would enjoy a beatific existence in the company of the gods because he had been a good and faithful slave to them. Slave is the right word ('chattel' is the word that Plato uses,[8] or, as Aristotle prefers to put it, 'an "ensouled" or living chattel',[9] or 'tool'[1]). But the gods are good masters and in them the blameless slave will find no longer masters but friends.[2]

Not all his disciples believed him because the common belief at the time was that 'when the soul leaves the body, it no longer exists anywhere, and that on the day when a man dies it is destroyed and set free; and as soon as it leaves the body . . . it flies away, dispersed like a breath or like smoke, and it is no longer anything or anywhere'.[3]

This common belief the Greeks did not find cheering, for it could only mean the total destruction and disintegration of the ego, the ultimate horror of man as individual in whatever part of the world he may live. Socrates' disciples wanted to believe that his intuition of personal survival was true, particularly as it was preached to them by him, for it meant that the just and

8. Plato, *Phaedo*, 62B.   9. Aristotle, *Politics*, 1.2.4 (1253b 33).
1. Id., *Nicomachean Ethics*, 8.11.6 (1061b 4).
2. Plato, *Phaedo*, 69E.   3. Ibid., 70A.

good would be released into a heaven where they, though 'chattels', would be graciously accepted as friends by their masters, the gods. So too the average Buddhist, both in the Buddha's day and now, looks for a happier and more prosperous incarnation in a future life as a reward for the merits he has won for himself in his present existence. He does not yet aspire to Nirvana because he cannot understand how what he has always regarded as essentially himself, the ego, 'the "I" that works in the world, thinks about itself, observes its own reactions and talks about itself is not the true "I" . . . [and that it] is doomed to disappear as completely as smoke from a chimney'.[4] No more could the disciples of Socrates: they did not realize that their own common belief was precisely what the Buddha had been preaching in India not so long ago, but not as a doctrine of despair but as the ultimate salvation and enlightenment. Even in India few could understand this austere doctrine, but at least the premises from which they started made it easier for them to understand: for they believed and had believed for centuries in reincarnation.

With *his* disciples Socrates had to start from the very beginning. These young men, whose morals the State had accused him of trying to corrupt, admired him first and foremost as the most brilliant dialectician of his day. Perhaps they did not know the other side of his philosophy, the seamy side that was all mixed up with secret rites and what would now be called 'theosophy', his deep commitment (if we are to believe Plato) to the Dionysian 'orgies' with all their unseemly drunkenness and crazy ecstasy. Perhaps they did not know of his visionary experiences which transmitted him to other worlds, some too marvellously beautiful for human sight to bear, some so frightful that it would have been better had they never been seen. That he had come to believe in the transmigration of souls they probably did know since the Pythagoreans had long proclaimed it, and this, to them, would

4. Thomas Merton, *New Seeds of Contemplation* (Burns & Oates, London, 1962), p. 6.

have been consolation indeed, for one and all of them were virtuous, at least as Socrates understood virtue.

But we would do well to say goodbye to Socrates since we can never be quite sure that the amazing visionary experiences Plato attributes to him are really his rather than Plato's own; and I have often had an uneasy suspicion that the illness which Phaedo attributes to him in the dialogue named after him and which prevented him from seeing his beloved master pass from the prison-house of his ageing body into the world of ideal Beauty, Goodness and Truth, was not perhaps a diplomatic illness, so outrageous do many of the utterances attributed to him appear to be.

Whatever the truth about Socrates may have been, there can surely be no doubt that Plato had a thoroughly divided personality: he was at war with himself. And the proof of it would seem to be that this is the very subject with which his last, longest, and surely nastiest dialogue, the *Laws*, begins: 'Every man is at war with himself.'[5] This, indeed, is the very nature of our human condition, 'and the victory of self over self is primary and the best of all victories just as the defeat of self by self is the most disgraceful and the worst. And this means that there is war within each of us against ourselves.'[6]

This, of course, is a truism in most religions. We find it in Buddhism, where we are told that 'the self is the lord of self', yet that even for a man whose 'self' is subdued such a lord is 'hard to come by'.[7] In the Hindu tradition the author of the *Bhagavad-Gītā* (6.6) puts it the other way round: 'Self is the friend to the self of him whose self is by the self subdued; but for the man bereft of self self will act as an enemy indeed.' Perhaps this does not sound very sensible, since though it is implied that there must be two 'selves' in man, it is not at all clear *what* they are. This seems to be typical of Hindu imprecision. Plato, at least, speaks of a higher and a lower soul,

5. Plato, *Laws*, Bk. I, 626D.
6. Ibid., 626E. Cf. *Republic*, 430E ff.   7. *Dhammapada*, 160.

the first of which he identifies with reason and/or the contemplative intellect, since even he does not always make this distinction clear. What he does, however, imply is that there is a *third* soul which is both the mid-point between the 'higher' and the 'lower' and the field of battle on which they fight. This field of battle is the meeting-point, the common ground, the *same* thing (above, p. 129) to both the warring factions. It is the Brahman of the Hindus, which is 'ever the same' in all beings, being the principle of eternity which can never change. This 'sameness' cannot be affected by any of the opposites, and so the man who, having realized this 'sameness', this identity with what is eternal in himself, sees everything else as the 'same' as himself, cannot be affected by pleasure or pain, victory or defeat, nor, for that matter, can he be affected by good or evil, for they are suffused with that Brahman which is ever the same. This Plato seems to have realized himself, for, in the *Phaedo*, he tells us that no soul can be greater or less than any other because, before it entered the body, it 'existed just as that essence exists which is called the essence of "what is" '.[8] True, you cannot say that it is simply 'what is': that is the ultimate step that only Parmenides dared to take in Greece. But you can say that 'it is most like the divine, the immortal, the "intelligible" (*noēton*), the uniform, the indissoluble, and that which is always most like itself in these respects'.[9] In other words it is an immortal, indestructible, and timeless monad, a very 'god', suffused in Absolute Beauty, Absolute Goodness, and Absolute Truth. Its union with the body is unnatural and must be dissolved.

In India this was precisely what the Sānkhya philosophers taught (pp. 112ff.), except that, while affirming that these spiritual monads must be timeless and eternal, they refused to admit that they could have any attributes at all, whether good or evil: it was only their association with matter and its three inherent qualities of 'purity', 'energy', and 'lethargy' that lent them the appearance of virtue and vice. In themselves they

8. Plato, *Phaedo*, 92D and ff.   9. Ibid, 80B.

had no attribute whatever: each one of them simply *is*, isolated, autarkic, and aloof.

As to matter, this was simply the world of never-ending change in which the three basic qualities were for ever combining with each other and then separating out again, forming both physical and moral organisms which never remained the same; for the whole infinite complex of matter was shot through by the law of *karma*, what we would call the law of cause and effect, which operated both on the physical and the moral plane with mechanical precision. Matter was not evil in itself: far from it, it was, as Teilhard de Chardin was to say millenniums later, 'the combined essence of all evil and all goodness'.[1] Admittedly, two of the basic qualities of matter bound the spiritual monad to the relentless wheel of Time, but the noblest of them, 'purity', 'goodness' (call it what you will), was there to help spirit to return once again to his splendid isolation. Hence to rail against matter, as Plato and the early Buddhists did, was ungracious, ungrateful, and silly. Poor old Brother Ass, as St Francis called the body, well, he might be stupid, but he really did try to do his best, and it was both wicked and perverse of his rider, the soul, to try to beat him into submission, as Plato sometimes did – as well he might since a donkey is not a living creature in its own right but simply the 'chattel' or property of its owner, just as man was a chattel of the gods, or as Plato was to say later when he had become thoroughly disgusted with the vast majority of his fellow-men, their 'puppet',[2] the doll with which these entrancing beings played.

This was not the way of the Indian Sānkhya. Certainly it was a misfortune that spirit ever got mixed up with matter, but matter could be kindly. She was vain no doubt and liked flirting with these pure, pure spirits who seemed to be so unaccountably fascinated by her, but once they had acknowl-

1. Pierre Teilhard de Chardin, *Hymn of the Universe* (Collins, London, and Harper, New York, 1965), p. 60.
2. Plato, *Laws*, Bk. I, 644D.

edged her charms she was perfectly prepared to send them off
to the eternal hermitage where they belonged. In any case, it
was all play-acting really. Matter put on the play, and it
might be a tragedy which would serve to purge spirit by the
emotions of terror and compassion (Aristotle's prescription).
This indeed was necessary, for pure spirit is far too pure to
have any such emotions himself. After all he cannot have
emotions since emotions are attributes, and since he has none,
he has to borrow them from matter, though he will be silly
enough at the time to think they are his own. Or matter may
prefer to dance for him, to beguile his passage through her
unstable abode. Then, when he is tired of it all, she will bow
herself out as any nice dancing-girl might.

'As a dancing-girl stops dancing once she has shown herself
to the audience, so does matter stop once she has shown herself to spirit. She finds all kinds of ways to help him, though
he is quite incapable of helping anyone; and although it is she
who has all the attributes while he has none at all, she works
for his sake though he himself has no purpose whatever. I
really think there is nothing more generous than matter. It is
enough for her simply to have been seen: then she will never
come within the range of spirit's sight again.'[3]

No such generosity was shown to matter by the god Plato
from his bodily prison. For it is the body itself that is the
enemy, filling us not only with passions, desires, and phobias
but also with all kinds of daydreams, ceaselessly chattering
away and leaving us no time for the sacred science called
philosophy. Worse still, it seems that poor old Brother Ass is
also responsible for war and for the acquisitive drive that has
produced capitalism.[4] So the true philosopher must behave as
if he were dead while yet alive.[5] ('Death was Charlie's trip',
you may remember.)[6] Crucify the body, then, as Charlie

3. Ishvarakrishna, *Sāmkhya-kārikā*, 59–61.
4. Plato, *Phaedo*, 66C–D, etc., etc.
5. Ibid., 67E.
6. See above, p. 67.

144

Manson crucified himself. If you do not, it will crucify you and there will literally be hell to pay.

'Each pleasure or pain has nails, and nails [the soul] to the body, pins it down, and makes it corporeal, so that it believes the things are true which the body says are true. For because it has the same beliefs and pleasures as the body it is compelled, I think, to adopt the same habits and mode of life, and can never depart in purity to the other world, but must always go away contaminated with the body; and so it sinks quickly into another body again and grows into it like seed that is sown. Hence it has no part in what is divine and pure and uniform.'[7]

Reincarnation, the wickedness of matter, the eternal beatitude of all those holy souls who had for ever cast aside the filth of the body, the appalling tortures of the damned, hatred of the common people who were too stupid to appreciate the nobility of the philosophic calling – Plato swallowed the lot. Why? Because he had *seen*. Hence he could say in all earnestness that the only people who had come to philosophize correctly were the Bacchi, the followers of the ecstatic and often orgiastic cult of the wine-god Dionysus.[8]

Whether or not Plato or his master Socrates was actually initiated into a mystery cult which taught reincarnation and the immortality of a soul which was of its nature a stranger to this world does not really matter very much. What does matter is that Plato clearly had visions of intense power and beauty which he attributes to non-human entities and which have nothing whatever to do with philosophy as normally understood. Most people are reasonably contented to be embodied: Plato could never be happy till he was 'en-godded' (*entheos*).[9] And it must have been when he was 'en-godded' that he *saw* those extraordinary 'myths' which illumine his dialogues with an almost supernatural light. He was literally enchanted and

7. Plato, *Phaedo*, 83D–E (H. N. Fowler's translation, slightly modified).
8. Ibid., 69C. 9. Id., *Phaedrus*, 255B; cf. 244B.

possessed, and his myths resemble nothing so much as the visions of William Blake – or a highly successful trip on LSD.

Perhaps the most powerful of these as well as the most 'psychedelic' is the vision attributed to Socrates, which he is alleged to have seen during those last hours before he drank the hemlock – those solemn hours so movingly described in the *Phaedo* but at which Plato was not himself present. As with Aldous Huxley and no doubt thousands of other 'positive' trips on psychedelic drugs, Socrates was transported to another world where colours were unbelievably brighter and more vivid. 'There the whole earth is of such colours, and they are much brighter and purer than ours; for one part is purple of wonderful beauty, and one is golden, and one is white, whiter than chalk or snow, and the earth is made up of the other colours likewise, and they are more in number and more beautiful than those which we see here.' So too the trees, the fruit, and the flowers shimmered with unearthly splendour and the common stones of the mountains had the lustre of our own most precious stones. In this more than psychedelic paradise dwell the gods who hold converse with the blessed and together they see 'the sun and moon and stars as they really are',[1] that is, an absolute Beauty and the absolute Good.[2]

The description of hell is more confused, as is only natural since matter itself is a source of confusion. There are rivers and lakes of mud and fire, among them the Acherousian lake where 'the souls of most of the dead go and, after remaining there for the appointed time . . . are sent back to be born again as living beings'.[3] The nature of their reincarnation is, of course, conditioned by their conduct in former lives. The violent, the drunken, and the glutton will, for reasons best known to Plato, be reincarnated as donkeys 'and suchlike beasts' (poor Brother Ass), the unjust, the tyrant, and the robber as wolves, hawks or kites, while those 'who, by nature

---

1. Id., *Phaedo*, 110C–111C.   3. Id., *Phaedo*, 113A.
2. Id., *Republic*, 516B, 517B.

or habit, have practised the social and civic virtues called
sobriety and justice but without the benefit of philosophy or
intellect (*nous*)' will be reborn 'into some such social and gentle
species as that of bees or wasps or ants'[4] – which seems appropriate enough. The conscientious bureaucrats who have
spent their lives regimenting human beings into a uniform
type, since it is obvious that the State must, so far as is
possible, imitate the totally uniform and One, will be rewarded
by being allowed to join an insect society so perfectly socialized
by Nature herself that they too may settle down as clockwork
automata, thereby laying down the burden of coercion[5] that
they had so nobly shouldered on earth. Today they might
equally well or better be born in the Soviet Union where at
least the workers have not yet developed the habit of starving
their bureaucrats to death as does the good proletarian worker
bee the fat bureaucratic drone.

The dangers of applying Plato's particular vision of the
One, which is at the same time the Beautiful and the Good, to
politics have already been expounded at great length by Sir
Karl Popper in his brilliant destruction of the myth of Plato
himself in *The Open Society and its Enemies* (Volume 1, *The
Spell of Plato*). Much as I should like to say something about
that ludicrously sinister gerontocracy presented to us by
Plato in the *Laws*, with its Dionysian Chorus of drunken old
men gazing up at the One and framing laws the sole object of
which is to homogenize the many (that is, you and me) in
order to harmonize us with the One, not to mention the
Nocturnal Council composed of more old men plus their
middle-aged boy-friends whose duty it is to watch over the
divine laws (and incidentally over each other), I must refrain.
What I can scarcely help doing, however, is to say something
about the great man's mysticism, its origins, and its goal. How
often have we been told by Christians that Plato arrived at a
'truer' conception of God because he realized, long before
St John, that the love of God was indeed possible, whereas the

4. Ibid., 81E–82B.   5. Id., *Laws*, Bk. II, 660A, etc., etc.

coldly rational Aristotle had roundly said that though we might aspire towards God, God was so busy thinking about himself that he had no time for the likes of you and me. That this seems to me to be quite untrue is one of the reasons I have attempted to write this book at all.

Plato wrote a lot about love. One of his dialogues, the *Symposium*, is entirely devoted to the subject, while a second, the *Phaedrus*, though purporting to be about rhetoric, is overwhelmingly devoted to the theme of love. Whichever was written first is of little consequence since the *Symposium*, which deals with love both human and divine, follows logically upon the *Phaedrus* where the love depicted is 'divinely human', that love of man for boy which the Greeks call *paiderasteia* – pederasty, meaning literally 'the love for boys' – but which we have come to call Platonic love after its most outstanding practitioner.

There can be no doubt about the reality of the 'spell' of Plato. He is a wonderful writer and both the *Phaedrus* and the *Symposium* are among the best things he ever wrote. The problem is: how *can* the same man have written these two delightful dialogues, so brimful of the love of earthly beauty and earthly life, as well as those many other dialogues which condemn matter and the body, which is the prison of the soul, as being the source of all evil including those purely spiritual evils like avarice and envy which man does *not* inherit from his animal forebears? The *Phaedrus*, I think, will give us the clue to the solution.

It is perfectly clear, on rereading the *Phaedrus*, that 'Socrates' is madly in love with the young Phaedrus. The dialogue is, however, so intensely vivid that one cannot help feeling that Plato is speaking out of personal experience. He is deeply and passionately in love with a young friend who is studying rhetoric under Lysias, the acknowledged master of that art in his day. Phaedrus, however, not only admires Lysias but seems to be strangely attached to him. 'Socrates' is jealous. He persuades the not too reluctant pupil to read him his master's discourse on love, and has little trouble in demolishing Lysias' arguments. He then points out with a good deal of satisfaction that they are trite. Lysias had, in fact, argued that the young could derive more profit from professors who were not given to falling in love with their pupils than vice versa. Lovers, he says, are mentally sick and quite unable to control themselves: they are corroded with jealousy and therefore keep their young friends from associating with anyone rich or clever enough to seduce them away from themselves: they are not really interested in their boy-friends as persons but merely as a means to attain their own selfish pleasures. As the boy grows older and his youthful beauty fades, they will grow tired of him, transfer their attentions to others now more beautiful and younger than he, and deeply resent it if the discarded object of their affection should ask for or even expect the favours they had lavished on him in the good old days.

All this 'Socrates' dismisses as commonplace and hopelessly 'square' – just the sort of thing you might expect from a professional barrister (which Lysias was). He ridicules Lysias' apparent detachment and makes it quite clear not only that he himself is passionately in love with Phaedrus (since it is unusual to call even one's best friend 'my darling and truly golden [boy]',[6] let alone 'dear Eros',[7] identifying the boy with the god of passionate love himself), but also that he is an inspired prophet, inebriated by a divine madness (*mania*) which is the source of the greatest benefits to man. This madness is the very opposite of 'sobriety', 'sanity', or 'temperance' (as the Greek word *sōphrosunē* has been transmuted into English via a clumsy Latin translation),[8] elsewhere one of the four cardinal Platonic virtues, the others being wisdom, justice, and courage. This being so, it will never be accepted by the average intellectual (*deinos*) but only by the truly wise, for the wise man must not only be a competent dialectician but 'engodded' and therefore truly divine.

6. Id., *Phaedrus*, 235E.   7. Ibid., 257A.   8. Ibid., 244A.

'Socrates' then proceeds to lecture the fascinated Phaedrus on the now familiar lines: the soul is in itself divine and a stranger to the body; it moves of itself, being moved by nothing else – ungenerated, beautiful, wise and good. The soul of man, however, can best be likened to a chariot drawn by two horses, with a charioteer to guide and restrain them. The charioteer is the contemplative intellect which contemplates the absolute Beauty, Goodness, and Wisdom above him. But the two horses are of unequal nature, the one being good and docile, while the other is fierce and refractory. A good charioteer will succeed in keeping the horses in equilibrium, but an incompetent one will be thrown off his balance, and so chariot, charioteer, and horses all come tumbling down to earth, losing their wings in the process, dragged down and down by the coarse nature of that refractory beast.

Now, in heaven, apart from the highest immortal essence which is absolute Wisdom, absolute Beauty, and absolute Good, there are also other archetypes of all the virtues, and indeed of all the good things we find on earth. But the fallen soul, unless it happens to have landed in the body of a philosopher, on looking round, can find nothing that reminds him of the eternal realm from which he has fallen except beauty – the beauty of human beings. If the soul has no part in philosophy it will be dragged towards the beautiful form it sees by the unruly horse which is all insolence and puffed up with pride: enflamed by what it sees, it is filled with the lust to possess and procreate, or, if the form is a boy, it gives itself up to unnatural lust.[9] If the thing of beauty has the form of a lovely boy and if the soul is that of a philosopher or one who is a natural lover of boys (*paiderastēsas*)[1] and of a philosophical turn of mind, it will remember the heavenly beauty it contemplated before its fall. The now embodied soul of the philosopher-pederast will be torn in two, dragged down by the evil horse to lust after and possess the beautiful boy, but restrained by the good one, who represents 'sobriety',

9. Ibid., 251A.   1. Ibid., 249A.

modesty, and 'true opinion', from committing so foul a deed. Torn between the two extremes of contemplation of beauty incarnate and the carnal desire to ravish and possess the 'en-godded' flesh, the philosopher's soul is thrown off its balance. At the sight of the boy a shock of recognition passes between the beauty that loves and the beauty that is loved, and the lover's soul boils over in an ecstasy of joyful pain. Separated from him, the 'en-godded' sage, inspired already by the divine madness that is yet the soul of wisdom, 'is perplexed and raves, and in this madness cannot sleep at night or remain in any one place by day. Filled with ungratified desire he rushes wherever he thinks he may see him who possesses Beauty. And when he sees him he is bathed in the waters of desire. The passages that were sealed up are opened, and the soul finds respite from the stings [of passion] and is eased of its pangs and tastes of the fruit of the sweetest pleasure available to it in present time. And so it will not willingly consent to be deprived of its beloved nor will it prefer anything to this beauteous boy, but it will forget mother, brothers, and all its comrades, neglect its property and care nothing for its loss, despise all the customs and decencies in which it had formerly taken pride, for it is now ready to be a slave and sleep wherever they will let it so long as it is as near as possible to its love.'[2]

The boy has become for the lover a true incarnation of the divine Beauty and is therefore worthy of divine honours. This may seem strange to us, however permissive our society may be, but it is interesting to note that the 'contemplation of boys' came to be accepted among the Sufis (as the Muslim mystics were called) of a later age who sought thereby to contemplate uncreated beauty through what they considered to be its most perfect projection on earth. Other techniques included singing and dancing, both of which were regarded as means for reproducing the uniformity and harmony which is the best that mortal men can do to rebuild a likeness of the supernatural One which is the goal of all their aspiration. The boy for them

2. Ibid., 251E–252A.

was like the 'spiritual monads' in the Sānkhya system in India. Like matter in that system, the Sufis were content to see him and be seen by him and, once their contemplation had been gratified, to withdraw in gratitude and humble veneration. Such was the theory of it at least: the practice could be very different.

This was not the way of Plato: for the 'pederast' is also a philosopher and, dazed though he may be by the divine madness, intellect must of necessity resume its leading role. It will not do to choose just any good-looking boy because he happens to have a pretty face, for this would amount to letting oneself be dragged off course by that wicked horse. He must confine himself to one whose outward beauty is matched by a corresponding malleability of soul. Accordingly, 'each man chooses his love from among the beautiful according to his character, and builds him up and adorns him like a statue as being a very god to himself, so that he can honour him and perform secret rites for him'.[3]

There is, I suppose, nothing particularly startling about this, for this is precisely the point of image-worship in India. The image is worshipped simply because it is the place that the god has chosen as his own particular home from which he can, pre-eminently, manifest himself to the faithful. So too the comely human boy represents the philosopher-pederast's god, his *ishta-devatā* or 'deity of his choice', as the Hindus put it, whom he may and should bow down to and worship. But the boy is not only divine, he is still a boy. And boys will be boys; and Plato, more than anyone, more even than the Jesuits, realized that boys must be indoctrinated to become what in eternity they are, not only perfectly beautiful but perfectly virtuous, and not only virtuous but virtuous in the manner of the philosopher's 'deity of his choice': they must be *made* to conform to Plato's own Idea of the Good. 'By persuading the boy [that is, if necessary, coercing him, as Plato makes perfectly clear in the *Laws*] and by attuning him to the wavelength of the god,

3. Ibid., 252D–E.

they lead him on to behave as the god behaves and to conform himself to his form.'[4] What happens, then, is this: the philosopher-pederast has recognized 'the deity of his choice' in the person of a handsome boy. The boy's divine soul shines forth through the beauty of his face and the grace of his young body, but, being still a boy, he does not know that he is divine, only his philosopher-lover knows; and so it is his sacred duty not only to bring the boy to a realization of his own divinity, but also to make him see the same divinity in his lover. In the boy the divine beauty manifests itself in bodily form through a kind of physical electricity, and this is transformed by the lover into a kind of spiritual electricity by the divine intellect that indwells the philosopher-lover's soul. The boy, then, can be 'willingly coerced'[5] into realizing his true godlike self through and in the same divine 'idea', 'form', or 'archetype' of absolute Beauty which indwells both himself and his lover.

The process by which this self-realization is brought about is slow and sometimes painful. The refractory horse is never far away, dragging the lover's soul towards the morass of carnal lust. Things get much worse, however, when the divine child himself falls in love with the lover, and sex begins to rear its ugly head. This, he realizes, is not just friendship but something uncanny he has never experienced before. He cannot bear to be separated from his lover and endures agonies when he is away. 'Like the lover, though less strongly, he yearns to see him, touch him, kiss him, and lie down with him.' And, as you might expect, one thing very soon leads to another (*poiei to meta touto tachu tauta*). Sure enough, the lover's refractory horse has a word or two to say to him and demands some little enjoyment in return for all the pains it has had to endure, 'but the boy's one doesn't have to say anything, and [the boy himself], bursting with passion and quite helpless against it, hugs and kisses his lover, clinging to him as to one who is madly (*sphodra*) fond of him. And so, when they lie down together, he would be in no position to refuse any favour

4. Ibid., 253B.   5. Cf. Plato, *Laws*, Bk II, 670D.

his lover might ask of him, if *that* is what he wanted. But the other horse and the charioteer tense themselves against all this by resorting to the virtues of modesty and reason.'[6]

All this is not only legitimate but, as we would now say, a sacrament, for 'neither human wisdom nor the divine madness can confer upon man a greater good than this'.[7]

How does all this square with Plato's condemnation of what he himself calls an 'unnatural pleasure'?[8] His considered opinion is laid down in the work of his extreme old age, the *Laws*, where it seems clear that what he considers to be 'unnatural' vice is not homosexuality as such, let alone pederasty (the 'love of boys'), but what is technically known as sodomy, what he himself calls 'sowing unfertile seed in males'.[9] This, like adultery and fornication with females, should be punished by depriving a man of his right to hold any office of state.[1] Heterosexual practices are solely allowed for reproductive purposes.[2] Pederasty, that is the love of boys, however, is on an altogether different level, as we have seen, since it has in it an element of the divine. For Plato it would be a sacrilege to confuse this 'divine' love with the wholly carnal and 'unnatural' act of sodomy, for the pederastic lover is primarily a man of contemplation (*horōn*), only secondarily a lover (*erōn*). But though it may be doubtful whether the ageing author of the *Laws* would wholly have approved of the passionate scene so vividly described in the *Phaedrus*, he *does* concede that homosexual practices which stop short of sodomy should not only be permitted by the law if they are indulged in in private, but should also be regarded as honourable (*kalon*).[3] There can, of course, be no question of consenting adults, as in Great Britain today, since pederasty, as its very name implies, means that one of the parties should *not* be an adult.

6. Plato, *Phaedrus*, 255E–256A.   7. Ibid., 256B.
8. Ibid., 251A; cf. *Laws*, Bk. VIII, 836C, 841D.
9. Plato, *Laws*, Bk. VIII, 841D.   1. Ibid., 841E.
2. Plato, *Phaedrus*, 251A; *Laws*, Bk. VIII, 839A.
3. Id., *Laws*, Bk. VIII, 841B. In the *Republic* (403B) kissing only is permitted.

What form of homosexuality does Plato in fact authorize between his philosopher and his divine boy? The answer must surely be that it is what has been clinically described as the 'full-body technique', but apparently, stopping short of orgasm.[4] Given Plato's detailed description in the *Phaedrus*, and making full allowance for the timely intervention of 'modesty' and 'reason', this much would seem to be permitted.

This may still seem a bit 'far out' to us, but the Greeks never had a Victorian age and in Plato's time at least homosexual love was taken for granted and respected. Had this not been so, the tyrannicides, Harmodius and Aristogeiton, a 'Platonic' pair of lovers if ever there was one, would hardly have been 'canonized' as national heroes. For Plato pederasty with the right boy, at the proper time and place and given the right dispositions (as Aristotle would have insisted, had he thought these matters worthy of serious attention), was a sacrament of union which, in its own way, symbolized the oneness of Beauty itself, which was in its turn a facet of the absolute One.

That Plato did regard pederasty as a kind of 'holy communion' seems proved by the myth in the *Symposium*. The myth as told by 'Socrates' is not his own: he had heard it from a prophetess from Mantinea who had access to divine secrets. Love, she said, was an intermediary between God and mortal man, a great 'daemon' then, for it is the function of daemons, precisely, to fill the gaps that apparently yawn between the immortal and timeless world on the one hand and our own world of birth, death, growth and decay on the other. It is love, then, 'that unites the All with itself', and it is love too that operates in all religious and magical rites – in incantations, sacrifices, initiatory rites, and in magic itself.[5] The god himself was begotten by Resourcefulness on Penury. Hence he is rough, dirty, unshod, nameless, sleeping on the ground, having nowhere to lay his head. All this he inherits

4. Or so it would appear from *Symposium*, 218B–219E.
5. Plato, *Symposium*, 202E–203A.

from his mother. On his father's side, however, he is always ready to help the good and beautiful; he is resourceful, virile, and always up to some new trick. He practises philosophy, and, because of rather than in spite of this, he is a skilled magician and sorcerer. Neither mortal nor immortal, he blooms and fades only to rise again in his full vigour. So too, being neither wholly wise nor wholly ignorant, he must be a 'philosopher' ('one who loves wisdom' but can never reach it).[6] As such he must always long for what is good and for beatitude, and beatitude means precisely 'to possess the Good for ever'.[7]

But how, 'Socrates' asks, can one make use of love in order to possess oneself of the Good? The prophetess's answer is disconcerting: you must give birth in the good either in body or in soul; for giving birth in either sense assures you some kind of immortality. If you are one of the vulgar herd you will marry a wife and bring up a family. This is a good of a sort since you live on in your children and this is a faint imitation of immortality. And it is for the very same reason that men seek fame for themselves: they seek to live on in the memories of men, and this too is a form of immortality. It follows, then, that love, which aspires to the good, is really the unquenchable longing of mortal men for immortality. Carnal man turns to woman so that he may live on in his progeny, but spiritual man is pregnant with spiritual offspring which no woman can supply. To be pregnant with spiritual immortality is indeed an awesome thing, and in order to bring it to birth the philosopher must submit to a slow initiation at the hands of the prophetess of Love. The first step is that so vividly described in the *Phaedrus*, to find one beautiful boy and to conform him to the divine which indwells both himself and you. Then you must see beauty in all bodies, casting aside your former 'beloved disciple' as being of little worth. From there you must go on to perceive the beauty of the souls that indwell all bodies, and then, divesting yourself of all this in its turn, you

6. Ibid., 203C–204A.   7. Ibid., 206A.

must face the 'mighty ocean' of the Beautiful, and then 'in a flash' you will see 'a beauty that is of its very nature marvellous, . . . first as what eternally is, neither coming to be nor passing away, neither growing nor wasting away', then as Beauty beyond space and time, beyond all relation or division of any kind, beyond all definition and understanding, but 'Itself by itself and having the same form as itself, that which eternally is, while all other things of beauty participate in it but in such a way that when all other things come to be and are destroyed, it becomes neither greater nor less nor is it affected by anything'.[8]

This is your final goal, but it all began with the contemplation of and communion with the graceful body of an 'engodded' boy, through the love and possession of whom you will finally come to possess that uniquely beautiful One who is past all understanding. This ineffable wonder you will have seen because you had first learnt how 'to love a boy rightly' (*orthōs paiderastein*). How strange it all is, this 'perennial philosophy', which some strive to attain by orthodoxy ('right belief'), others by orthopraxis ('right practice'), while yet others, with Plato at their head, win through to it by 'orthopederasty' ('the right way to love a boy').

Is something wrong? one cannot help asking. The fact that Plato (or 'Socrates') should himself choose to appear in the combined role of philosopher and magician-pederast is neither more nor less shocking than the religious practices attributed to (and claimed by) some 'left-hand' Tantric sects in India.[9] In the context of Greek rationalism it *is* shocking, for Plato seems to be trying to hold two positions at once: firstly he makes a sharp distinction between body and soul, and secondly he makes use of the body and, if we are to believe the *Phaedrus*, of 'full-body' homosexual practices, as a means to achieve contemplation of absolute and wholly discarnate beauty. From the Western 'either/or' point of view this amounts to intellectual dishonesty, but from the Indian 'both/

8. Ibid., 210E–211B.   9. Above, p. 101.

and' point of view it is not only commonplace but the very foundation of every kind of Yoga technique. Whatever the metaphysical theory behind any particular Yoga may be, the principle of the technique remains the same: so far from denying any reality to the body, you *use* it by diverting it from its natural animal functions and forcing it to behave in a way that is unnatural to it in order to make it play its own part in divorcing itself from spirit with which it is temporarily united in what is, at a deeper level, a still more unnatural alliance. As in jujitsu, you use your enemy's strength in order to defeat him. This is as true of shamanism as it is of Yoga: both assume that man is an immortal spirit imprisoned in a mortal frame: he is two things, not one. It is, then, the function of the immortal element, while still in this body, to control and direct it, if necessary, by main force. This means that man's goal can only be to dehumanize himself: he must convince himself that he is a god – or a devil. Pascal was only half right when he said that man is half angel and half beast, and that if he tries to identify himself entirely with the angel, he may find that the beast (Plato's refractory horse) will turn and rend him and that he will finish by being wholly bestial. Plato's Muslim counterpart, Al-Ghazālī, having been brought up as a Muslim and therefore within the framework of a religious orthodoxy in which the Devil played an important part, saw that man is not only an angel and a beast but also a devil: and the Devil's prime function is to deceive. As Plato himself knew, absolute Truth can never be fully understood by man: he can only contemplate it at a distance, guided (or so he believed) by 'right' opinion or 'right' belief (*doxa*). But what is 'right' belief? The history of philosophy from Heraclitus to Hegel shows that it means no more than that 'what I believe on my own authority is true'. This is dangerous: and modern linguistic philosophy is right to prick these philosophical bubbles, but once the bubbles congeal into *religious* solids mere philosophers are quite powerless to do anything about it.

Plato tried to fuse human wisdom (*sōphrosunē*) with the

divine madness, and the result was a fusion of the mutually exclusive systems of Heraclitus and Parmenides with more than a dash of shamanism thrown in. In such a system, which is in effect the 'perennial philosophy' that 'All is One and One is All', all things must be ultimately both good and evil. As we have seen, in Plato's case the contemplation of the One logically, that is, according to 'right' or 'correct' opinion or belief, resulted in the ruthless indoctrination and coercion of the many from the cradle to the grave. Plato's Republic as finally revised in the *Laws* has been almost perfectly realized in the Soviet Union, where 'wrong' or 'incorrect' opinion is either a criminal offence or a case for psychiatric 'reform'.

In Plato's case, if not in that of the Soviet Union, this passion for indoctrination is a venial sin, but it springs from the one mortal sin that has, ever since the 'Fall', poisoned the life of mankind – the desire not only to be but to have. Plato had this sin in an extreme form. Whether it was a boy or the absolute Good and absolute Beauty which are at the same time the absolute One, his attitude was always the same: he saw the beautiful, and he fell down in adoration, but, having adored, he immediately set about winning the beloved object for himself by absorbing him into himself and remaking him into the likeness of himself. This is the message of the *Phaedrus* despite all that clever talk about how the true lover can never be jealous (he has no need to be since his beloved is already bewitched). Plato's ultimate aim in pederasty, as in philosophy, is to *possess* the object of his love. He sins against the second Buddhist commandment, 'This is not mine'. He is ravished by the beauty of his boy and rewards him by 'ravishing' him intellectually in his turn. Sometimes he seems to do the same to the Absolute, for his God is the 'God of the philosophers and scientists', who was *not* the god that brought tears of joy to Pascal on that memorable night of Monday, 23 November 1654. For Pascal's God is capable not only of ravishing you with his beauty but also of ravishing you – raping you, that is – by the sheer force of his relentless will.

You cannot possess God: you cannot 'have' him like Plato had his lovely teenage boy. You can only be 'had' by God, and that is something Plato could never understand. Plato's One was in reality a projection upwards of Plato's own ideas, just as his ideal state as depicted in the *Laws* was its downward projection. Above, the utterly pure and aloof God of Marcion, the second-century heretic, whom Tertullian so fiercely attacked: below, the enforced uniformity of modern Soviet man.

No, it is not the ghost of Heraclitus nor yet the phantom of Parmenides that bestrides the earth today: it is rather the spectre of Plato, who used the ideas of both to provide a model for a perfect clockwork state where All should be One under the guidance of uniquely enlightened seers, and who has, indirectly, that is, through the thought of like-minded Hindus, bewitched with his divine madness so many of the well-to-do who might otherwise have been reincarnated as bees. Charles Manson, too, fell under this fateful spell and dealt out summary justice that might have surprised the Nocturnal Synod of Plato's weird Republic but could scarcely have shocked their minds, so thoroughly conditioned were they to equate shock with sin.

5

OUR FATHER ARISTOTLE

'All is One and One is All.' This is the eternal refrain of the 'perennial philosophy', the truth of which became translucently apparent to Aldous Huxley as he lay bemused under the influence of mescalin, the distilled juice of the divine cactus. This is the philosophy that has been summoned to testify to the 'truth' of every kind of religious syncretism, used to eviscerate all the *positive* beliefs of each and every religious tradition, used by Engels to turn the basically economic thinking of Marx into a new kind of 'mysticism and incomprehensible transcendentalism',[1] used by Teilhard de Chardin to transform Christianity from its roots in atoning ('at-one-ing') self-sacrifice in the most literal sense of that word into a Platonic mishmash in which 'holy' matter is alternately worshipped and spurned, used again with ruthless logic by Charlie Manson to butcher and hack to pieces those shadowy reflections of the One who were deluded enough to plead for their silly little individual lives before he plunged them into the ineffable Oneness of the All. And all this in the name of a 'philosophy', the slogan of which ('All is One') is literally meaningless.

It was, of course, Aristotle who first pricked this huge, inflated bubble. And it would be for this one inestimable service alone that he richly deserves to be hailed by all who care for truth without a capital letter, rather than Platonic 'Truth' with that tell-tale capital, as our father, friend, and guide.

It would, of course, be ridiculous to pretend that Aristotle was not himself interested in the 'truth', that is, the ultimate

1. Frederick Engels, *Dialectics of Nature* (E.T., Moscow, 1954), p. 91.

reality that lies at the heart of all appearances. He was – almost passionately so. But he knew as well as Plato – and in practice a good deal better – that all that even the best philosopher could do, even the 'Shakespeare of science' as Iris Murdoch so oddly calls him, was to present what he had come to believe to be true in as intelligible a way as possible.

As to the One and the All he has this to say, and, for our present purposes, it must suffice:

'Now since the term "being" (*to on*, "what is") can be used in many ways, the most pertinent question with which to begin will be: *how* those who assert that all things are one, understand this proposition. Do they mean that "all things" are one substance (*ousia*, "being-ness"), or are they thinking in terms of "How many?" or "What sort of"? Or, again, are they asserting that all things are *one* substance (as one man or one horse or one soul) or in terms of "What sort of [one]"? – For this too is a "one" – as, for example, "white" or "hot" or any other quality of this kind [all being one in so far as they are white or hot or whatever]. For there is all the difference between these various propositions and all are impossible to maintain.'[2]

Logically, of course, Aristotle is absolutely right. How can 'all things' be 'one' in *any* sense? Nor does it help if you substitute 'the All' in the singular for 'all things', since 'the All' is a possible answer to the question 'How much?' For instance, you ask me, 'How much do you want?' and I answer, 'The lot'. Thus 'the All' or 'the lot' is what we call a 'quantity', which is the English transliteration of the Latin *quantitas*, which is a translation of Aristotle's much more direct *to poson*, 'the "how much?"' But then Latin, poor language that it is, has, like Sanskrit, no definite article with the result that the English-speaking world which derives nearly all its abstract nouns from Latin seldom knows what it is really talking about.

Again what has quantity or size (that is, anything about which you can ask the question 'How many?' or 'How much?')

2. Aristotle, *Physics*, 185a 21–27.

must be infinitely divisible; and what is divisible cannot be the absolute One.

Here we must stop, for to follow up Aristotle's arguments and to try to explain his marvellously complicated yet beautifully clear way of thinking, defining, qualifying the definition, distinguishing, and then distinguishing again among the distinctions already made, would take us much too far afield and end up by reducing the unfortunate reader to tears or just plain boredom; for, according to Aristotle, even the absolute Good can be 'a bore'.[3]

We must, however, quote Aristotle's own conclusion about this vexed and vexing question of the One and the many since it is basic to his whole way of thought. 'On this point, indeed,' he says, '[previous philosophers] were already getting into difficulties and had to admit that the One *is* the many – as if it were inadmissible for the same thing to be *both* the One *and* the many, provided, of course, that they are not diametrically opposed; for the One is one either potentially or actually.'[4]

Thus Aristotle can think both in terms of 'both/and' *and* in terms of 'either/or'; and the key to this paradox is supplied by those magical and essentially Aristotelian terms, 'potentiality' and 'actuality'. Perhaps, then, if Aristotle is the intellectual father of the West, he is also, by proxy, stepfather of the East.

Aristotle differs from Plato in that his method was essentially scientific. Given the time when he lived and the very rudimentary stage that science had then reached, he was the first Western philosopher to apply, so far as was possible, Professor Monod's now famous 'principle of objectivity'. Unlike Professor Monod, however, he realized that there were certain factors in human behaviour that eluded purely scientific enquiry: among these was ethics. In the physical sciences, however, the principle of objectivity must rule, for it is the sign of a bad scientist to stick to any view he may hold if new evidence turns up to refute him. This point he

3. Id., *Nicomachean Ethics*, 8.6.4 (1158a 25). Greek *lupēron*, more accurately, perhaps, 'distressing'.   4. Id., *Physics*, 186a 1–3.

makes clearly after his discussion on the habits of bees, whose behaviour fascinated him. 'But', he quite rightly and modestly says, 'the facts have not been sufficiently ascertained; but if at any future time they are ascertained, then we must believe the [new evidence supplied by] the senses rather than theories. As to theories, well, we should believe them too provided that their conclusions are in accordance with the [newly discovered] phenomena.'[5]

It cannot be said, then, that Aristotle was ever wilfully disloyal to the principle of objectivity which must be strictly observed in the exact sciences so long as he was dealing with purely physical matters. That his geocentric view of the universe was unquestionably accepted for centuries is no fault of his, for he is no more responsible for what Aristotelians were to do with his essentially empirical thought than is Marx for what the Marxists have done to him. Had he been alive today he would have been somewhat pained to find Pierre Teilhard de Chardin denouncing his allegedly 'static' view of the universe while extolling a dynamic one which, he claimed, was more in accordance with modern science. On a closer inspection of Teilhard's work he might have been amused to find that Teilhard was in fact reaffirming his own teleological view of the universe *against* the considered opinion of the scientific establishment.

It has always been something of a mystery what Teilhard learnt (if anything) at his Jesuit theological seminary. He *must*, I suppose, have read Aquinas, but it is quite clear that he never bothered to read Aquinas's master in philosophy, *the* Philosopher, as Aquinas rightly and reverently calls him, that is, of course, Aristotle himself. Had he done so, he would have realized that Aristotle was an evolutionist before his time, though, like Teilhard himself, not of the Darwinian species but the Lamarckian one. For Aristotle took as his point of departure the observed fact of change, and the analysis of change and the classification of the various types of change

5. Id., *Generation of Animals*, 3.10 (760b 30).

were the subject-matter of all his physical treatises. Like
Teilhard's, his whole approach was teleological, that is to say,
he believed that the universe had a purpose and that it was all
the time growing into its own perfection: 'Action for an end
[lit. "the 'for the sake of something' "] exists in things which
come to be and are in nature.'[6] And again: 'God and Nature
make nothing to no purpose.'[7]

God or nature: so here we are again at the old identification
which the earliest Greek philosophers had made when they
broke with the old gods of Homer and Hesiod, the same
identification which runs throughout the Upanishads and
was made explicit in the West by Spinoza, the god 'who does
not speak and has no care'.[8] Has Aristotle really nothing more
to offer than this? We shall see.

So interested was Aristotle in the end (*tel-os*) and fulfilment
(*en-tel-echeia*, 'entelechy') of all things that he never seriously
interested himself in their beginning. The Greeks of his time
all assumed that the universe was eternal: it had always existed
in some form though it never remained the same. If pressed
on the subject of creation, Aristotle would probably have
replied that if you insisted that there was a beginning, it was
up to you to prove it. Supposing, however, you had proved it,
then perhaps we could say that 'in the beginning' there was
matter only, one in the sense that it is the substratum without
the existence of which nothing at all could ever come to be,
but many in the sense that, though in itself it is so indefinite
that it might be considered as Not-being rather than Being, it
is nonetheless 'a substance (*ousia*, "being-ness") or very nearly
so'[9] since it is pure potentiality, that is to say, it can be transformed into absolutely anything. In itself 'it has no *separate*
existence but is always bound up with a contrariety from which
the so-called elements come into existence'.[1]

The elements, for the ancient Greeks as for the ancient

6. Id., *Physics*, 199a 8.　　7. Id., *On the Heavens*, 1.4 (271a 34).
8. *Chāndogya* Upanishad, 3.14.3.　　9. Aristotle, *Physics*, 192a 6.
1. Id., *Coming to Be and Passing Away*, 329a 25–7.

Hindus, were fire, air, water, and earth; and the whole physical universe was thought to be a more or less complex combination of these. But the elements were themselves complex, each being composed of two factors drawn from the even more primary pairs of opposites: the hot and the cold, the wet and the dry, fire being the combination of the hot and the dry, water of the cold and the wet, and so on. Primary matter, then, is totally indefinite; but without it nothing that is clearly definable, like the four elements, can come to be. It is very, very like the Chinese Tao:

> The Way that can be told is not an Unvarying Way;
> The names that can be named are not unvarying names.
> It was from the Nameless that Heaven and Earth sprang;
> The named is but the mother that rears the myriad
> creatures, each after its kind.[2]

As being that which cannot exist on its own (since it is totally indefinite), matter can only be conceived of in thought. Yet in the world which we perceive through our senses, it can be transformed into anything by combining with what Aristotle calls 'form'. Everything, then, that exists in this world of 'appearance' is a combination of matter and form, 'form' being that which makes a thing what it is as distinct from anything else. In China the Neo-Confucians hit upon almost exactly the same idea,[3] and for nearly eight centuries this Aristotelian analysis of being was a compulsory subject in the Chinese civil service examination.

When the Christians speak of God creating the world out of nothing, they have, so far as I can see, no biblical authority for doing so except for 2 Maccabees 7:28, where we read that 'God made all things out of "things that are not" (*ex ouk ontōn*)', a definition of primary matter which Aristotle would surely have accepted – with the necessary qualifications, of course.

2. *Tao Tê Ching*, 1.1 (Arthur Waley's translation).
3. See Carsun Chang, *The Development of Neo-Confucian Thought* (Vision Press, London, 1958), pp. 260–3.

However close to sheer nothingness matter may be, it is the substratum, or, to translate the Greek word more literally, 'that which lies under' the whole structure of the universe. As modern science is coming to realize more and more clearly, it is still as elusive as it was to Aristotle or as Māyā was to the Hindus. Yet, despite its resistance to definition, it is the basis on which the ladder rests up which that particular and superlatively complex combination of matter and form called man must climb, if he is ever to say goodbye to matter for ever and come into the presence of that 'living Being who is eternal and superlatively good',[4] which is God.

In a very early work, 'The Struggle against the Multitude', Teilhard de Chardin gives a highly imaginative account of how he conceived of the universe 'in the beginning'. As usual with Teilhard there is nothing conventionally Christian about this passage but it is amazingly true to the spirit of Aristotle – the real Aristotle whom he did not know, yet who speaks through his mouth in the following words:

'In the beginning there were, at the two poles of existence, God and pure multiplicity (*la Multitude*). Even so, God was all alone, because this pure multiplicity which was *in a state of absolute dissociation* did not exist. For all eternity God saw the shadow of his unity in a diffused state of disarray beneath his feet; and this shadow, *fraught as it was with every possibility of producing something*, was not another God, because, *in itself*, *it did not exist*, nor had it ever existed, nor could it ever have existed, because its essence was to be infinitely divided in itself, that is to say, *to tend towards nothingness*. Infinite in extension, infinitely rarefied, this pure multiplicity, annihilated as to its essence, slept at the antipodes of Being, which is one and concentrated.

'It was then that Unity, *overflowing with life*, joined battle through [the process] of creation with the multiple, which, *though non-existent in itself*, opposed it as a contrast and a

4. Aristotle, *Metaphysics*, 12(11).7.9 (1072b 29–30).

challenge. To create, as it appears to me, means to condense, concentrate, organize, unite.'[5]

This is pure Aristotle as the italicized passages should make clear. Indeed, had Aristotle not been convinced, along with most of his contemporaries, that the universe had always existed, this is precisely how he would have described creation: matter, 'in a state of absolute dissociation' and 'tending towards nothingness', receiving from God, who is pure 'form' without any alloy of matter, something of 'form' in however rudimentary a way.

That matter should receive form at all would probably never have occurred to Aristotle had he not believed that over against primary matter, which in the physical world is never dissociated from form because *in itself* it is little more than a hypothesis which can only be conceived of in the mind, there stood an absolute Form, itself devoid of matter, but capable of enabling matter to partake of form in increasingly complex ways. In a passage that would have astonished Teilhard, coming, as it does, from so suspect a source, Aristotle says:

'Admitting that there is something divine, good, and desirable, we admit that there are two principles (matter and contrariety), the one contrary to it [the divine], the other such that of its own nature it is inclined to desire and yearn for it. . . . Form cannot desire itself, for it is not defective; nor can contrariety desire it, for opposites are mutually destructive. The truth is that what desires form is matter, as the female desires the male, and the ugly the beautiful.'[6]

For Aristotle there can be no question of matter 'joining battle' with form, as Teilhard poetically puts it in his little creation myth. Matter longs for form because only through form can it come to life. Matter longs for form because she

5. Pierre Teilhard de Chardin, *Écrits du temps de la guerre* (Grasset, Paris, 1965), p. 114; cf. E.T. in *Writings in Time of War* (Collins, London, and Harper & Row, New York, 1968), p. 95. My italics.

6. Aristotle, *Physics*, Bk. I.9 (192a 16–23).

herself has nothing: she simply longs to 'be' in however rudimentary and restricted a way. Aristotle is not devoid of a poetry of his own.

The concept of matter which I have tried to summarize we owe entirely to Aristotle. He called it 'wood'. I wonder why. Why not water, for instance, which can so easily be transformed from the wet and cold into the wet and hot as steam, and the cold and dry as ice? Perhaps the answer is that wood is living matter which grows and decays, yet even when 'dead' can be transformed into so many different and complicated forms. Moreover, it is the 'matter' not only of the carpenter but also of the builder, and the building up of a house from various shapes and sizes of wood is very much Aristotle's idea of the building up of matter which is incomprehensible in itself into an intelligible and complex form which, in his day, was probably beautiful as well as useful. In the perfectly constructed house the wood found only one of the many fulfilments ('entelechies') it potentially possessed. And was this too the idea that was at the back of the mind of that ancient seer in India who sang out to his God:

> What was the *wood*? What was the tree
> From which heaven and earth were fashioned forth?
> Ask, ask, ye wise in heart, on what did he rely
> That he should thus support these worlds?[7]

Aristotle gave the answer: matter – and form.

Matter and form are not the same as Plato's soul and body: they complement each other and are not necessarily at variance with one another. In this world, at least, neither can exist without the other. Form is the active principle, matter the passive, and in the human being, therefore, it is the male who gives form to the embryo while the female supplies the matter. Hence the role of the female is subordinate to that of the male, and this principle must be observed in family relationships: 'The husband rules because of his superior competence and

7. *Rigveda*, 10.81.4.

in whatever is proper to a man, but all matters that are more suited to a woman he hands over to his wife.'[8]

The whole universe and every individual part of it naturally works towards its own fulfilment: its destiny is its own perfection. Thus the perfection of a man will necessarily be different from the perfection of any other animal, for man is distinguished from the other animals by the fact that he possesses an additional faculty which they do not possess – intellect (*nous*). But man, nevertheless, is part of Nature, and, in spite of the fact that Aristotle had said that 'God and Nature make nothing to no purpose',[9] thereby, apparently, identifying God with Nature, Nature in fact *does* make mistakes, just as human beings do in their respective professions.

'Mistakes *are* made,' Aristotle says, 'even in the crafts and professions. The grammarian may make a mistake in writing and a doctor may prescribe the wrong medicine. Hence it seems clear enough that mistakes can be made in the order of Nature. If, then, there are occasions when, in the exercise of their own speciality, professional men and craftsmen achieve their purpose (their "for the sake of something") in the right way, and if, when mistakes do occur, whatever was attempted was done for the sake of some [purpose] but failed to come off, so too something similar must obtain in the sphere of Nature as a whole. And so, monsters [for instance] will be failures of purpose in Nature itself. [They will be cases in which one's purpose, which is the fulfilment of all one's potentialities for good, will be thwarted.]'[1]

Potentiality, which to all intents and purposes is another word for matter, is, according to Teilhard, the 'combined essence of all evil and all goodness'. Potentiality is nothing until it is 'actualized', that is, realized in activity as 'energy'.[2]

8. Aristotle, *Nicomachean Ethics*, 8.10.5 (1160b 34–5).

9. Above, p. 165.

1. Aristotle, *Physics*, 199a 33–199b 5.

2. The Greek word is *energeia* (lit. 'in-act-ness', 'in-doing-ness'). The word has been traditionally translated as 'actuality' or simply 'act', both deriving from the Latin of St Thomas Aquinas.

Hence, in principle, 'actuality' – the realized potentiality – must be superior to mere potentiality. But, as Aristotle points out, evil is an undeniable fact: in Nature as well as in man.

'It has become apparent', he says, 'that in Nature the opposites of individual good things inhere in those good things themselves, and so we have not only order and the beautiful but also disorder and the vile. Moreover, there are more evil things than good and more shoddy ones than beautiful.'[3]

Each of us, in other words, has the ability to reach his own fulfilment, but most of us do not attain to it. Indeed, since Aristotle was totally unaffected by the current craze for re-incarnation and knew nothing of the doctrine of purgatory (which he might well have welcomed, had he known of it), it seemed obvious to him that a man must live out his full life's span if he is to reach his own 'right' fulfilment. Those who died young could not, therefore, achieve their appointed end in its complete and 'well-rounded' form. [4]

But evil can be more positively defined than this: its very essence is strife[5] and disorder.[6] This may be assumed to be true throughout Nature. Human beings, however, since they have intellect, also have the freedom to choose between good and evil,[7] and this, somewhat paradoxically, means that the actualization of a potentiality (which is itself neutral) in an evil way will be worse than the potentiality itself. This Aristotle makes perfectly clear:

'That "actuality" is better and more to be esteemed than a potentiality for good will become clear from the following arguments. Everything we speak of as potential [or able to develop into something] is equally able to develop into its opposite. For example, when we say that something is able to enjoy good health, it is at the same time able to be ill since it

3. Aristotle, *Metaphysics*, 1.4.2 (984b 33–985a 2).
4. Id., *Nicomachean Ethics*, 10.7.7 (1177b 25–6).
5. Id., *Metaphysics*, 12 (11).10.7 (1075b 8).
6. Ibid., 1.4.2 (985a 1).   7. Ibid., 5 (4).14.5 (1020b 24–5).

has both potentialities within it; for the same potentiality may result in either good health or sickness, in being at rest or in motion, in building up or pulling down, or in being built up and falling down. So opposites can be potentially present at the same time in anything, but any two opposites cannot possibly be so present at the same time and together. I mean the actualization and realization of these potentialities cannot be present at one and the same time, as, for instance, enjoying good health and being ill. Therefore one of these realized opposites must necessarily be good, but the mere potentiality behind them may equally well be both or neither. Therefore actualization [and realization] is better. But in the case of evil things the final result (*telos*, "end") and its realization are worse than the potentiality; for that which is merely potential [and able to develop into something] is able to develop into [one or other of] both opposite qualities.

'Clearly, then, evil does not exist apart from *things*; for, of its very nature, evil must come after mere potentiality [which can be realized as either good or evil]. Hence there is not [and cannot be] any evil or going astray (*hamartēma*) or indeed anything that has ever perished in beings that exist "from the beginning" and are eternal: for to perish, to pass away, and to be destroyed are indeed evils.'[8]

In man the greatest evil is, on the physical plane, to be destroyed, in other words, death; for life is a good in itself, for we share it with God. On the moral plane the good manifests itself as virtue or moral excellence, which is an acquired state or 'habit' (Latin *habitus*, which translates Greek *hexis*, a 'having' or a 'being had') that prepares you for a purely spiritual life where all is 'form', and physical matter is finally left behind. Hence it is also called a 'perfection' or 'fulfil-ment' (*tel-eiōsis*). It is this that evil destroys, if it can: if it cannot, then it deviates from it:[9] and the word Aristotle uses here for 'deviation' is *ekstasis*, 'ecstasy'! This would seem to be

8. Ibid., 9 (8).9.1–3 (1051a 4–22).
9. Id., *Physics*, Bk VII. 2–3 (246a 10–16; 246b 20–247a 4).

an indirect hit at Plato's theory of the separation of the soul from the body in 'en-godded' ecstasy.[1]

Evil then is the destruction of physical life at death and the destruction of one's 'right mind' by being 'beside oneself': it is strife, and it is disorder. More significantly, it is the development of potentiality, which is something entirely neutral, being pregnant with both good and evil and itself akin to nothingness, into something worse and inferior to potentiality itself – something more vague and impalpable even than primary matter. It is the destruction and dissipation of the soul into pure nothingness – indeed into a minus quantity beyond nothingness.

One of the words that Aristotle habitually uses to describe evil is *hamartia* or *hamartēma*, 'straying from the road', 'missing the point', and hence 'failure' in general. The word was adopted into Christianity to translate the various Hebrew words rendered into English as 'sin'. This is not what Aristotle means by the word. For him it falls between bad luck in wrongdoing and acts that are intrinsically wrong, whether perpetrated with malice aforethought or not. For example, the man who is simply unlucky in wrong-doing may seriously injure an adversary when he had only intended to teach him a lesson by injuring him very slightly: this is bad luck since the injury inflicted greatly exceeds what was intended. But when an injury is inflicted intentionally but in ignorance of its intrinsic wickedness, this will be a *hamartēma* which might, then, be translated as 'a mistake due to ignorance of the current standards of what is good and what is evil'. It is what Catholics call venial sin, a concept they derive from Thomas Aquinas who took it over, as he did most things, from '*the* Philosopher', his 'father', Aristotle. If, however, an injury is inflicted with full knowledge that it is wrong but without deliberate intent, this will be an offence against justice. For instance, acts of violence committed in a fit of anger or when

1. Aristotle himself speaks of 'manic ecstasy' (*manikē ekstasis*) in *Categories*, 10a 1.

under the influence of drink or drugs, are certainly acts of injustice, but this does not mean that the man in question is, by
that one unpremeditated act of injustice, unjust himself; for
a man can only be held responsible for what he does, if he
both knows of the wickedness of his action and has fully made
up his mind to do it. When, however, a man knowingly commits a serious crime and is bent on going through with it, then
he is both unjust and straight wicked.[2] In Catholic terminology
he has committed mortal sin and will go to hell – unless, of
course, he genuinely repents and sees the wickedness of what he
has done. For Aristotle it would mean that he has strayed far
away from the path that leads to his true end and fulfilment.

The ethical path traced out by Aristotle for the good man,
which is very much that of the enlightened humanist anywhere and everywhere, cannot be allowed to detain us here,
since good conduct is only the condition of final self-fulfilment
and beatitude. What, then, according to Aristotle, is the true
end of man?

The end of man, obviously, if we take the word 'end' in its
everyday sense, is death. This, for the ordinary man, meant
that he was simply snuffed out, his 'breath of life' returning
to the air from whence it had come. For the Hindus the
merging of this individual 'breath of life' into the universal
'Breath of Life' meant being merged into the Absolute,
Brahman. Like the ordinary Greeks of their own time the
ancient Hindus believed that 'after death there is no consciousness'. But what the Greeks did not understand was that
the only consciousness they knew, ego-consciousness, the controlling centre of which is somewhere in the brain and which
must therefore die when the body dies, is not the only form of
consciousness. There is also a deeper centre, which C. G.
Jung called either the 'self' or, in his posthumous *Memories,
Dreams, Reflections*, 'personality no. 2', which has access to
what he called the 'collective unconscious' which is common
to all men and does not die. *This* 'self is wholly indestructible:

2. Aristotle, *Nicomachean Ethics*, 5.8.6–8 (1135b 11–25).

of its very nature it cannot be annihilated', for, like 'the immovable heart of well-rounded truth' of Parmenides, it *'is* all together, now, one and coherent': there is no duality in it.

'For where there is any semblance of duality, there does one see another, smell another, taste another, speak to another, hear another, think of another, touch another, understand another. But when all has become one's very Self, then with what should one see whom? With what should one smell, taste, speak to or hear whom? With what should one think of or touch whom? With what should one understand whom? *With what should one understand Him by whom one understands this whole universe?'*[3]

The last sentence, which I have drawn from one of the earliest Upanishads, seems to point to what Aristotle understands as the end and fulfilment of man.

In the *Phaedo* Plato had said that the philosopher should behave as if he were already dead:[4] he should kick away his vile body in which he is imprisoned, with joy, and this he can best do by leading a life of asceticism. In Buddhist terms, he should seek to attain Nirvana while yet alive, and when physical death actually overtakes him, then he should, like the swan, give vent to a paean of pure joy, since he can already catch a glimpse of the blessings that await him in the other world.[5] This snapping of the universe in two was not to the taste of Aristotle, for as his Christian 'children' were to say: 'Grace perfects nature.'

Aristotle knew nothing of grace: and had he done so, he would have seen in it only the whim of a totally unstable 'god' of a peculiarly arrogant barbarian tribe. What he knew about was *Nous* – let us call it 'Mind' for the moment – and this he had learnt from Plato, who in his turn had inherited it from earlier philosophers. There was Mind in man, and, as his own researches in natural philosophy had convinced him, there was Mind in the universe too. Never a man to jump to hasty

3. *Brihadāranyaka* Upanishad, 4.5.13–15.
4. Above, p. 144.   5. Plato, *Phaedo*, 85A–B.

conclusions, he kept the two spheres in which Mind operated separate so far as he was able. The first he discussed principally in his little treatise *On the Soul*; the second he was bound to touch upon in all his works on physics, for it was through his research into the physical world that he became convinced that behind the physical world, as he observed it – the world, the only common property of all the parts of which was movement and change – there must be an Unmoved Mover who could not change.

But let us consider first what he has to say about man in his treatise *On the Soul*. The first and obvious thing about man is that he is an animal, but he is not *just* an animal; for he has a faculty which the animals lack – the power to think – just as the animals have faculties that plants lack, living creatures though they be: they have the power of moving from place to place and they have senses with which they can apprehend the outside world. So too man surpasses the other animals by his ability to think. So if you were asked what was the end or fulfilment of man, you would say, presumably, 'to think': and you would be right up to a point. But of this later.

If man is a thinking animal, what do we mean by his soul? Is the soul a stranger to the body and imprisoned in it, as Plato supposed, or is it merely what keeps the body alive, as the Hebrews first thought? The soul, as Aristotle goes on to explain, has various faculties which it inherits from its evolutionary forebears – the nutritive faculty, sense-perception, the faculty of movement from place to place, and imagination, which it seems to share with the higher animals. Beyond these, however, it has reason and thought, and this, you might think, was its highest faculty and its 'end'. You would be wrong, for beyond all this there is the 'contemplative Mind',[6] of which we shall have to say something later. The soul then is seen to be a composite substance (*ousia*, 'being-ness') like the body, but it cannot be identified with the body. The body is a substratum ('something lying under'), which is another way of

6. Aristotle, *On the Soul*, 2.3 (415a 1–12).

saying matter. But this is not primary matter, but matter that
has already acquired a highly complex 'form'. The body itself
is a 'form' to what is inferior to itself, presumably the parts
that constitute it; but it is not the fulfilment of the whole man,
for this can only be achieved by the soul which 'holds it
together', for, were it not for this, its elements 'would be torn
apart, there being nothing to stop them'.[7] Hence we must say
that the soul too is a 'substance', that is 'the form of the
physical body which has life only potentially': it is then both
the form and the fulfilment of the body, fulfilment being to
potentiality what form is to matter.[8] To put it still more
precisely, Aristotle says it is *to ti ēn einai*[9] of the body. Literally
translated this means 'the "what was it to be?" ', a phrase that
has worried translators of Aristotle ever since he coined it.
Since the phrase is frequently coupled with *ousia*, 'being-
ness' ('substance'), it has often been paraphrased as 'essence'.
Professor D. W. Hamlyn, the latest translator of the treatise
On the Soul refuses to fob us off with a mere paraphrase and
presents us with 'what is it for it to be what it was?' which
sounds very much like nonsense.[1]

It seems to me that there is no real difficulty here at all.
Aristotle, as one might expect, meant exactly what he said:
'What was it to be?' – to which the answer is 'It was to be
. . . X', leaving 'X' unidentified for the moment.[2] The phrase,
however, so far from obscuring Aristotle's thought, throws a

7. Ibid., 2.4 (416a 6–7).   8. Ibid., 2.1 (412a 16–21).
9. Ibid., 412b 11. The phrase is very common in Aristotle's later
works.
1. Hamlyn's justification for his translation will be found on pp.
85–6 of his translation (D. W. Hamlyn, Aristotle's *De Anima* (Clarendon Press, Oxford, 1968)). His justification of this apparently meaningless phrase is ingenious, but to an amateur like myself it seems to
cause new difficulties rather than solve old ones. He concludes by
saying: 'There is no doubt that it means *essence*.' Why then did
Aristotle have to invent yet another word meaning *essence* unless he
meant to express an idea for which 'essence' was inadequate?
2. An exact parallel to the phrase occurs in *Nicomachean Ethics*,
1165b 30: *aneu de toutōn ouk ēn philous einai*, 'but without these

flood of light on to it, for it implies the simpler question: 'What was it?' Or, to put it more personally: 'What were *you* before you were conceived in your mother's womb?' Answer: 'Nothing.' Or to be more precise: 'There was a certain grade of matter in my mother's womb yearning for the "form" that my father would supply.' For the father is form to the mother who is matter,[3] and matter longs for form.[4] Then follows the next question in this Aristotelian catechism: 'What were you, then, to be?' And sure enough the answer is given towards the end of the book where we read: '[The thought] about the "what is it?" is true [only] in relationship to the "what was it to be?"'[5] Or, to put it more personally again: '*What* am I?' Answer: 'I am [myself] only in so far as I am in accordance with what I was to be.' In other words, 'in so far as I exist at all I am that which from the moment of my conception I was destined to be – the fulfilment and completion of that which I eternally *am*'.

The essence of man is the contemplative intellect as distinct from the practical intellect; and the contemplative intellect operates in a sphere where there is no matter, only form; no potentiality, only fulfilment. It is to the practical intellect what the soul is to the body: it is its perfection and fulfilment, and just as the soul governs the body, so does the contemplative intellect govern and direct the practical one so long as the latter is in the body: at least that is what it should do if there is no deviation from the straight path which leads from 'I am nothing' to 'I am what I was to be'. Hence the practical intellect which directs the body must become passive in its relationship to the contemplative intellect because the latter alone is totally free from matter in so far as matter is the principle and locus of change.

things *it would not be* [possible for them] *to be* friends'. The conditional sense is demanded by the context. The question to which this clause would answer, would be precisely *ti ēn einai*? 'What was it to be [for them]?' Answer: 'It was [for them] to be friends.'

3. See above, p. 169.   4. See above, p. 168.

5. Aristotle, *On the Soul*, 430b 28, and Hamlyn's note.

Meanwhile the practical intellect, which can only remain practical so long as it distinguishes between itself as thinker and the objects of its thought which it is its business to co-ordinate and direct, finds that as it approaches its fulfilment, it too has become an object of thought. If it is an object of thought itself, then, in this respect at least, it must be identical with everything it has ever thought about. It realizes that the very act of thinking is identical with the things it thinks about: thinker, thinking, and thought coalesce and become one. *But* the thinker and the thinking that have *seen* that all things are one in the thinking of thought, have now become the object of thought itself. The omnipotent and omniscient thinker, who now realizes that he understands nothing until he has become identified with every conceivable object of thought, now sees that he is an object of thought himself. He is slipping out of this world which has its firm base in the near-nothingness that is matter into the world of 'forms' where he himself has become an object of thought. The monistic vision fades in which 'All is One and One is All'; and, from being the lord and master of his own little kingdom of identity and 'sameness' (*to auto*), he is calmly informed by Contemplative Intellect that so far as he is concerned he is simply the equivalent of matter in a world into which purely physical matter has never been able to intrude.

'Since there is in the whole of Nature something which serves as matter to every kind of thing (and it is this which is potentially all of them), while on the other hand there is something else which is their cause and, as it were, their "maker" (*poiētikon*) in so far as it "makes" all things – rather like a craft or profession in relation to the matter [which is proper to itself] – it necessarily follows that these differences must exist in the soul too. So there will be one kind of intellect which will be capable of *becoming* all things, and another which will be able to "*make*" all things (for this will be its inherent disposition (*hexis*), as you might say), just as light ["makes" all colours]. For in a way light "makes" colours which were

179

potential only into actual colours. This intellect is something quite separate: it cannot be affected by anything nor is it mixed with anything, for in its essence it is pure actuality, pure activity, pure energy.[6]

'Now that which "makes" is always more honourable than that which submits to the making, just as the first principle (*archē*) is more honourable than matter. . . . But there can be no question of its thinking at one time and not at another. It is separate, a thing alone, just what it is [and nothing else], and this alone is the deathless and eternal. But we cannot [normally] bring it up into consciousness, for it cannot be affected by anything, whereas the intellect that can be so affected is perishable. Without *this* [the "craftsman" intellect], it cannot think anything at all.'[7]

I have quoted this passage in full because it is on the basis of these words alone that St Thomas Aquinas built his grandiose structure of the 'active' and 'passive' intellects which must have puzzled and bored generations of Catholic seminarians. How could it be otherwise? For Aristotle has now entered into the uncharted realm of things eternal; and, master-craftsman that he is, he must try to express a 'form' that is totally separate from matter in words that might conceivably make sense to lesser 'forms' still bathed in matter, that is, you and me. What, then, is he saying?

'What were you?' . . . 'What were you to be?'

'In the beginning was the Intellect: and the Intellect was related (*pros*) to God: and the Intellect *was* God. Through It all things came to be: and without It no thing has ever come to be.'

These are the opening words of the Gospel according to St John, as literally translated as it is possible to do.

'In the beginning was the Logos.' The untranslatable word

6. 'Pure', etc. Three alternative translations of the one word *energeia*. The word 'pure' is added for emphasis; it is not in the Greek.
7. Aristotle, *On the Soul*, 430a 10–25.

'Logos' I have here translated as 'Intellect', for no other reason than to bring it into line with Aristotle's thought – in spite of the fact that Aristotle speaks of *Nous*, not *Logos*. The words differ, but the meaning is, I think, the same; and Mr Edward Hussey has probably come as near to pinning it down as possible. The Logos is 'the true account of the law of the universe':[8] and this 'account' is both reasonable and reason itself. It is identical with the *Nous* of Aristotle, which, following St Thomas Aquinas, I have hitherto translated as 'intellect' or 'mind' for lack of a better word. We can, of course, call it Mind (with a capital letter to indicate that it does *not* mean 'mind' as normally understood); we can, with Sri Aurobindo, India's Teilhard de Chardin, call it 'Supermind'. But it doesn't matter very much what you call it, for 'the names that can be named are not unvarying names'. And what Aristotle (and the Upanishads and the *Tao Tê Ching*) is talking about is precisely 'an unvarying Name'.[9] Aristotle, the master-scientist, who had spent all his life analysing and cataloguing every conceivable combination of matter and form, everything that comes to be and passes away, has at last found that which neither comes to be nor passes away but simply is in the *mind* of man – *not* his heart as the Upanishads and, along with them, almost all the mystics in all religious traditions would have it. He is, of course, right, since not only does the heart die but when it dies the whole of the body dies along with it, including what we normally call the mind and what St Thomas Aquinas calls the 'passive intellect' in his valiant attempt to translate the Greek *pathētikos nous*. '*Pathētikos*' is, of course, the origin of the English word 'pathetic', and *this nous* – *this* mind – is indeed 'pathetic' in every sense of the word: it is pathetic and much to be pitied because it is perishable and must die when the body dies. Of itself it can do nothing; it cannot even think unless activated by that other 'craftsman' mind which always *is*, both as 'first principle',

8. E. Hussey, *The Presocratics*, p. 40.
9. *Tao Tê Ching*, 1.1.

the 'beginning' (*archē*), and as 'that which was to be', the end.

'In the beginning': these are the words with which the Bible opens, as does the Gospel according to St John. For Aristotle this would also mean 'in the first principle', by which he would understand 'in pure form'. And this is only fitting since form is prior to matter in the sense that matter cannot exist without it, for the 'what it was to be' of man is 'what he is' in eternity. This does not mean that man *is* God, since in his treatise *On the Soul* Aristotle is talking about man, not God. The fact that he uses much the same terminology about God in the *Metaphysics* has nothing to do with the case. Man may be *like* God in that, in his 'craftsman' mind, thinker, thinking, and what is thought are all one, but he is not *the* Unmoved Mover, only one unmoved mover among many. He is a craftsman and his craft is to think through the passive, mortal mind, whose 'craft' is to *become* all things by empathy – and the Greek word is absolutely correct in this context. But how can we translate it? Basically the Greek root *path* means 'to have something done to one'; it is used as the passive of *poiein*, to 'make' or 'do', for instance, 'Do not do to other people anything that would make you angry if you were similarly done to by others',[1] that is, 'if you were treated like that by others'. 'Becoming all things' is, of course, one of the many pantheistic slogans the imprecision of which irritated Aristotle so much. Why, then, does he suddenly become imprecise himself? He does not. What he says is that your ephemeral, mortal mind which is snuffed out at death has the power to become all things in what is common to all of them, that is, to be acted upon by an eternal and timeless agent. Activated by the 'craftsman' mind in which the act of thinking and the act of being thought are literally one, the passive mind, being receptive by nature,[2] is flooded with the pure light it receives from the absolute unity of the 'craftsman' mind where thinking and what is thought are all one. It is now

1. Isocrates, *Nicocles*, 61.   2. Aristotle, *On the Soul*, 429a 15.

open to two separate activities or energies. On the one side it is activated by the 'craftsman' mind which is *a* one,[3] not *the* One; on the other by the forms-in-matter which are the objects of sense-perception. In a flash of intuitive insight the matter that veils the external forms disappears and so only continuous and coherent forms remain: and in this sense it can be said that the passive mind '*becomes* all things', for it is through the light of the 'craftsman', 'creative' mind that it perceives all things as in some sense one, for 'the soul is *in a sense* all things that *are*. . . . But it cannot be the things themselves; for it is not the stone that is in the soul, but its form.'[4]

In the light of what Aristotle says, we can understand such sayings from the Upanishads as :'Whoso thus knows that he is Brahman becomes this whole universe. Even the gods have not the power to cause him to un-Be, for he becomes their own self.'[5] Unfortunately they have, for the poor, pathetic, passive mind *is* perishable, and, having seen the vision of all things as they are in the light of eternity, it will think it really *is* that other Mind, the craftsman and maker, and it will then think that it is omnipotent and omniscient, beyond good and evil. But, after the sudden flash, the craftsman withdraws, leaving behind, maybe, a megalomaniac passive mind, whether it be a Meister Eckhart in good or a Charles Manson in evil. Aristotle *knew*.

So much for man. What of God?

On the subject of God or the gods, Aristotle had an open mind. He found it reasonable to suppose that divine beings existed who were immortal since this had always been the common belief of mankind,[6] but he was not sure, for 'they may well have been what Xenophanes said'.[7] That is to say, the gods as described in Greek mythology can hardly have been true gods, for 'Homer and Hesiod have attributed to the gods everything which brings shame and reproach among men:

3. Ibid., 429b 28.   4. Ibid., 431b 21–432a 1.
5. *Brihadāranyaka* Upanishad, 1.4.10.
6. Aristotle, *On the Heavens*, 270b 1 ff.   7. Id., *Poetics*, 1461a 1.

theft, adultery and fraud'.[8] What Aristotle understood by gods were the movers of the heavenly spheres whose circular, rotating motion seemed to be regular, uniform, and eternal, thus imitating on the physical plane the unmoving One who was the changeless cause of all change. This 'Unmoved Mover' must be the equivalent in the universe of the 'crafts-man', creative mind in man, but this does not mean that they are the same, for even that part of the mind of man which is immortal as a separate, unmade substance only becomes creatively active after its association with a particular type of matter; in the case of human beings the 'form' is supplied by the seed of the male, the 'matter' by the female. In general terms it is possible to speak of man as the principle of man; but, as Aristotle insists, there is no such thing as 'man' in general, only particular men.[9] Hence the 'creative mind' which alone can survive physical death must be a *separate* essence, one among many, a 'one' in itself, but not *the* One, very much like the spiritual monads of the Sānkhya system in India. But what is the relationship of these individual 'ones' to the Unmoved Mover, or the Changeless Maker of Change, to the separate eternal monads which are the essence of a given man and which alone are changeless and immortal, and how does the totally Unmoved manage to impart motion at all?

The answer would appear to be that just as matter longs for form as the female longs for the male, so do all compounded beings long for the Unmoved, Unmade and Uncompounded. Hence there are *three* ingredients involved: in human terms, body, mind (*nous*), *and*, as the unifying principle, longing, yearning (*orexis*),[1] and passionate love (*eros*).[2] The mover in all cases will be the element of attraction and attractiveness that draws the changing, compound being to its source and form, the potential to the actual and real. But, as we have seen, the potential can be wrongly actualized. If this happens, it

8. E. Hussey, *The Presocratics*, p. 13.
9. Aristotle, *Metaphysics*, 12 (11).5.4 (1071a 21).
1. Ibid., 12(11).5.1 (1071a 3).   2. Cf. ibid., 12 (11).7.4 (1072b 4).

will be converted into an evil which is worse than the purely potential itself, for it becomes less than the matter which gave rise to it: it is a minus quantity, so to speak, but a minus quantity that is, by the mere fact that it has become actual, furiously active, the very principle of strife and disintegration.

Aristotle gives two illustrations of what he means. Take the example of health: you have two possible forms of actualization – health and illness; then you have the matter in which these contraries may be actualized – the body. Either of the contraries may be actualized, but the craft or profession concerned with bodily health is the medical profession, and it is this that 'moves' the body in the direction of health. In this case the 'craftsman' mind is the craft or profession of medicine, 'for', as Aristotle says, 'health is, in a sense, the craft of medicine'. So, too, in the matter of building a house, you have the form, a shape of the house that is to be built – the architect's blueprint, if you like; 'a certain kind of disorder' – the building-site; and bricks – the matter out of which the house is to be built. The 'craftsman' mind will therefore be the technique of building itself or, if the house is to be beautiful as well as merely useful, the art of architecture. In this case too the 'form' of the house, that is, the idea of the house as it is present in the architect's mind is, in a sense, the art of architecture, since it is the art or craft that is the 'unmoved' principle of motion that gives actuality or reality to the actual house when built.[3]

So too with man. The opposites or contrarieties corresponding to 'health and illness', or the 'house to be built' and 'a certain kind of disorder', are not mentioned, and it is simply said that 'man generates man'. In another treatise, however, much the same parallel is maintained: 'The male provides the "form" and the "principle of movement", while the female provides the "body" and the "matter".'[4] The corresponding art or craft, then, must be the 'art of love', and this, according

3. Ibid., 12 (11).4.7–8 (1070b 24–34).
4. Id., *Generation of Animals*, 1.20.10 (729a 10–11).

to the other two examples, must 'in a sense' be the same as one of the two unmentioned opposites, which corresponds to 'health' and the 'blueprint of the house' in the architect's mind. The 'art of love' will, then, be the same as the father's idea of the child that the act of coition will actualize and bring into existence. But, given that any potentiality can be actualized in a good or evil way, it would seem plain that, though the good and natural actualization of a human being must also be a human being, the reverse may also prove to be true, and the result will be not a normal human being but a 'monster', either a physical 'monster', like a spastic, or a moral 'monster' – or at least one who is potentially so; for it must be remembered that every new form that arises in nature or in the arts itself becomes 'matter' to a higher and more complex form which, in the natural order of things, will be a faithful reproduction of its archetype, but which may also be a deviation from the norm, a 'mutation' for better or for worse. In other words a potential monster will become an actual monster if it is exposed to conditions appropriate to the formation of monsters as would seem to be true in the case of Charles Manson.

Matter longs for form, as we have seen, just as the female longs for the male. So too does the whole universe long for the most perfect Form, which, though unmoved itself, is the principle of all motion and all change. Matter while still incompletely formed – and matter as matter always is incomplete and indefinite – must long for the Perfect and Changeless because it alone is unmoved and has the principle of movement within it because of its irresistible power to attract. Can this be defined a little more closely, if only by analogy?

Aristotle has a very mundane illustration of what he means. The Unmoved Mover must be supremely lovable and desirable in itself: hence it causes movement by simple attraction: it activates desire in all subordinate forms still attached to matter and not totally 'separate' as they must be when they have reached their perfect fulfilment. It 'touches' them without being touched itself; for it, like the 'craftsman', creative mind in individual men, must be an 'agent', that is, something or someone that acts on something else, *does* something to something else, whereas the other as yet unperfected form is 'passive', that is, acted on: something is being done to it without its doing anything at all. And so, says Aristotle, 'we sometimes say that a bore touches [or affects] us, but we do not affect him'.[5]

I do not think it is wrong to translate the Greek *ton lupounta*, 'one who causes pain', as 'a bore' since this seems to me to illustrate almost perfectly what Aristotle has in mind. For surely the essence of a bore is that he bores into your vitals causing you exquisite pain and making you squirm in misery without being able to do anything about it, while he remains unmoved and unmovable in his relentless detachment. Perhaps this is what the Devil does to his victims in hell. With the Unmoved Mover, however, Aristotle's God, things are very different: he moves us by an attraction so great that we are fired by longing and passionate love, though we by no means assume that our love is returned. We do not know and we have no right to care, for perfect love asks nothing in return.

Once again we seem to be very near the Sānkhya philosophy of India: matter yearns for spirit, and spirit acts on her by its force of attraction, its immutable perfection. Matter, it is true, is always active in the sense that she is never for a moment at rest, but, in so far as she is fascinated by spirit, she is passive: something is being done to her. Spirit, then, while being quite motionless itself, moves her as Aristotle's Unmoved Mover moves the whole universe of both pure spirits or minds (the 'creative' minds of all men fulfilled) as well as all that is still tinged with matter.

Aristotle's God is to the whole universe what the 'craftsman', creative mind is to the passive mind and the body which it controls so long as these exist. He is a magnet of attraction,

5. Id., *Coming to Be and Passing Away*, 1.6 (323a 33–4).

which in a timeless and spaceless world holds everything together both 'within' the universe and 'outside' it. The universe itself, which, according to Aristotle's way of thinking, must be a perfect sphere (had he, one wonders, some intuitive insight into the curvature of space envisaged by modern physics?), contains all its appropriate matter, which, though perpetually changing, always remains quantitatively the same. In ordinary language, then, one would have to speak of God and the other 'creative minds' as being *outside* the universe, but this can only be a figurative way of talking. All you can say is that 'outside the universe (lit. "heaven") there is neither place nor void nor time. . . . Hence, whatever is there, is of such a nature as not to be in any place nor does time cause it to age; nor is there any change in any of the beings whose allotted sphere of operation lies beyond the outermost motion. Changeless and impassible, and possessed of the best and most self-sufficient life, it so abides in fulfilment (*diatelei*) for all eternity.'[6]

Aristotle then arrives almost where the Upanishads begin: 'This is the Self, exempt from evil, untouched by age or death or sorrow, untouched by hunger or thirst: this is the Self whose desire is the real, whose idea is the real.'[7] This is the Unmoved Mover and it is God.

He is eternal, pure 'substance' or Being-ness, pure actuality, activity, and energy. That which is yearned for and that which is thought of move all that yearns and thinks: but, both being eternal and pure Being-ness, they are identical. We all yearn for what we think is good for us, but it is only when we know what is our real good that we desire it rationally. Hence rational thought must precede our yearning on our side too; for it is the act of thinking that arouses desire; and desire, when once aroused, can only be for the supremely good and what is supremely desirable in itself.[8] This is therefore the 'what was

6. Id., *On the Heavens*, 1.9 (279a 12–23).
7. *Chāndogya* Upanishad, 8.1.5.
8. Aristotle, *Metaphysics*, 12 (11).7.2–4 (1072a).

it to be?' of the whole universe;[9] it is quite literally the Omega
Point of Teilhard de Chardin, the point of convergence of the
whole universe, and it is also its starting-point: 'for the *first*
"what was it to be?" has no matter, for it is pure self-fulfilment
and consummation – *entelecheia*.'[1] It is not only 'in the beginning' because it *is* the beginning, but also 'at the end' because
it *is* the end: hence it literally encompasses and holds together
(*periechei*) the whole universe, itself the timeless and spaceless,
holding, as it were, in its immortal and ever-living hands the
eternally revolving and perfect sphere, the 'immovable heart
of well-rounded truth', as Parmenides called it. But the
universe is not immovable as Parmenides had supposed, but
eternally rotating on its own axis and so perfectly spherical
that it is impossible to say whether it is moving or not, for
'it is complete [and perfect] from all sides, like the mass of a
well-rounded ball, and evenly balanced every way from the
centre',[2] as Parmenides had put it. This eternal movement,
which is the nearest thing to rest but still under the influence
of space and time, fringes on eternity where all spirits and
minds are one creative, 'poetic' (*poiētikos*) Mind. Held in the
well-loved hands of Him who is eternally at rest but who
impels all things to move 'each according to its nature for years
unending',[3] it imitates the totally Unmoved Mover as best it
can. All this, too, had been prefigured in India in the Upanishads and expressed in paradox. Indeed the *Ishā* Upanishad,
which contains the quintessence of all Upanishadic teaching,
came very near to apprehending the truth as Aristotle saw it
by the exercise of his 'craftsman', creative, making, poetic
mind. In the opening lines the Upanishad announces the truth
as it sees it:

> This whole universe must be pervaded by a Lord –
> Whatever moves in this moving world . . .

But it then goes on to say in paradox:

9. Ibid., 12 (11).8.18 (1074a 36).   2. E. Hussey, op. cit., p. 89.
1. Ibid.   3. *Ishā* Upanishad, 8.

It moves. It does not move.
It is far, yet It is near:
It is within this whole universe,
And yet it is without it.[4]

Or, as Aristotle would explain, being perfectly actual and
eternally fulfilled, 'it does not move', but in so far as it is also
the first mover, it does move in the sense that it is the first
mover from which all movement must ultimately derive.

But the Upanishad too becomes more explicit:

He, the wise Sage, all-conquering, self-existent,
Encompassed that which is resplendent,
    Incorporeal, invulnerable,
Devoid of sinews, pure, unpierced by evil:
All things he ordered, each according to its nature,
    For years unending.[5]

What could be more Aristotelian than this? The wise Sage,
Aristotle's 'intellect', 'thought', or the 'Thinking of Thought',
who is the same as the Unmoved Mover, though seen from a
different viewpoint, 'encompasses' the 'incorporeal, invulner-
able' domain of all those intelligences separate from matter
which are for ever 'what they were to be', and 'orders all things,
each according to its nature, for years unending'.

This too is the Christian God as proclaimed in the Book of
Revelation: ' "I am the Alpha and the Omega [the First and
the Last]" says the Lord God, who is, who was, and who is to
come, the Ruler of All.'[6]

And it is the God of the Koran too: 'He is the First and the
Last, the Outward and the Inward; and of all things he is the
Knower.'[7]

Not only as first intelligence is he necessarily the 'Knower
of all things', but he is also the 'Ruler of All' and 'orders all
things, each according to its nature'. That Aristotle's God, the

4. Ibid., 5.   6. Revelation 1:8.
5. Ibid., 8.   7. Koran, 57.3.

Unmoved Mover, must also be ruler of all and therefore fully transcendent seems plain, but is he also the 'Inward', the Immanent God, mentioned though not emphasized in the Koran, who indwells the very texture of the Upanishads?

Whether he is both did not seem obvious to Aristotle, and so he says: 'We must consider too in which way the nature of the Whole possesses the good and the superlatively Good; whether as something separate and [existing as] itself by itself, or as order, or again in both senses as is the case of an army. For its well[-being] both is *in* the order and *is* the general. But it consists principally in the general; for the general is not dependent on the order, but the order depends on him. All things, indeed, are ordered together in some way, but not all alike.'[8] In the world of spirit and mind where all things that 'were to be' actually *are*, 'all things participate in the whole', the whole itself being the total and appropriate order of its 'general' whose perfect unity it 'incarnates' (or should we not rather say 'ensouls'?), but there are still those souls which have wilfully strayed from the way that leads from 'what it was to be' to their actual being, and these will be dissolved back into primary matter and beyond, where they will be lost without trace or name.[9] These, as Teilhard de Chardin has somewhat heartlessly put it, 'are simply paying for the forward march and triumph of all. They are casualties, fallen on the field of honour.'[1] But Aristotle was not only wiser than Teilhard de Chardin, he could also think lucidly, using not only his titanic scientific intellect without recourse to Platonic myths, but also his intuition which saw the consummation of all things in the supremely One, supremely Aware, supremely Good, unchanging and unchanged, which puts Teilhard's pseudo-science, pseudo-theology, and pseudo-philosophy to shame. All that Teilhard can claim to have done is to have refurbished Aristotle's own architectonic master-

8. Aristotle, *Metaphysics*, 12 (11).10.1–2 (1075a 12–17).
9. Ibid., 12 (11).10.4 (1075a 23–5): cf. above, pp. 184–5.
1. P. Teilhard de Chardin, *Human Energy*, p. 50.

piece of convergent reality in a manner more pleasing to our modern taste for the turgid and imprecise. Moreover, Aristotle seems to me to have been of an altogether more humane disposition, as we shall very soon see.

Aristotle knew, I said a few pages back. This is true; for, after describing the Unmoved Mover, the 'Thinking of Thought', for which all beings long, as being also 'that without which [all] well-[being, all well-thinking, all well-doing] cannot exist, and which cannot be conceived of otherwise than as simple – the first Principle upon which the whole universe depends', he added that 'we too can experience *for a short time* a mode of living similar to that [life which is] supremely good'.[2] He did not ask much, and what little he asked, he received. And that was enough: for, by this short vision (or visions) Aristotle was confirmed in his belief in the Beatific Vision in which pure Being was seen as pure Thought and pure Joy – the *Sat Chit Ananda*, as the Vedantins in India have traditionally described *their* 'total experience'. For not only is what Aristotle experienced, for a short time only, supreme Being and supreme Thought: it is also supreme Joy. Indeed the actuality, activity, and energy of what is itself pure actuality without the faintest trace of potentiality – pure being without any alloy of becoming – is joy. Better still, it is 'pleasure' (*hēdonē*); for Aristotle, unlike the whole ascetic side of Plato and the ascetic tradition as we find it represented to some extent in all the mystical traditions of the major world religions, was not averse to any earthly 'good' since each relative 'good' is simply another way of saying the actualization and fulfilment of the 'what was it to be?' in the 'what it is' in the eternal Now. 'Hence', he goes on to say, 'wakefulness, perception, and thought are what is most pleasurable, joyous, and sweet (*hēdiston*), whereas hopes and memories are only so through them'. Hope can only be a virtue in that it looks forward to a future state, and memory can only be sweet in that it 'recollects and recalls a moment of beatitude in the past', whereas

2. Aristotle, *Metaphysics*, 12 (11).7.6–7 (1072b 14–15).

to be fully awake – to be fully a Buddha (for that is what the
word *buddha* means) – is supreme 'enlightenment' and perfect fulfilment. This is, then, what Aristotle means by 'thinking' (*noēsis*). Far from being a state beyond dreamless sleep,
as the Upanishads would have us believe, it is a state of
supreme alertness – the Buddhist enlightenment – and so,
perhaps, in this 'absolute' context, we should translate *nous*
not by 'thought', but by 'awareness' or 'the aware'. This may
make Aristotle's meaning clearer. So let us say with him:
'Awareness in itself is the awareness of what is supremely
good in itself, awareness in an absolute sense (*malista*) of
what is absolute. Now the Aware One (*Nous*) is aware of
itself through participation in what it is aware of; for, by
touching it and becoming aware of it, it is itself that of which
it is aware, so that the Aware One and what it is aware of are
the *same*, for that which is receptive of what it is aware of and
of being-ness is the Aware One', just as, for the Hindus, the
awareness of Being (*sat-cit*) is Being itself. 'And in that it
possesses [itself] (*echōn*) it is all energy, activity, and actuality
(*energei*)' – these three-in-one being represented by the single
Greek word *energeia* – which is 'pleasure', the pleasure that
God takes in himself, his simple love of himself as awareness
of himself as Being in itself. And this is the Aristotelian
Trinity, which seems to differ little, if at all, from the *Sat Chit
Ananda* of the Hindus and the Christian Trinity, which it
seems to describe at least as well as either Augustine or
Thomas Aquinas. But while the Christian saints could
scarcely have arrived at the idea of the Trinity at all without
relying on what they regarded as being a divine revelation and
wrestling with the problems that that revelation seemed to have
left unsolved (and this is the way of revelations, for God or
'the gods seem to love the obscure, yes the gods seem to love
the obscure'[3]), Aristotle reached the same fulfilment, end,
and consummation by sheer hard thinking, without needing
to be 'en-godded' by any Platonic daemon.

3. *Aitareyya* Upanishad, 3.14.

'And so', he continues, 'it will be this [energy, activity and actuality, which is joy] rather than that[4] [Aware One which is receptive of what it is aware of and of Being] which seems to be·the [truly] divine which the Aware One *possesses*. And it is contemplation that is supremely joyous and supremely good. If, then, it is thus that God possesses the good in eternity, even as we can so do on occasion, it is wonderful indeed: if even more so, then it is yet more marvellous. But this is just how it is. And [in him] there is life too: for the actuality, activity and energy of the Aware One is life, and the Aware One is itself that energy and actuality. Actuality as it is in itself is indeed the supremely good and eternal life of the Aware. And so we roundly affirm that God is a living being, eternal and supremely good, and that in God there is life and coherent, eternal being. For that *is* God.'[5]

If I understand this passage aright (and it is more than probable that I do not), then Aristotle will mean that what is supremely divine in God himself, who is, by definition, both the Unmoved Mover and the Thinking of Thought or the supremely Aware One, is neither this Being nor this Awareness-thought but his sheer actuality, his energy, and his activity which constitutes his joy – the joy he *possesses* in himself and which is his by nature and by right for all eternity and in which we, through our own craftsman, creative, 'poetic' minds, can, on occasion, share.

In the *Taittirīya* Upanishad which we quoted above (p. 119) we read:

---

4. Reading (with W. D. Ross) *ekeinou mallon touto*, but taking *touto* to refer to *energein* understood from the immediately preceding *energei*, and *ekeinou* as referring to *dechtikon tou noētou*. The correct translation, however, seems to be quite uncertain. See W. D. Ross, *Aristotle's Metaphysics*, Vol. II (Clarendon Press, Oxford, 1924), pp. 380–1.

5. Aristotle, *Metaphysics* 12 (11).7.7–9 (1072b).

In the beginning this universe was Not-being only;
    Therefrom was Being born:
[And being] itself made [for itself] a self:
    Hence it is called 'well-done'.

Translate this into Aristotelian terms, and you have the following: 'In the beginning this universe was potential matter only; therefrom was form-in-matter born. "What was it, then, to be?" It was to be a "craftsman", creative awareness-mind, and this was the "self" that it "made" and became. Hence it is called "well-done" – the perfectly actualized being-awareness-joy that it always "was to be".'

And so, the Upanishad adds: 'What this "well-done" really is, is the sweet taste[6] that pervades the whole universe. Once a man has tasted this, he is suffused with joy. For who could breathe, who could live, were this joy not suffused throughout space? For this alone brings joy.'[7]

We have followed Aristotle in his search for the essence of man and next in his pursuit of the existence of God; and we have seen how, after proving to himself at least that God existed, he saw that he must be Being-Awareness-Joy, probably at about the same time that the Hindu seers arrived at this formula in India. He saw him primarily as the Unmoved Mover (a privilege which is his alone), and as the 'Thinking of Thought' or rather the 'Awareness of Awareness itself' in which man too can share as did Aristotle himself; and in this he saw the highest possible pleasure and a joy to end all other joys because it is itself the end and fulfilment of all partial joys.

We have followed him as he relentlessly tracked down that elusive awareness in the soul of man and in the 'Supermind' of God – to use Sri Aurobindo's phrase. We have followed him, then, both in his psychology (the 'science of the soul') and in

6. Cf. id., *Nicomachean Ethics*, 10.9.4 (1179b 15): 'They will have no idea of the good and the truly sweet unless they have tasted it.'

7 *Taittirīya* Upanishad, 2.7.

his physics and metaphysics (the science of nature and of what lies beyond it). We must now complete the account of 'our father's' quest and follow him in his search for the Absolute through his 'ethics' (the admittedly inexact 'science of human behaviour').

For Aristotle man is essentially not only a thinking animal but a social one.[8] No more than his Jewish prototype, Adam, was he made to live alone. Hence the idea of the Indian Sannyāsin, the hermit-ascetic, appeared a trifle absurd to him; for 'it would, perhaps, be slightly ridiculous to represent the truly blessed man as a hermit, for no [right-thinking] person would choose to possess all good things entirely on his own, for man is a social creature and designed by nature to live with others'.[9] And to live with others, if it is to be tolerable at all, must mean to live in harmony with them. Hence the importance Aristotle attached to friendship, not indeed to Plato's strange divinization of one particular kind of love, but to friendship between good men and how this can vary according to the age, rank, family ties, and tastes of any given pair of friends.

The eighth and ninth books of the *Nicomachean Ethics* are entirely devoted to friendship and are sandwiched in between a preliminary account of the nature of pleasure and a more detailed one which leads up to the supreme pleasure of contemplation. As in all things in this world, there are degrees of pleasure of which the lowest are monstrous deviations from the 'mean', the straight and narrow path between excess and deficiency, while the highest leaves even the golden mean itself far behind as it reaches out in yearning towards the absolutely perfect Being we have already sufficiently discussed. Between the lowest and the highest friendship plays an intermediary part. Through loving your neighbour as yourself you will learn to love what is most noble in yourself: and that is divine.

8. Aristotle, *Politics*, 1.1.9 (1253a 3).
9. Id., *Nicomachean Ethics*, 9.9.3 (1169b 17ff.).

You may like or 'love' a person for three reasons: either because he is good, or because you derive pleasure from his company, or because he is useful to you. This last type of friendship Aristotle considers to be so obviously base that we need not let it detain us. That it can be accounted as friendship at all is due to man's boundless capacity to deceive himself, for 'everyone loves not what is really good for himself, but what appears to be so'.[1] What friendship really means is to 'wish another good for his own sake',[2] not for your own or for any profit or pleasure you may derive from him.

Aristotle has often been blamed by Christians for his supposedly cold and detached conception of God. Unlike the Christian God, his God is represented as a kind of super-Aristotle, thinking pure thought in a more or less solipsistic eternity. This seems to me a very one-sided representation, and I think it is belied not only by what we have said hitherto but also by the fact that in the *Ethics* it is precisely through his analysis of friendship and the selfless pleasure that can be derived from it that Aristotle approaches God in a purely human way – the way, both human and humane, that was so typical of Confucius and his followers in China.

It is true that Aristotle says that there can only be true friendship between like and like, and God is so remote from man that to speak of love or friendship between the two would be, if not blasphemous, then at least absurd; for 'we say that friendship can only exist when it is returned, but the "friendship" we feel for God does not admit of any such return, nor can one in general speak of loving or liking God; for it would be absurd for a man to say that he loved or liked Zeus'.[3] The gap between God and man is so wide that so long as God remains God and man a mere mortal, God will be wholly unapproachable because he is wholly 'separate'.[4] But this is only half the story, for Aristotle believed quite as much

---

1. Ibid., 8.2.2. (1155b 25).   2. Ibid., 8.2.3 (1155b 31).
3. Id., *Magna Moralia*, 2.11.6 (1208b 28–32); cf. *Eudemian Ethics*, 7.3.4 (1238b 29).   4. Id., *Nicomachean Ethics*, 8.7.5 (1159a 5).

as did St Paul that 'our present perishable nature must put on imperishability and this mortal nature must put on immortality'.[5] Here and now, of course, our unlikeness to God is so great that to speak of God as 'friend' would be ridiculously inappropriate, for in this context Aristotle is speaking of friendship between equals. But there are quite other kinds of 'friendship', such as a child's love for its parents; and this kind of love Aristotle *does* compare to the love of men for their gods,[6] adding that in this respect Homer was quite right to call Zeus 'father', since our own father is the author of our very 'being'[7] and therefore entitled to our own love and respect to a superlative degree.[8] This, then, is a relationship of total dependence, for the 'What was it to be?' has not yet become that supreme 'craftsman' Mind and 'Awareness of Awareness' that it will one day be because that is in eternity what it *is*: it has not yet become 'like God'.

Friendship, however, in the strict sense of the word implies equality and likeness in virtue,[9] and for the true friend it will be enough to love without necessarily expecting to be loved in return,[1] though no friendship can last unless it is mutually based.

'Eros' is the word used for sexual attraction, and the main difference between 'eros' and 'philia', the kind of friendship that is wholly self-giving, is that you can normally only be in love with one person at a time, while the gift of self can be distributed to more than one, though Aristotle, with his usual caution, thinks not too many. This, I think, is where Aristotle's *Ethics* links up with his *Metaphysics*, for in the latter work, as we saw, God is passionately loved and yearned for: he is the object not only of all your thought and awareness but of all your love and desire. You are, in other words, head

5. I Corinthians 15:53.
6. Aristotle, *Nicomachean Ethics*, 8.12.5 (1162a 4).
7. Ibid., 8.10.4 (1160b 28); 8.11.2 (1161a 17).
8. Ibid., 8.14.4 (1163b 16).
9. Ibid., 8.8.5 (1159b 3).   1. Ibid., 8.8.3 (1159a 28).

over heels in love with him because you recognize in him, if
not the author of your own fulfilment, then at least the fulfilment of all fulfilments of which yours is but one. Friendship
is a schooling in this art of understanding and love: 'it desires
the being and life of the friend for his own sake.'[2] This means
that your friend is another self to you,[3] just as a child is another
self to his parents though separated from them[4] as one fulfilled 'craftsman' awareness-Mind is separated from all others
though held together by the attractive effulgence of God.

If your fulfilment must consist in passionately longing for
God with all that is immortal in yourself, then you must learn
to love your own true self which does not pass away when the
body dies. This means that you must be utterly serious with
yourself, for this serious 'you' 'is at one mind with itself and
yearns for the same things with all its soul. . . . It desires to
live itself and to be preserved for ever – and most of all that
part of it with which it thinks and is aware (*phronei*). For to *be*
is a "good" for the serious man, and everyone desires good
things for himself; and no one would choose to *possess* everything in the world if that meant *becoming* somebody else (for
only God possesses the [whole] good now [and always]):
[rather he would choose] to *be* whatever he may happen to be.'[5]

There is a Muslim tradition which says: 'Who knows
himself, knows his Lord.' Aristotle knew all about this too.
He knew that each individual must know himself as he is in
eternity, a divine spark of pure awareness which far exceeds
all other things that go to make up his being including the
passive mind, which is a mere tool in the hands of the 'craftsman'. 'It would seem, then, that *this* is what each of us
is, inasmuch as it is the sovereign and better part. It would
then be pointless for a man not to choose his own life but that
of somebody else; . . . for what is proper to each by nature is
the most excellent and pleasant and sweet for each. And for
man this is life in accordance with his mind (*nous*) inasmuch

2. Ibid., 9.4.1 (1166a 5).   4. Ibid., 8.12.3 (1161b 29).
3. Ibid., 9.9.10 (1170b 6).   5. Ibid., 9.4.3–4 (1166a 14–23).

as this, more than anything else, is man. Therefore this life will be the most truly happy and beatific.'[6]

Thus, then, in the *Metaphysics*, in the treatise *On the Soul*, and in the *Ethics*, Aristotle presents us with three aspects of the Absolute: Being; Awareness-Mind; and the sweetness of the highest pleasure possible – Joy. These are three and yet they are One, and each and all of them are to be 'tasted' by each one of us in his own way, but not in *absolute* separation, rather separately and at the same time coherently together; 'for what is in the Now is some kind of whole'.[7]

I have said above (p. 31) that Aristotle is the Balzac of philosophy, just as he is the intellectual father of all of us who seek to reach our own fulfilment in ourselves and in our relationships with one another and with God in an eternal Now where nothing of value can ever pass away. And so let us leave the last word to Balzac himself, the Aristotle among novelists, who saw, through all the apparent discords of our storm-tossed world, 'the immovable heart of well-rounded truth', the vision of the inspired Parmenides:

'The true light appeared, lighting up the creations which had hitherto seemed arid to them; and then they saw the source from which all the worlds – terrestrial, spiritual, and divine – derive their impulse.

'Each world had a centre towards which all the points of its own sphere inclined. And these worlds themselves were points which inclined towards the centre of their species. Each species had its centre turned towards the vast celestial regions which themselves communicated with the inexhaustible, radiant *mover of all that is*.

'And so, from the greatest to the least of the worlds, and from the least of the worlds to the smallest particle of the beings that compose it, all was individual, and yet all was one.'[8]

6. Ibid., 10.7.9 (1178a 2–8).   7. Ibid., 10.4.4 (1174b 9).

8. Honoré de Balzac, from *Séraphîta*, in *La comédie humaine* (Bibliothèque de la Pléiade, Gallimard, Paris, 1937), Vol. X, p. 583 (Balzac's italics).

'What, then, was it to be?' The complete end and fulfilment of each atom of matter that had ever received 'form' in its yearning for changeless Being that is yet the source of all change – the Unmoved Mover, who is also the 'Awareness of Awareness' and, supremely, the sweet taste of inexhaustible Joy.

6

GOD: MAD OR BAD?

THIS YEAR OF GRACE 1654
Monday, 23rd November, day of St Clement pope
and martyr and others in the martyrology.
Vigil of St Chrysostom martyr and others.
From about 10.30 p.m. until about half past
midnight.

FIRE

God of Abraham, God of Isaac, God of Jacob,
not of the philosophers and the scientists.
Certainty. Certainty. Feeling. Joy. Peace.
God of Jesus Christ.
Deum meum et Deum vestrum
[My God and your God].
Forgetfulness of the world and of all things
except God.
He can only be found in the ways taught in the
Gospel.
Greatness of the human soul.
Righteous Father, the world has not known you, but
I have known you.
Joy, Joy, Joy, tears of joy. ———————————
I separated myself from Him. ———————————
Derelinquerunt me fontem aquae vivae—————
[They have abandoned me, the fountain of
living water].[1]

———

1. Jeremiah 2:13: 'Since my people have committed a double
crime:/they have abandoned me,/the fountain of living water,/ only to
dig cisterns for themselves,/leaky cisterns/that hold no water.' Cf.

> My God, will you leave me? ——————————
> May I not be separated from him for ever.

———————————————————————————————

> This is eternal life, that they should know Thee, the
> one true God and him whom thou hast sent, Jesus
> Christ.
> Jesus Christ ——————————————————————
> Jesus Christ ——————————————————————
> I have separated myself from him. I have fled him,
> renounced him, crucified him.
> May I never be separated from him! ——————————
> He can only be kept by following the ways taught in
> the Gospel.
>   Renunciation, total and sweet.[2] ——————————

Of all accounts of a positively *Christian* mystical experience
this is one of the most famous and certainly the most impressive. It is so because of its terse precision and quite as
much for what it does *not* say as for what it does. Take, for
comparison, a typology of the essential ingredients of mysticism recently drawn up by the late Professor W. T. Stace,
whom one of his admirers has extolled as 'the current philosophical authority on mysticism' – for no other reason, as far
as the uninitiated can understand, than that he is reputed to
have said of mystical experience in general and LSD experiences in all their notorious variety: 'It's not a matter of its
being *similar* to mystical experience; it *is* mystical experience.'
The remark as it stands is fatuous. Stace nevertheless did
attempt to draw up a typology of mysticism drawn from a
variety of secondary sources, the chief of whom he refers to
anonymously as N.M., an American 'intellectual' (as one
might expect) who, following in the footsteps of Aldous

ibid., 17.13: 'Hope of Israel, Yahweh!/All who abandon you will be
put to shame,/those who turn from you will be uprooted from the
land,/since they have abandoned the fountain of living water.'
    2. Pascal, *Mémorial*, in *Oeuvres complètes*, pp. 553–4.

Huxley, had swallowed a dose of mescalin and, like Huxley, had been granted a revelation of things 'as they really are'. Stace's conclusions are summarized under six heads:

1. The Unifying Vision – all things are One. The Unitary Consciousness; the One, the Void; pure consciousness.
2. The more concrete apprehension of the One as an inner subjectivity, or life, in all things. Nonspatial, nontemporal.
3. Sense of objectivity or reality.
4. Feeling of blessedness, joy, happiness, satisfaction, etc.
5. Feeling that what is apprehended is holy, or sacred, or divine. This is the quality which gives rise to the interpretation of the experience as being an experience of 'God'. It is the specifically religious element in the experience. It is closely intertwined with, but not identical with, the previously listed characteristic of blessedness and joy.
6. Paradoxicality.[3]

I suppose that it can be taken for granted that Professor Stace, as a modern philosopher, had not bothered himself overmuch with so outdated a philosopher as Aristotle (writers on the philosophy of the magisterially opaque Hegel rarely do), but as the much-advertised 'current philosophical authority on mysticism' he might have felt some obligation to find out just what that marvellous man had to say on the subject. Aristotle would scarcely have been impressed by Stace's categories, most of which he was quite acute enough to have observed himself – and demolished, or rather explained in intelligible terms.

As to category 1: 'All is One.' He had already explained that this could scarcely be true in any sense (p. 163).

Category 2: For Aristotle this is simply untrue. The 'inner subjectivity, or life, in all things' was the 'Awareness of Awareness', the 'Thinking of Thought', which he attributed

3. W. T. Stace, *Mysticism and Philosophy* (J. B. Lippincott, Philadelphia, 1960, and Macmillan, London, 1961), pp. 131 and 79.

both to God and the 'craftsman, creative mind', which alone
are immortal and unchanging. All else is primal matter, the
'what did not exist' of 2 Maccabees 7:28; for as God himself
says in the Koran (as the Muslims believe): 'All things perish,
except His Face.'[4] The philosopher-mystic Al-Ghazālī
elaborates this in these terms: 'They all perish at some time or
another; or rather they are perishing for all eternity since they
cannot be conceived of in any other way. All things except
God, when considered in their essence *qua* essence, are pure
not-being. If, however, they are considered from the aspect in
which existence permeates them from the primal Reality, they
are seen to exist not in their own essence, but through the
aspect (lit. "face") which accompanies Him who gives them
existence.'[5] Al-Ghazālī knew his Aristotle.

Category 3: By a 'sense of objectivity or reality' Stace
apparently meant that the mystic is utterly convinced of the
absolute truth of his experience as against the relative truth
of our day-to-day knowledge derived from sense-perception.[6]
Aristotle would have described this as the disentanglement of
'form' from matter. He knew perfectly well that to 'become
the All' means not what it literally says, but rather to receive
into your 'passive' mind the forms of all things. You do not
become a stone, but the form of a stone is impressed on the
tablet of your mind (p. 183). This is not objectivity as normally understood, let alone Professor Monod's 'principle of
objectivity'; it is merely a restatement in psychological terms
of Aristotle's idea of the priority of form over matter. As to its
'reality': the 'realities' *known* and *seen* by self-styled mystics
seem to vary a good deal. Both St Francis of Assisi and Charles
Manson *knew* and *saw*, but the results were not (in our
relative world at least) precisely the same.

As to category 4: 'Feeling of blessedness, joy, happiness,

4. Koran, 28.88.
5. See R. C. Zaehner, *Mysticism Sacred and Profane* (Clarendon
Press, Oxford, 1957), p. 157.
6. See my *Drugs, Mysticism and Make-believe*, pp. 91–2.

satisfaction, etc.' You do not have to be a mystic in any normal sense of that word in order to experience these highly pleasurable sensations. Many people, I am assured, feel precisely this in the sexual act, more particularly if this act culminates in what Charlie Manson's 'Family' called the 'total experience', which leads to a 'transvaluation of all values' into values that seem either very much better or very much worse than the values they replace. But let us be done with quibbling over words, for whatever 'seems' is mere appearance; it has nothing to do with the 'total experience' of Reality. Heraclitus knew all about this, and Aristotle tried to sort him out (p. 163).

So on to category 5: The 'holy, or sacred, or divine'. Aristotle is usually content with the word 'divine' – 'godlike' – that is, what you have in common with God or the gods. But it all depends on what you mean by God. For Aristotle, plainly, it was the 'god of the philosophers', for as all good Catholics know through their erstwhile ideal, St Thomas Aquinas, as opposed to the profoundly sceptical apostle from whom he presumably borrowed his name, he was to become *the* Philosopher, whose credentials presumably were more impressive than those of *the* Apostle, Saul of Tarsus, who, on his own admission, was 'the least of the apostles' and hardly deserved to be called by that name.[7] The God of *the* Philosopher, however, was scarcely the God of *the* Apostle. He was the Unmoved Mover who drew all beings to himself simply by being the supreme object of all longing and all passionate love. He was not for ever buffeting, chastising, and hounding his rational creation, as the accounts of all religions that believe in him never tire of telling us. As Pascal makes very clear, the God whom *he* had seen and experienced was not *this* God – the only God, I am afraid, whom Aristotle might be said to share with W. T. Stace – but the 'God of Abraham, God of Isaac, God of Jacob', a very different kettle of fish, if we may be permitted an irreverent comparison.

7. 1 Corinthians 15:9.

God: Mad or Bad?

Now that we have, I hope, with the fatherly aid of our Master Aristotle, brought some little order into the imprecision of Professor Stace's categories of what he conceives mysticism to be, let us see how Pascal emerges from his artful scrutiny.

Having made it quite clear that what he has experienced and seen has nothing to do with the 'God of the philosophers', it is not surprising that we hear nothing about the One. True, Pascal's own God of Abraham, Isaac and Jacob, had made it at least as clear as the God of the Koran that he was One: 'Listen, Israel: Yahweh our God is the one Yahweh.'[8] But this meant no more than that he was the one almighty Lord, Creator of heaven and earth, as opposed to the multitude of pagan gods who made no such claims. It did most emphatic-·ally not mean that he was the 'One without a second' from which all plurality *appears* to proceed as does the spider's web from a spider, as the Upanishads say.[9] Far less did it mean that he was that One who was also the Form of the Good which Plato intuitively recognized and Parmenides defined, to the lasting distraction of the Platonist fringe that always hovers around the hard Aristotelian core that is the foundation on which our whole Western civilization is built up. With such a God, Pascal's God had nothing whatever to do. Yet despite this grave deviation from the orthodoxy of the 'perennial philosophy', Pascal scored a bull's-eye on Stace's category no. 3, 'sense of objectivity or reality'. '*Certitude. Certitude.*' – 'Certainty. Certainty.' – is what he said, and he said it twice, adding a full stop after each affirmation in case you should think that he was speaking metaphorically or in jest. 'Feeling, Joy, Peace.' . . . 'Joy, joy, joy, tears of joy.' Yet again a bull's-eye in category no. 4. As to the 'holy, or sacred, or divine', this can scarcely be denied him since the whole *mémorial* is one concentrated, coherent paean to *his* God, Jewish idol though he may be in the starry eyes of the 'earnest seekers' after the 'All is One' of that perpetually elusive and many-headed

8. Deuteronomy 6:4.   9. *Mundaka* Upanishad, 1.7, etc.

hydra Aldous Huxley has taught us to equate with the 'perennial philosophy'.

But there is a great deal that Stace omitted to mention and which he would have found, had he chosen to consider the case of Pascal of which he can scarcely have been unaware. I do not, of course, mean Jesus Christ, who, from his point of view, would merely be a Christian's imposition of his own particular idol on to an essentially monistic background, nor do I refer to the intrusion of the Gospel, which is open to the same criticism. Nor yet do I wish to draw attention to the 'greatness of the human soul', a *folie de la grandeur* which would rank Pascal, if interpreted out of context, with the Hindu monists (or 'non-dualists', as they prefer to be called), the mainstream of Zen Buddhism, Plato and the Platonists of every shape and size. But Pascal was not quite this, for he realized full well that man is always at war with himself, his 'misery', which is caused by his passions, for ever striving against his 'greatness', which derives from his mind. And in this he seems to follow Plato in the *Phaedrus*, with its myth of the recalcitrant horse for ever dragging its docile companion and their charioteer into the maelstrom of base desire, and he is at one with him too in making a sharp distinction between body and soul, but, being a Christian, he pulls himself up in time, for man is neither angel nor beast. Should he aspire to be either, he is a fool, for 'when all is said and done, he is only a man, that is say, as capable of little as of much, of everything as of nothing: he is neither angel nor beast, but man.'[1] This, at least, is Aristotelian and, therefore, Catholic Christian.

No, the essential factor that Stace omits from his typology of mysticism is Pascal's 'forgetfulness of the world and of all things except God'. And it is precisely here that Stace and all his fellow-devotees of the 'perennial philosophy' wilfully, we uncharitably suppose, neglect the one essential criterion that distinguishes the religious mystic from the nature mystic and the participant in the average successful 'trip' on LSD. For

1. Pascal, *Pensées*, in *Oeuvres complètes*, p. 1133.

the latter see the world in brighter colours, brought to life, as it were, and enhanced, as did 'Socrates' in the *Phaedo*, while the former withdraw their senses from the objects of sense with a view to reaching their inmost self which is timeless and eternal. To achieve this aim asceticism of some sort is usually practised. This can and often does take extreme forms such as the gruelling mortification practised by both Hindu Sannyāsins and the Christian desert fathers, not to mention Charlie Manson's forty-five-mile walk in the blazing desert sun. Such excesses, however, are reproved both by the author of the *Bhagavad-Gītā* and by the Buddha himself, both of whom recommended moderation in all matters that concerned the body.[2] So, for that matter, did Aristotle, who very sensibly said that the contemplative needs no external means with which to pursue his craft, for these, so far from helping him, will merely get in the way.[3]

'Forgetfulness of the world and of all things except God.' Few mystics, except the Buddhists, would quarrel with either limb of this proposition. In the case of the second one the Buddhists would doubtless demur at the use of the word 'God' at all. Others would be glad to accept the word for lack of anything better, but they would inwardly understand 'the God of the philosophers and scientists', who is at least respectable. Out of respect for Pascal, I would hope, they would politely feign to ignore his 'God of Abraham, God of Isaac, God of Jacob', since, from what they might have read about him, it would be absolutely clear to them that he was not respectable at all. And if they had read extensively with unblinkered eyes, they would probably think that he was a hopelessly psychotic case – either mad or bad, or more likely both.

Since, at the age of twenty, I was converted to a religious way of experiencing things by what I would now call an acute case of nature mysticism while reading and rereading the more obscure and purely 'magical' poems of Arthur Rimbaud, I

2. See my *Drugs, Mysticism and Make-believe*, pp. 81–2.
3. Aristotle, *Nicomachean Ethics*, 10.8.6 (1178b 3–5).

suddenly *saw* very much as the much-quoted R. M. Bucke had *seen*, and with much the same results. With the naïvely preposterous Bucke, whose very name was unfamiliar to me at the time, I experienced what he calls 'cosmic consciousness', seeing all things as One; and I *saw* that 'this consciousness shows the cosmos to consist not of dead matter governed by unconscious, rigid, and unintending law; it shows it on the contrary as entirely immaterial, entirely spiritual and entirely alive; it shows that death is an absurdity, that everyone and everything has eternal life; it shows that the universe is God and that God is the universe, and that no evil ever did or ever will enter into it; a great deal of this is, of course, from the point of view of self consciousness, absurd; it is nevertheless undoubtedly true.'[4]

Had I read this passage at the time, I should have agreed with every word of it. I no longer believed in God since, along with Aleister Crowley and E. M. Forster, I had been brought up in Tonbridge School, a most undistinguished Anglican establishment at that time where what would now be called 'religious education (R.E.)' was shared between an Anglo-Catholic and a broad churchman whose broadness was so broad as to be indistinguishable from total agnosticism. Religion for me, then, became an incoherent farce (and in those days (1930) religion for me meant Anglican Christianity). Hence, to this day, it has continued to appear so to me unless the whole tragico-comic charade is bound together by a golden cord of mysticism which assures me, even in my frequent periods of cynical doubt and near-despair, that 'the what I am to be' is what I eternally am – a living awareness, yearning for but never attaining to that supremely joyous Awareness of deathless Being which Aristotle, after a lifetime of patient, logical, discursive thought, affirmed in the strongest possible terms *is* God.

Like Bucke I concluded from one single experience (though

4. R. M. Bucke, *Cosmic Consciousness* (23rd ed., E. P. Dutton, New York, 1966), pp. 17–18.

it lasted far longer than his) 'that the universe is "God" and
that "God" is the universe, and *that no evil ever did or ever will
enter into it*'. When I turned from the Classics to Oriental
Languages I had the immense gratification of finding out that
this is precisely what the ancient Hindus thought and what
Hindus continue to think and that this same vision was
repeated in the glowing language of the Persian Sufi poets,
particularly in Rūmī, the 'en-godded' Platonic poet-prophet of
the East. Apparently I was not wholly mad, but sane enough
to know that this was not the sort of thing you discussed with
others because they would almost certainly think you *were*
mad – and amoral and totally irresponsible. But, after reading
the Upanishads and a great deal of Rūmī, I realized that I had
been initiated into a great mystery by the teenage prodigy,
Rimbaud, and that this mystery was as ancient and as lofty as
the Himalayas themselves. I had no reason or inclination to
bother my foolish head any more with a puny little hill the
Jews were pleased to glorify with the name of Mount Sion,
let alone with the so-called Mountain of the Transfiguration,
the traditional site of which is, I believe, well below sea-level.
What I felt was exactly what Bertrand Russell felt and tried
(unsuccessfully) to describe on 16 August 1918. He did it
better, more honestly, and more lucidly than any of the
inspired and 'en-godded' nature mystics in the West, from
Plato himself to Aldous Huxley and that en-godded and en-
drugged apostle of LSD, Dr Timothy Leary, whose lucid
ravings formed the kernel of my last book, *Drugs, Mysticism
and Make-believe*.

'It is quite true what you say,' Russell wrote to Lady
Ottoline Morrell, 'that you have never expressed yourself –
but who has, that has anything to express? The things one
says are all unsuccessful attempts to say something else –
something that perhaps by its very nature cannot be said. I
know that I have struggled all my life to say something that I
never shall learn how to say. And it is the same with you. It is
so with all who spend their lives in the quest of something

elusive, and yet omnipresent, and at once subtle and infinite. One seeks it in music, and the sea, and sunsets; at times I have seemed very near it in crowds when I have been feeling strongly what they were feeling; one seeks it in love above all. But if one lets oneself imagine one has found it, some cruel irony is sure to come and show one that it is not really found. . . .

'The outcome is that one is a ghost, floating through the world without any real contact. Even when one feels nearest to other people, something in one seems obstinately to belong to God and to refuse to enter into any earthly communion – at least that is how I should express it if I thought there was a God. It is odd, isn't it? I care passionately for this world, and many things and people in it, and yet . . . what is it all? There *must* be something more important, one feels, though I don't *believe* there is. I am haunted – some ghost, from some extra-mundane region, seems always trying to tell me something that I am to repeat to the world, but I cannot understand the message.'[5]

In trying to convey the message that would not be transmitted Russell found no word to express his 'inborn' intuition except God – and he didn't believe in God, not, I suspect, even in Aristotle's God, with whom he must have been familiar. Nor was he prepared to submit to the 'total experience' of that god whom Spinoza had identified with Nature nor the see-saw god of Heraclitus whose up is down and whose down is up, the principle of eternal ambivalence, who would tell us, if he dared, that good *is* evil, and evil *is* good. Russell passionately believed in right and wrong and spent his entire life in combating what he thought to be wrong. He could never see the diabolic smirk behind the radiant smile of the God he so nearly touched. He had not soared into the heavens of pure beatitude nor plumbed the depths of Aristotle's sub-material hell as Rimbaud had. He had not seen

5. *The Autobiography of Bertrand Russell*, Vol. II (Allen & Unwin, London, and Atlantic Monthly Press, Boston, 1968), p. 90.

that these are the two sides of the same coin. He could not see
that –

> Elle est retrouvée.
> Quoi? – L'Éternité.
> C'est la mer allée
> Avec le soleil.

can never be separated from:

> Là pas d'espérance,
> Nul orietur.
> Science avec patience,
> Le supplice est sûr.[6]

Even I, whose eyes had been opened by Rimbaud himself,
did not fully understand this. All I knew was that I *was* in
eternity and that the shifting sea was merged in the unchanging brilliance of the sun. As to the darker, Satanic side, I
would have agreed that 'no evil ever did or ever will enter' the
universe which was identical with God. What did I care that
one of my best friends was going through the hell of what
would now be called a depressive psychosis? Blind, silly fool:
it was all his stupid imagination. Why hadn't he too got the
sense to *see*? Did I pity him? Not one bit. Just about as much,
I suppose, as Charlie Manson pitied Sharon Tate and her
unborn child.

> O saisons, ô châteaux!
> Quelle âme est sans défauts?[7]

These were the magic words that opened my eyes. I will not
even try to translate them, because magic is contained in the
sounds themselves, as any self-respecting Hindu guru will
tell you: the meaning, if there is any, is just a 'verbalization',
a 'name'.[8] The reality is It: sea and sun, the One!

6. Above, p. 63, where an English translation is supplied.
7. Arthur Rimbaud, *Oeuvres complètes*, pp. 140, 238.
8. Cf. *Chāndogya* Upanishad, 6.1.4–6.

In such a state it is quite as easy to be utterly callous about the actual individual sufferings of individual people close to ourselves as it is in our normal state to be callous about the innocent victims massacred daily in Vietnam, in what was once East Pakistan or in what was once called Biafra.

Aristotle has been frequently censured for having calmly accepted slavery as the natural condition of inferior men as being no more than 'ensouled tools'. But why this should be held against him in particular I have never understood, since it was the common assumption of all the ancient world, both Jewish and Greek. It was accepted by Jesus and sanctioned by Paul, it was accepted by Muhammad and had already received the seal of approval from Yahweh, the Lord God of Israel, himself: 'They shall be your property and you may leave them as an inheritance to your sons after you, to hold in perpetual possession. These you may have for slaves; but to your brothers, the sons of Israel, you must not be hard masters.'[9]

'Righteous Father', 'Just Father', Pascal had said when he wept for joy during those two unforgettable hours he lived in direct contact with the God and Father of his Lord, the Jew Jesus Christ: he did not say 'Holy Father', let alone '*Good* Father', since he was in the presence of the *total* God as he had revealed himself to Israel, his chosen people, not of the God of the philosophers – of Aristotle, St Thomas Aquinas, and, of course, Plato, whose radiant image Miss Iris Murdoch has so valiantly striven to clothe with some kind of quasi-human flesh and blood.[1] But we are not at the moment interested in Miss Murdoch's Idea of the Good, but in Pascal's God, who is not good but just.

' "Good Master, what have I to do to inherit eternal life?" Jesus said to him, "Why do you call me good? No one is good but God alone" '[2] we read in the Gospel according to St Luke.

---

9. Leviticus 25:45–6. Cf. also Deuteronomy 15:12ff., which lays down conditions for *Jewish* slaves.

1. Iris Murdoch, *The Sovereignty of Good, passim.*

2. Luke 18:18–19; Mark 10:17–18.

What did Jesus mean by 'good'? Obviously not what either
Plato or Aristotle were talking about, radically different though
their views on the subject were. Even in the matter of slaves,
those 'ensouled tools' of Aristotle, Aristotle was far more
humane than Yahweh was to the foreign slaves of Israel –
their 'natural' slaves as the barbarians were natural slaves to
the Greeks. 'They shall be your property': and that, apparently,
is that. You do not argue with Yahweh, as Job was later to
learn; for Yahweh is naked power. 'It is a dreadful thing to fall
into the hands of the living God',[3] as the Epistle to the
Hebrews says. And this is precisely what the 'election' of
Israel means.

If there is any humanity in the Christian and Catholic
religion we owe it quite as much to Aristotle as to the slaughtered Lamb of God. We may have become co-heirs with Israel
in the New Covenant of this capricious God – stepsons, that is,
and no longer slaves. But what difference has it made, since
not only has our mother, the Holy Catholic Church, treated us
like 'ensouled tools', just as the Persian tyrant treated *his* sons,[4]
but she has also turned upon the true heirs of the Old Covenant and consistently treated them as a tainted thing apart (and
naturally enough since, being unambiguously chosen, they *are*
apart). Once power fell into her far from unwilling hands she
wreaked her vengeance on them for steadfastly refusing to
admit that a new prophet had arisen in Israel who made the
unheard-of claim to be the Son of God. 'Slaves' to the Law
the Jews might well be, but even slaves can be loved, as
Aristotle pointed out, not as slaves, of course, but because a
slave, 'tool' though he may be, is entitled to some degrees of
affection, friendship, and love simply because he is a human
being. 'As a slave you cannot love (*philia*) him, but as a man
you can; for there seems to be some kind of just relationship
between every human being and every other one who is
able to participate in *Law* and *Covenant*: how much more,

3. Hebrews 10:31.
4. Aristotle, *Nicomachean Ethics*, 8.10.4 (1160b 29).

then, in this matter of love in so far as he too is a human being.'[5]

Here speaks a human being, as humane as he is human, as much a stranger to the raging God of Israel as he was to the 'en-godded' magician, Plato. How strange that he should speak of 'law' and 'covenant', using the same Greek words that Paul used in that tortuous Epistle to the Romans in which he seems to identify the Jewish Law with sin, only to separate them out again with all the ingenious ambiguity that is so characteristic of the man.

But if Aristotle can testify to the Law and the Covenant in prophetic terms he would be the first to disavow, so can Elijah, the prophet of that raving God, hint at the sweetly reasonable voice of him who was to become *the* Philosopher of Holy Catholic Church. If any of the readers of this book has been forced to read the historical books of the Old Testament at school, he will no doubt remember the story of the wind and the earthquake and what used to be called 'a still small voice':

'There came a mighty wind, so strong it tore the mountains and shattered the rocks before Yahweh. But Yahweh was not in the wind. After the wind came an earthquake. But Yahweh was not in the earthquake. After the earthquake came a fire. But Yahweh was not in the fire. And after the fire there came the voice of a gentle breeze.'[6]

I like to think that the 'voice of a gentle breeze' was the voice of Aristotle who, through the 'ensouled tool' that was Thomas Aquinas, did much to smooth down the African harshness of Augustine's stern bequest. But that is a passing fancy, for we must now leave the lowlands of human reason and ascend to the Holy Mountain where the savage Lord of

5. Ibid., 8.11.7 (1161b 5–8).

6. 1 Kings 19:11–12 (Jerusalem version, but substituting 'voice' for 'sound' following the Septuagint. For 'gentle breeze' the AV and RSV, of course, have 'still small voice'. The New English Bible, with its usual infelicity, has 'a low murmuring sound', which, however faithful to the Hebrew, is wonderfully flat in English).

Armies rages in the horror of the storm. But before we do this, let us seek him out in India, for he can rage there as furiously as he ever did on Sinai. He speaks through the mouth of Kabīr, claimed as a saint by Hindus, Muslims, and Sikhs alike. He is a Thug:

> God is a Thug: and Thuggery's what he has brought to the world!
> Yet how can I live without him, tell me, my motherly friend.
>
> Who is the husband? Who is the wife of whom?
> Ponder on that in your inmost heart.
>
> Who is the son? And who is the father of whom?
> Who is it who dies? Who is wracked with torment?
>
> Says Kabīr: 'What of it? I'm pleased with the Thug as he is.
> For once I recognized the Thug, the Thuggery vanished away'.[7]

God is a Thug! . . . The Thugs are or were a Hindu religious sect who believed that they had received a divine mandate from the dreaded goddess Kālī to waylay, rob, and strangle whomsoever the goddess might indicate to them. This they did with precision and ritual punctiliousness. 'He meditates his murders without any misgivings, he perpetrates them without any emotions of pity, and he remembers them without any feelings of remorse. They trouble not his dreams, nor does their recollection ever cause him inquietude in darkness, in solitude, or in the hour of death.'[8]

Charles Manson might have learnt much from the Thugs had the British imperialists not been so narrow-minded as to

7. Freely adapted from a literal English translation that my friend, Professor Charlotte Vaudeville of the Sorbonne, was kind enough to send me.

8. Quoted in Hastings, *Encyclopaedia of Religion and Ethics*, Vol. XII (T. & T. Clark, Edinburgh, and Charles Scribner's Sons, New York, 1921), p. 260.

suppress them. As it was, he had to make do with the Bible, where he found much to console him, particularly in the Book of Revelation. Indeed, one of his 'favourite passages from Revelation 9 was [verse 21, which reads]: "Neither repented they of their murders, nor of their sorceries, nor of their fornication, nor of their thefts" – words he would quote over and over again, preparing his worshippers to kill.'[9]

Of course Charlie dragged these words out of their context, but this is a vice to which practically all scholars are addicted, and Charlie was not a scholar, at least in the generally accepted sense of that word. Nor can he be blamed for interpreting the Book of Revelation in terms that seemed to fit most closely into his philosophy; for this has for centuries been a game at which many older and wiser men have played, though rarely with such deadly effect. It is not, then, altogether surprising that the Greek Church showed some reluctance in admitting this sanguinary portrayal of divine vengeance into the canon of Holy Scripture. Some people were rash enough to think that all that blood-and-thunder stuff had passed with the passing of the Old Covenant. They were wrong, as history has proved.

That the Bible should have inspired Charles Manson to evil should surprise no one who has not been indoctrinated into interpreting it along nice, orthodox lines. To the man who approaches it with a completely open mind it is bound to seem what it is: a 'bloody' book in the literal sense of that word. Is Manson to be blamed for interpreting it in his own peculiar way when the Dutch Reformed Church justifies the policy of *apartheid* on scriptural grounds? Or is Anthony Burgess just playing to the gallery when in his masterpiece, *A Clockwork Orange*, he describes Alex's reaction to the Good Book in these words:

'I would read of these old yahoodies (Jews) beating each other and then drinking their Hebrew vino and getting on to the bed with their wives' like hand-maidens, real horrorshow

9. E. Sanders, *The Family*, p. 149.

(good). That kept me going, brothers. I didn't so much dig the later part of the book, which is more like all preachy talk than fighting and the old in-out.'[1]

No, he is telling the literal truth, however displeasing it may be to the professionals in 'preachy talk'. And if they don't want to believe Charles Manson and Anthony Burgess, perhaps they will not totally disregard the considered opinion of C. G. Jung in the introductory pages to his *Answer to Job*:

'The Book of Job', he wrote, 'is a landmark in the long historical development of the divine drama. At the time the book was written, there were already many testimonies which had given a contradictory picture of Yahweh – the picture of a God who knew no moderation in his emotions and suffered precisely from this lack of moderation. He himself admitted that he was eaten up with rage and jealousy and that this knowledge was painful to him. Insight existed along with obtuseness, loving-kindness along with cruelty, creative power along with destructiveness. Everything was there, and none of these qualities was an obstruction to the other. Such a condition is only thinkable either when no reflecting consciousness is present at all, or when the capacity for reflection is very feeble and a more or less adventitious phenomenon. A condition of this sort can only be described as *amoral*. . . .

'I shall not give a cool and carefully considered exegesis that tries to be fair to every detail, but a purely subjective reaction. In this way I hope to act as a voice for many who feel the same way as I do, and to give expression to the shattering emotions that the unvarnished spectacle of divine savagery and ruthlessness produces in us.'[2]

And if the 'preachy' people will not listen to Jung, then per-

1. Anthony Burgess, *A Clockwork Orange* (Penguin Books, Harmondsworth, 1972), p. 64. I have replaced Burgess's futuristic slang with more understandable English words.

2. C. G. Jung, *Answer to Job* (Routledge & Kegan Paul, London, 1954), pp. 3–4; *Collected Works*, Vol. 11 (Routledge & Kegan Paul, London, and Princeton University Press, Princeton, 1959), part 2B

haps they will not be too proud to listen to one of their own number who paid for *his* preaching with his life.

'Why is it', Dietrich Bonhoeffer asks, 'that in the Old Testament men tell lies vigorously and often to the glory of God (I've now collected the passages), kill, deceive, rob, divorce, and even fornicate (see the genealogy of Jesus), doubt, blaspheme, and curse, whereas in the New Testament there is nothing of all this? "An earlier stage" of religion? That is a very naïve way out; it is one and the same God.'[3]

'One and the same God': the *saevus deus*, the 'savage, raving, raging, berserk God' in whom Tertullian rejoiced and whom his adversary, Marcion of Pontus, rejected.

Marcion was a Gnostic; and, like all Gnostics and Platonists, he rejected the whole of matter as evil. Though he was a sincere convert to Christianity, he remained a Platonist at heart, and his ideas on creation seem to be based on Plato's account of creation in the *Timaeus*. Very briefly this account may be summarized as follows.

In eternity there exists a whole world of timeless and unchanging forms, perfect and incorruptible. Apart from these there is a divine Artisan, 'maker' and 'father', perfectly good in himself, indeed overflowing with goodness, since he wished to reproduce a perfect copy of the perfect world of forms which he eternally contemplates. The perfect world, apart from its changeless perfection, is also characterized by harmony and justice: everything just *is*: or, in the language of mortal men, everything is just as it should be and there is no possibility of error in it. But in order to produce his copy the Creator God had to use materials of some kind, and the only material available was matter; and matter was chaos. How he produced order out of chaos is a long story. It must, then, suffice to say that he first created the soul of his copy and then its body, which he formed out of matter. Knowing full well that any-

3. Dietrich Bonhoeffer, *Letters and Papers from Prison*, enlarged edition (E.T., SCM Press, London, and Macmillan, New York, 1971), p. 157.

thing that partakes of matter must come to be and pass away,
he created lesser gods – the heavenly bodies, sun, moon, and
stars – so that they should form the copy as best they could,
thus preserving himself from all responsibility for evil.[4]
Needless to say, the copy turned out to be a pretty shoddy
affair, and shoddier than all the rest of the physical universe
which, being a perfect sphere and perfectly regular in its
circular motion, was a reasonable copy in time of the perfections of eternity. It turned out to be man, formed as he was of
gross, chaotic matter on the one hand and an immortal soul on
the other which he derived from the soul of the copy-world
(our world, that is to say) which had been created by the good
God himself. Hence we have the same pattern we have already
met with in the *Phaedo*: man is an immortal soul imprisoned
in a material body which is governed by the disorderly passions of anger and lust. In itself the body is irretrievably evil.

This, no doubt, was Marcion's view of the world before he
became a Christian. What attracted him to Christianity must
have been the goodness he saw in Jesus Christ. His Christ was
more like the Buddha than the historical Jesus as we know him
through the Synoptics and to some extent through St John
too: he had come to save the immortal souls of men *from* the
world, he had not come to sanctify the whole man, body as
well as soul. To a Platonist this latter idea would be unthinkable. How, then, could a Platonist and a Gnostic actually
embrace Christianity the central doctrine of which is that God
was actually born of a woman, lived in a body, eating and
drinking, sweating and suffering like anyone else, for about
thirty-three years, was tortured to death, shedding real human
blood, and finally rose from the dead in bodily form only to
start eating and drinking again? The answer is not far to seek.
St Paul had done it all before: he managed to believe at the
same time that God took on real human flesh and was crucified
for the salvation of men and that the flesh as such, being subject to decay, could not be saved in any way that made sense.

4. Plato, *Timaeus*, 42E

In the middle of the second century AD, when Marcion became a Christian, Christian doctrine had already been formed on lines dictated by St Paul, who had never known Jesus the man, and, to judge from his letters, which account for nearly a third of what was later to become the canon of the New Testament, cared precious little about what *sort* of man he was. All he knew was that Jesus Christ was God made man, that that God-man had been crucified, had risen from the dead, and ascended into heaven. *His* Christ was a blinding flash of light and a voice saying, 'Saul, Saul, why are you persecuting me.' Jesus Christ, the God-man, had indeed been crucified, but he had risen in a 'glorified' body – the body Peter, James, and John had been privileged to see at the Transfiguration, a body of dazzling white light – not the resurrected body as described by the four Evangelists. For *that* body Paul had no use at all, much less for his own. He hated it, bullied it into submission in the best ascetic-Gnostic tradition, and cried out to be released from it: 'Who will rescue me from this body doomed to death?'[5] *This* was the Christ that must have attracted Marcion into the Catholic Church.

During Marcion's lifetime the books that go to make up the New Testament as we know it almost certainly all existed (Tertullian in his book *Against Marcion* quotes them all except 2 Timothy, Titus, James, and 2 John), but they had not been drawn up as a canon, that is to say, the Catholic Church had not pronounced as to which were divinely inspired and which were not. Now Christian Gnostics were no new thing, but Marcion was not like the others. He did not seek to allegorize the Bible or to build up fantastic cosmogonies modelled on Plato's *Timaeus* as others had already done. Rather he set out to do what the Church herself had failed to do, namely, to present the Church with a body of scripture to set over against the Jewish Bible. In this, he must have thought, he was doing the Church a service, but Marcion was a philosopher with a Platonic cast of mind, and he was keenly aware that Plato's

5. Romans 7:24.

God was above all the 'Idea of the Good', that is immutable
perfection not too closely defined, but 'Good' he certainly was.
And this view he found confirmed by Christ himself: 'No one
is good but God alone.' This phrase occurs in all the three
Synoptics, which Marcion plainly compared with each other
and with John. Presumably, after much deliberation, he
decided that Luke alone was a true account of the mission,
death, and resurrection of Jesus. John's gospel, despite its
forthright condemnation of this world and of the flesh, must
have been ruled out of court from the beginning because it is
John who insists most unambiguously that the Logos was in
fact 'made flesh', and it is John again who insists on the reality
of the physical body of the risen Christ, he alone telling us
how that born sceptic, Thomas, refused to be convinced until
he had actually put his hand into Jesus' side where it had been
split by a soldier's spear to make sure that he was really dead.
None of this was at all Platonic, so John must be ruled out.
Mark, presumably, was not considered seriously since the
doctrinal content of his gospel must have seemed to Marcion
pretty thin. That left Matthew and Luke. Both had dis-
advantages, for both gave long and detailed accounts of how
the birth of Jesus had been announced to the Virgin Mary and
how she had actually conceived and given birth to a human
child whom she had been instructed by the Angel Gabriel to
call Jesus. None of this was to Marcion's liking and, like any
old pedant in search of an 'original' gospel, *Bhagavad-Gītā*
or whatever, he must have decided that Luke's gospel, being
less harsh than Matthew's, was the only true gospel. Unfortunately, however, wicked men had tampered with the original
text and interpolated a lot of spurious matter into the authentic
story (by which, of course, he meant what, in his opinion, the
story must have been), and he therefore proceeded to remove
from Luke everything that he thought must be spurious, including, of course, all that nonsense about the Virgin Birth;
for, as any sensible Gnostic will tell you, the eternal God
cannot conceivably be born.

Having rejected the three other gospels and tidied up Luke to his liking, Marcion proceeded to take a good look at the rest of what was beginning to be accepted as specifically Christian scripture as distinct from, but complementary to, the Jewish scripture – what we call the Old Testament. He immediately realized that Paul was very much up his street. He accepted all the major Epistles from Romans to 2 Thessalonians, but rejected what we have come to call the 'pastoral' Epistles to Paul's close friends, Timothy, Titus, and Philemon, because they were concerned with the practice of Christianity and not with doctrine, and Marcion was primarily a philosopher interested in discovering the Christian 'Truth'.

In our own day Miss Iris Murdoch has spoken of how the ordinary person is liable to be 'corrupted by [the] philosophy' of the likes of Professors Ryle, Hampshire, and Ayer.[6] This opinion she shares with Tertullian, Marcion's implacable adversary, who claimed that 'all heresies are under condemnation, because all of them take their stand upon the resources of subtle speech and the principles of philosophy'.[7] In this they are agreed, but in nothing else, for Tertullian savagely attacks the very principle that Miss Murdoch so wistfully defends, the Platonic conception of the 'Idea of the Good', which is, in fact, Marcion's God.

Marcion, however, took holy scripture seriously. Clearly, what the Church was already accepting as specifically Christian scripture had been tampered with, but why? and at whose instigation? As a convert and an intellectual, Marcion was bound to read not only the Christian writings, but also the Old Testament of which these were supposed to be the fulfilment. His reactions, I imagine, must have been very similar to Jung's and to those of Alex in *A Clockwork Orange*. The God of the Old Testament was simply savage (*saevus*, 'raving, raging, berserk'). Unlike Jung, he could not admit that

6. Iris Murdoch, *The Sovereignty of Good*, p. 97.
7. Tertullian, *Adversus Marcionem*, 5.19.7, ed. and tr. Ernest Evans, (Clarendon Press, Oxford, 1972), Vol. II, p. 633.

this is precisely what God is in his terrible aspect, since, as a good Platonist, he could not admit that evil could issue from one who was supremely good, let alone could he revel in it as Alex did and as Yahweh himself appears to do in most of the prophetic books. He saw that this God was savage, but he also saw that in his own mean little way he was also just, if by justice you mean never giving anyone the benefit of the doubt. He was just but he was not good, whereas the God he had discovered in the New Testament was the absolute Good of Plato.

Presumably he had read Plato's *Timaeus* and was familiar with the idea of the 'Demiurge', the Creator God who tries to reproduce a perfect copy of the timeless Good in time. Ultimately he failed, but he passed the buck of his failure on to the 'gods' whom he had himself created, thereby preserving his own pure, pure purity and irresponsibility. With this model in his mind, he took a very hard look at the Old Testament, which, as a convert, he had to take seriously. What he saw was what Jung saw, 'a God who knew no moderation in his emotions . . . eaten up with rage and jealousy', in whom 'insight existed along with obtuseness, loving-kindness along with cruelty'. As you might expect from a raving savage, this God was not only 'vengeful'[8] and 'atrocious',[9] but inconsistent, full of contrary qualities, highly volatile and unstable.[1] He was for ever changing his mind, making laws only to announce later that he hated those who obey the very laws he has made. He makes laws concerning the Sabbath day and institutes the Jewish feast days, and then, for no reason at all that any human being can understand, he suddenly announces in a fit of rage: 'Your new moons and sabbaths and great day I cannot abide: your fasting and workless days and feast days my soul hateth', and again, 'I hate, I have rejected, your feast days, and I will not

8. Ibid., 4.20.7; Evans, Vol. II, p. 367, etc.
9. Ibid., 4.39.3; Evans, Vol. II, p. 483.
1. Ibid., 2.21.1ff.; Evans, Vol I, pp. 142–5, and overtly or covertly *passim*.

smell in your solemn assemblies.'[2] It is true that after these outbursts of fanatic anger this God sobers up, and repents of what he has done or threatened to do much as a savage might do after a drinking bout. All this Marcion saw in the Old Testament and almost certainly much more which Tertullian does not mention because it·is too awful a mystery for anyone to begin to understand, I mean, this God's putting the city of Jericho under a ban which meant that all the men and women, whether young or old, were to be massacred together with their oxen, sheep and donkeys.[3] On the subject of this particular case of divinely inspired aggression and genocide Tertullian is mute.

What did Marcion make of all this? He must have concluded with horror that Plato had been hopelessly wrong. The Creator God, Plato's 'Demiurge', so far from trying to make a perfect copy in time and space of eternal truths, was totally unaware of the eternal, utterly good God above him. He thought that he was indeed the highest principle, that he was just, and that he would create a world in which strict justice would reign; but his justice was so vitiated with pettiness, weakness, and incoherence[4] that it was impossible to say whether he was good or evil. The answer, of course, was that he was both, as Tertullian boldly proclaims. He does not deny that this God himself had said: 'It is I who create evils', and 'Behold I send evils against you', nor does he deny that he repents of his 'wickedness' (*malitia*), because as a just God he takes vengeance on the wicked.[5] At his most sincere he admits that *his* God, the God who reveals himself *both* in the Old Testament and the New, is *not* good but just.[6] This Marcion could not accept, seeing, as he did, that Yahweh's justice was not justice at all by human standards; for it was a mean sort of justice, malicious, vengeful, and, of course,

2. Ibid., 5.4.6; Evans, Vol. II, p. 529.   3. Joshua 6:17–21.
4. Tertullian, op. cit., 2.25.1; Evans, Vol. I, p. 155, etc.
5. Ibid., 2.24.2–4; Evans, Vol. I, p. 151.
6. Ibid., 4.13.2; Evans, Vol. II, pp. 590–1.

savage. This God, unfortunately, existed all right; and the superlatively good God who dwelt in timeless peace above him had sent Jesus to deliver man from his odious Law, with which he, the Eternal, timeless Good, had had nothing to do. This the apostle Paul had made abundantly clear in his Epistle to the Romans (or so, at least, Marcion thought). Tertullian, whose character was nicely modelled on the vengeful aspect of his God, seems to have liked Paul little more than he liked the philosophers, and even goes so far as to call him the 'heretics' own apostle'[7] and the apostle of Marcion himself.[8]

For Marcion, then, there are two gods, not one. There is the God of the Law, the God of the Jews, and there is the supremely good God, 'the most kind and gentle',[9] who dwells above him, utterly serene in his timeless bliss,[1] contemplating himself, one must suppose, in a timeless trance. Hence, because of his very nature, action of any kind is repulsive to him, and it is only because he *is* so 'gentle and kind' that he finally wakes up from his trance, and seeing the havoc that the other 'raving' God is wreaking among men, decides he must send his messenger Jesus secretly and unannounced to redeem them from their bondage to the tyrant and from the flesh which is his nasty creation.

Having deduced all this from his study of the sacred sources, Marcion realized that it must have been the God of the Law himself who was not above lies and deceit,[2] or perhaps his servant Satan, who had tampered with the new dispensation which he had secretly sent down through that 'atrocious' Creator's realm without the Creator at first realizing what was happening. That the new dispensation was something totally different and not proclaimed beforehand by the prophets, as the Catholics so absurdly declared, was proved by history

7. Ibid., 3.6.4; Evans, Vol. I, p. 181.
8. Ibid., 4.34.5; Evans, Vol. II, p. 451.
9. Ibid., 5.13.9; Evans, Vol. II, p. 591.
1. See ibid., 5.17.2; Evans, Vol. II, p. 615.
2. Ibid., 3.8.2; Evans, Vol. I, p. 193.

itself. Jesus was the Saviour all right, for that is what his name means, but he was not the Christ, the 'Messiah', the 'anointed one', whom the Jews expected; and the proof was that the Jews, quite rightly from their point of view, refused to recognize him as such.[3] The Catholics could drag bits and pieces of the Old Testament out of their context to their heart's content, but this did not and could not alter the fact that the Jews found the claims of Jesus to be their Messiah quite laughable, whereas his claim to be the Son of their God was simply blasphemous. They were absolutely right: Jesus was not the Son of *their* God but the Saviour of man *from* their God. He was the spiritual 'son' (if that was the right word) and the 'anointed one' of the supremely good God, who was so overwhelmed by compassion for the sufferings of man at the hands of the Creator that he so far violated his own eternal nature as to send Jesus to the human race to tell them the truth both about himself and the crazy errors of the Creator. As Tertullian rightly saw, Marcion's radical plan was 'to make Christ a stranger to the Creator', to 'alienate'[4] him, to separate him off once and for all from the atrocious God and the atrocious book with which he had deceived the Jews. If the Jews refused to abandon the God whom they regarded as particularly theirs for the 'gentle' wraith the good God had sent among them, then they might expect to be treated as the Creator had ordered them to treat the Canaanites. That they should ever have tried to submit to his terrible laws was no fault of theirs, since they knew very well what to expect the moment they disobeyed him: they would be exiled, tortured, persecuted, and finally exterminated unless they submitted and grovelled to the tyrant who had chosen them. This is the penalty the Jew must pay if he remains steadfast and loyal to the savage God who, as Marcion would *not* see, was at the same time a God of forgiveness and love.

Unfortunately we only know Marcion from the accounts of

3. Ibid., 3.6.4; Evans, Vol. I, p. 183.
4. Ibid., 2.29.1; Evans, Vol. I, p. 167.

his enemies; but even so, a fairly clear picture of his religion emerges. Among Gnostics he is unique in that he accepts the Old Testament and the New as both being divinely inspired. (It was, by the way, due to him that the Church decided it *had* to draw up a canon of scripture, that is, it had to declare that certain scriptures were inspired revelation and rule out the rest because Marcion had drawn up his own canon which could not go unchallenged.) For Marcion all scripture was inspired, but by two very different gods, one the supremely Good who inhabited an eternal Now, the other the savage Creator who could only see infinity as an endless prolongation of time.[5] Unlike other intellectual heretics, he did not laugh the Old Testament out of court,[6] he took it very, very seriously indeed. He simply could not accept, as Jung did, that God could be 'a persecutor and a helper in one' and 'a totality of inner opposites'.[7] This the Jews had always accepted, since they had experienced in their own flesh the fearful consequences of disobedience to this savage yet strangely holy God. They knew and still do in their flesh and bones that sooner or later any wilful attempt at assimilation with the 'Gentiles' will meet with the most ghastly punishment at the hands of the Gentiles themselves. Like Tertullian they know you cannot understand the ways of the Creator. Isaiah and Job and all the prophets bear witness to this:

> Who could have advised the spirit of Yahweh,
> what counsellor could have instructed him?
> Whom has he consulted to enlighten him,
> and to learn the path of justice
> and discover the most skilful ways?[8]

You have got to accept him on his own terms or not at all. It is

5. This is implied in 5.17.1, though Tertullian himself speaks of an eternal present in 3.5.2 (Evans, Vol. I, p. 179).
6. Ibid., 5.6.10; Evans, Vol. II, pp. 540-1.
7. C. G. Jung, *Answer to Job*, p. 10; *Collected Works*, Vol. IX, part 2B.   8. Isaiah 40:13-14.

not for us, Tertullian adds, after quoting Isaiah, to 'say, "God ought not to have done that", or "He ought to have done this instead" – as though anyone knew what things there are in God except the Spirit of God'.[9] You cannot rationalize God any more than you can rationalize Christ.

Marcion, as thorough-going a dualist as you could wish for, not only split God in two, he also split Christ in two. The supremely good God's Christ had already appeared as Jesus, not as a truly human being indeed, since the flesh is no more than a sack stuffed with dung,[1] as the Marcionites never tired of saying, but as a fairly substantial wraith appearing out of nowhere, and certainly not from the 'sewer of a womb', through 'the unclean and shameful torments of child-bearing, and after that . . . the dirty, troublesome and ridiculous management of the new-born child'.[2] Marcion's Christ was far too pure for any such filthiness. As a wraith, too, he cannot have been really crucified, but he did reappear after the crucifixion, not as a man (since nobody recognized him), but as the wraith he had always been, since Luke plainly says that after his appearance to the two unnamed disciples on the road to Emmaus he 'vanished from their sight',[3] and this is scarcely what you would expect from a man with real flesh and blood. The good God's Saviour, then, *has* appeared as a wraith that behaved as if it were human but was not really human, bringing the Gnostic message that salvation could only be attained out of this body and in *dis*obedience to the Law.[4]

As to the God of the Law, his Christ has not yet come. He is the Christ prophesied by Isaiah (7:14), whose name would be Emmanuel, not Jesus, and whose mission would be one of

9. Tertullian, op. cit., 2.2.4–5; Evans, Vol. I, p. 89.

1. Ibid., 3.10.1; Evans, Vol. I, p. 199.

2. Ibid., 3.11.7; Evans, Vol. I, p. 203.

3. Luke 24:31. For Marcion's pruning of Luke, see, E. Evans, op. cit., Vol. II, pp. 643–4.

4. See E. Evans, op. cit., Vol. I, pp. x–xi, where he quotes Irenaeus' account of Marcion and his 'shameless blasphemy'.

war not peace.[5] This presumably is how Marcion interpreted
the horrors of the Book of Revelation, which he rejected outright as having nothing whatever to do with the good God,[6]
but probably everything to do with the raving Creator who
revels in that sort of thing, as indeed did Charles Manson who
found much comfort in that book. One wonders, then, whether,
had Marcion had his way with the Christian Church, Manson
would have gone to quite the extremes he did.

Marcion's account of the two Gods has a certain neat logic
about it, and basically Tertullian understands him far better
than would the Greekish liberal Christians of his time, like
Clement of Alexandria, himself almost as much of a Platonist
as Marcion himself. One had to be reasonable about these
things and allegorize the Old Testament away as much as
possible. Tertullian would have none of this: he accepted
Marcion's challenge and not only admitted but gloried in the
fact that God's mercy had to be counterbalanced by his
terrible judgment and his implacable vengeance. Tertullian
might not have approved of Jung, but Jung would certainly
have agreed with Tertullian. As a living presence, God is both
terrible and unspeakably tender. This the Jews have always
accepted without flinching. This too is what Catholic and
Protestant Christianity is all about, this is the message of Islam,
as it is (on occasion) of the Upanishads and the *Bhagavad-
Gītā*. Once God comes forth from eternity into time he is both
a raving, 'atrocious' savage and the Merciful, the Compassionate. And *this*, not Marcion's spotlessly pure and good God, is
the God who filled Pascal's heart with certainty, joy, and
peace. 'Nature' mysticism is not particularly mysterious.
Pascal's is, for whatever he experienced on that memorable
night, it must have contained an element of sheer wonder at
the unspeakable majesty of God in which his fury was seen to
be suffused with his mercy and love. Most Christian mystics
have felt this too, but they are never quoted by our irrational

5. Tertullian, op. cit., 3.12.1ff.; Evans, Vol. I, p. 205.
6. Ibid., 3.14.3–4; 4.5.2; Evans, Vol. I, p. 213; Vol. II, p. 271.

rationalists and dehumanized humanists. I greatly fear that Miss Murdoch, too, is pursuing as unsubstantial a Good as Marcion's Christ; for Plato's idea of the Good is so unrelated to man as he actually is that it might just as well not be there. Surely the greatness of Aristotle lies precisely in this, that he has bridged the gulf between matter and spirit in a way that no Platonist even wants to do. The secret of the success of Teilhard de Chardin is that, without knowing it, he has simply revamped Aristotle's basic view of the cosmos in the sort of terminology that appeals to the more half-baked intellectuals of today. Aristotle, too, had his own ideas of evil and they are not at all unlike those of Georges Bernanos as expressed in his masterpiece *Monsieur Ouine*.[7]

Drugs, Mysticism and Make-believe was the title of my last book; and it attempted to describe the modern world, and its rejection by the dissatisfied sons and daughters of a self-satisfied, money-proud bourgeoisie. Of course the young are right to want to escape from the sheer, smug, mechanized boredom which is the atmosphere which holds their horrid little identical homes together. They all know what they want to escape from, but have they any idea what they want to escape *to*? Not really, I am afraid, for in their schools and colleges they have been taught how *not* to think, and the motley band of Hindu and Japanese gurus who thrive on the sheer *naïveté* and blank stupidity of a sizeable majority of modern youth tell them that thought itself is evil (Krishnamurti, himself a highly Westernized intellectual, is particularly good at this). Basically what they are looking for is peace of mind, the Buddhist Nirvana: sometimes they find it, and good luck to them. But what they will not face, because they have seen it rather too often on their television screens, is what Bonhoeffer called 'the wickedness of evil'. They want the timeless blessedness allegedly supplied by Marcion's oh! so kind and gentle God, because they dare not face that frenzied God who storms and rages throughout the Old Testa-

7. See my *Drugs, Mysticism and Make-believe*, pp. 147–62.

ment, is tamed and muted in the Apocrypha and the New,
only to reappear with a literal vengeance in the Revelation
of St John the Divine which brings this terrible book to an
end.

Most of us are Marcionites at heart since we really believe
that Jesus Christ put paid to all that seething wrath by his own
self-sacrifice and submission. *His* Passion – his suffering and
death – somehow appeased that wrathful monster and reconciled him with his own creature, man, the creation of whom he
had once bitterly regretted. For did he not say to Noah: 'The
end has come for all things of flesh; I have decided this, because the earth is full of violence of man's making, and I will
efface them from the earth.'[8] As Marcion pointed out, the
savage God, being himself unstable, is always changing his
mind. He thought that by sending his only begotten Son to be
done to death on earth he would bring salvation for many.
Quite obviously no such thing has happened. Since the
'Christ-event', to borrow the modern jargon, nothing whatever has changed. Man is just as wicked, mediocre, and stupid
as he ever was. And the reason is, I suspect, that we are all
Marcionites (or Buddhists, there is not very much difference)
at heart. We do not believe in the reality of the raving God,
despite the fact that those few of us who have any intelligence at all realize that he is raving within ourselves all the
time.

It is to Tertullian's eternal credit that he recognized these
truths from the very scriptures he held sacred. The New
Testament was the natural fulfilment of the Old: God chastises
whom he loves. And it does indeed seem a strange sort of love
for a father to torture his own son to death. But what Oscar
Wilde wrote in Reading jail is very true indeed:

> Yet each man kills the thing he loves,
>   By each let this be heard,
>   Some do it with a bitter look,

8. Genesis 6:13.

Some with a flattering word.
The coward does it with a kiss,
The brave man with a sword!

It is with the sword that Yahweh kills, the 'sharp sword' of the rider on the white horse whose name is 'Faithful and True', the 'Word of God', whose 'cloak is soaked in blood', sent to strike the pagans and to 'tread out the wine of Almighty God's fierce anger':[9] Jesus Christ himself during his ministry on earth had said: 'It is not peace I have come to bring, but a sword.'[1] No wonder Marcion chose the gentle Luke rather than the fierce Matthew, for Luke substitutes 'division' for the sharp, concrete, cutting sword.

There is indeed a sharp division between those religions whose characteristic form of religious practice is prayer and adoration of Pascal's 'God of Abraham, God of Isaac, God of Jacob' on the one hand and religions in which sitting postures designed to find the God within you are thought to be the most appropriate way of approaching the Deity. These might aptly be called the 'religion of the philosophers and scientists'. The division between the two is, perhaps, at its sharpest in their attitude towards evil. For the three great monotheistic religions who worship the God of Abraham (whom Islam claims as its true founder), the God of Isaac (whom Christians worship as the 'Lamb of God', sacrificially slaughtered in the savage God's good time as the only really meaningful sacrifice, for which the ram slaughtered in Isaac's stead was only a substitute), and the God of Jacob, also known as Israel, whose God-sanctioned deceit led to God's choice of his faithful descendants to be his chosen people – these religions regard sin as basically meaning disobedience to an utterly incomprehensible God, while those who adhere to the 'God of the philosophers and scientists' regard sin as being in some way identical with matter. These include not only most Hindus, the Jains, the early Buddhists, and the Manichees, but also

9. Revelation 19:11–15.   1. Matthew 10:34. Cf. Luke 12:51.

Plato and the Platonists, the real heretics of Greek philosophy
in that, so far from identifying the One with the many as is
sometimes falsely alleged of them, they rather identified the
One with pure, pure Spirit, the 'Idea of the Good', and the
many with matter and the body, that hateful conglomerate of
living filth where the same filthy organs serve for the voiding
of evil-smelling excreta, which are the real carnal man, and
for the further reproduction and proliferation of more and
more animal filth for ever and ever. All this was as foreign to
the Hebrews as it had originally been to the Greeks, and we
owe it to our father Aristotle that he restored the unity of
matter and form, body and soul, which Plato had shattered,
thus bringing the Gentiles back into line with traditional
Hebrew thought and preparing them for what would have
seemed to him the perfect solution to whatever doubts remained in his master-builder's mind, the incarnation of the
Logos, 'the true account of the law of the universe',[2] in Jesus
of Nazareth, the carpenter whose craft it was to mould wood –
the very word Aristotle had chosen to represent his 'matter' –
into ever nobler and better forms. How fitting that this skilled
young craftsman should be chosen by his 'father', the Unmoved Mover, to *be* 'the true account of the law of man'. He
it was who was not only to put the coping-stone on to the Law
and the Prophets but also to show that, if Aristotle in any way
erred, it was in that he had not emphasized as strongly as he
might have done that you cannot always reach your total self-
fulfilment without first going through an act of total self-
abnegation.

The whole ascetic tradition, whether it be Buddhist,
Platonist, Manichaean, Christian, or Islamic, springs from that
most polluted of all sources, the Satanic sin of pride, the
desire to be 'like gods'. We are not gods, we are social, irrational animals, designed to become rational, social animals,
and finally, having built our house on solid Aristotelian rock,
to become 'like a god', our work well done. Then we can say

2. E. Hussey, *The Presocratics*, p. 40.

goodbye to poor old Brother Ass as he lies dying, our faithful servant till the last, obstinate little Brother Ass, whom we had to beat and shove around from time to time because he is after all a pretty silly little ass and sometimes thinks he knows the way home better than we do ourselves. There was never really any harm in him and we will know this when his gentle eyes are closed in death, a little saddened perhaps that we cannot take him with us to the promised land of all good things, perfected in the Joy of the total Awareness of Being which is our final end.

Or perhaps we can, for with that raging, savage God – who pushes us around as we pushed our own irritating little donkey around, simply because we *are* his children, and children, being children, cannot help making mistakes – with him all things are possible. Surely God, who made so improbable a beast as the ostrich 'giving her no share of common sense',[3] can bring old Brother Ass to his own perfection in what-ever state is most fitting for him in that unimaginable world where all things for ever *are* 'all together, now, one and coherent'.

No, it is not the body that is evil but the soul which mis-directs it, seeking only to use it for its own advantage and pleasure. For the soul to be at war with the body is an un-natural and wicked state of affairs; for, as Aristotle says, 'such persons are at war with themselves, desiring one thing and willing another, lacking all self-control. They choose what is pleasant enough but actually harms them instead of what they really think is good. . . . Wicked men seek the company of others, *but run away from themselves.* . . . They feel no affection for themselves, since they lack anything that is in any way lovable. Hence they can neither share joy with themselves nor can they have compassion on themselves. Their soul is in a state of civil war, one part of it suffering, out of sheer wicked-ness, from being unable to get hold of certain things, while another part of it is pleased. One part drags them this way,

3. Job 39:17.

while the other drags them that way, intent, it would seem on shattering them to pieces.'[4]

St Paul, of course, had the same trouble: 'I cannot understand my own behaviour. I fail to carry out the things I want to do, and I find myself doing the very things I hate.'[5] Aristotle knew quite as much about what is now called 'alienation' as did St Paul. The alienated man is in a state of civil war with himself, and this is the very definition of evil. It is also madness or schizophrenia (if you prefer it in Greek).

Why, then, are we mad and bad? Because 'it is not against flesh and blood that we have to struggle, but against the Sovereignties and the Powers who originate the darkness in this world, the spiritual army of evil in the heavens'.[6]

But who created these sinister Sovereignties and Powers? Why, that savage God of course. He created them and their grim commander Satan as angels of light, but they rebelled and were cast out from the presence of God so that they were free to plague the sons of men. But since God was omniscient, why did he not prevent it? Because it would appear there is evil in the very heart of God; for he whose Spirit is most Holy has also 'under his control the spirit which is not holy'.[7] You cannot put the blame on man or even on Satan: you have to blame, if blame you must, him who is alone responsible, God, the Creator of heaven and earth, 'who makes peace and creates evil things'.[8] For 'the same God smites, and also heals; he kills, and also makes alive: he brings down, but also raises up; he creates evils, but also makes peace'.[9] The Dead Sea Scrolls have the same story to tell; we read it again in the

4. Aristotle, *Nicomachean Ethics*, 9.4.8–9 (1166b 7–22).

5. Romans 7:15.

6. Ephesians 6:12. I have changed the Jerusalem Bible's 'human enemies' into the more literal 'flesh and blood'.

7. Tertullian, op. cit., 4.26.10; Evans, Vol. II, p. 411.

8. Isaiah 45:7. I follow the Septuagint translation as does Tertullian, op. cit., 2.14.1, although Tertullian admits that the Greek word for 'evil' can occasionally be used in the sense of 'discomforts and injuries'.   9. Tertullian, loc. cit.

Koran and the *Bhagavad-Gītā*; and we recognize the same God in the Hindu Shiva, the Absolute, who, like Yahweh, manifests himself alike in tenderness and terror. You will even find it in Zoroaster's *Gāthās*, where the warring twins, the Holy Spirit and the Evil One, are themselves subject to a higher power, their father who is the Wise Lord. This whole idea was taken over by the Dead Sea sect and proclaimed in no uncertain terms:

'He has created man to govern the world, and has appointed for him two spirits in which to walk until the time of His visitation: the spirits of truth and falsehood. Those born of truth spring from a fountain of light, but those born of falsehood spring from a source of darkness. All the children of righteousness are ruled by the Prince of Light and walk in the ways of light, but all the children of falsehood are ruled by the Angel of Darkness and walk in the ways of darkness.

'The Angel of Darkness leads all the children of righteousness astray, and until his end, all their sin, iniquities, wickedness, and all their unlawful deeds are caused by his dominion in accordance with the mysteries of God. . . .

'But the God of Israel and His Angel of Truth will succour all the sons of light. For it is He who created the spirits of Light and Darkness and founded every action upon them and established every deed [upon] their [ways]. And He loves the one everlastingly and delights in its works for ever; but the counsel of the other He loathes and for ever hates its ways.'[1]

Why, in the name of Marcion's God, does he create an Angel of Darkness whom he 'loathes and for ever hates its ways'? Is it we who are either mad or bad, or both? Or is it he? Marcion would no doubt have asked Tertullian; and Tertullian would almost certainly have replied 'both' – from a purely human point of view. But God is not human, and it is impious to question his ways. So 'he should be accepted without argument, to be worshipped and not judged, to be obeyed rather

1. G. Vermes, *The Dead Sea Scrolls in English* (Penguin Books, Harmondsworth, 1965), pp. 75–6.

than discussed, and even feared for his severity. For what could be more to a man's interest than regard for the true God, under whose control he had come, so to speak, because no other god was there?'[2] No wonder the author of the Epistle to the Hebrews wrote: 'It is a dreadful thing to fall into the hands of the living God.'[3] The same savage God who had revealed himself to the Jews was later to reveal himself to their Arab cousins through the 'en-godded' lips of the Prophet Muhammad. He is the same God all right, threatening and promising, the Merciful and Compassionate, but also the Vengeful and the Tyrant (*jabbār*), the Best of Deceivers,[4] who leads astray and guides whom he will. He is every bit as much the Lord God of armies as was Yahweh, but in his new Arabian disguise he was infinitely more successful, spreading a more up-to-date version of the old Jewish Law among the Gentiles, using that very sword that Jesus Christ himself had promised to bring. In the process he dealt the death-blow to the Zoroastrian faith, which, at that stage, alone among all the religions of the world, stuck to the absolute Goodness and Creativity of God, now pitted against another eternal principle, Ahriman, the Evil One, the destroyer and deceiver. Such relative rationality was no match for the Merciful and Compassionate One in whose heart burnt the insatiable Wrath that could 'create many *jinn* and men for hell',[5] where they will abide for ever roasting in the blazing fire.

Meanwhile he had not been idle in India, where Marcion's serene God seemed to be having it all his own way. He erupted in personal form as the great God Shiva, already known in the *Rigveda* as the divine archer, pursuing a solitary course, shooting his arrows at whom he will. Later he is black, swarthy, murderous and fearful, a robber, cheat and deceiver, lord of thieves and robbers.[6] This was the god that was to rise

2. Tertullian, op. cit., 2.1.2–3; Evans, Vol. I, p. 87.

3. Hebrews 10:31.   4. Koran, 3.47.   5. Ibid., 7.178.

6. See R. C. Zaehner, *Hinduism* (Oxford University Press, London, 1962), pp. 43–4.

to the rank of supreme God. He is terrible yet, like Yahweh, he is also mild. He is gruesome, haunting cremation-grounds, with matted hair and smeared with ashes. His necklace is of skulls and there are serpents in his hair. He is 'Lord of the dance', and when he dances he becomes raving mad – dancing the cosmos into existence and dancing it back again into chaos. Rushing down the mountain-side he dances in his frenzy, surrounded by a rout of goblins, creatures half-human, half-animal, who urge him on in his mad career. Yet it was this same gruesome, hideous, cruel, and raving God, whose symbol was the erect phallus, who aroused the passionate devotion of his worshippers, who said of him that he was Love itself, the answer to that yearning, passionate love that moved Aristotle's cosmos on to its final consummation.

How strange is the heart of man, and how unbelievable are the ways of God!

But before bringing this chapter to its close we cannot refrain from introducing Shiva's rival, the God of the *Bhagavad-Gītā* who, incarnate in the form of Krishna, reveals himself to Arjuna, not as Marcion's gentle God wrapped away in the silence of the infinite but as his Creator God of the Law in all his blazing savagery. The theophany is overwhelming and Arjuna is terrified at what he sees. Scarcely knowing what he says, he cries out in terrified amazement:

> Gazing upon thy mighty form
> With its myriad mouths, eyes, arms, thighs, feet,
>   Bellies and sharp gruesome tusks,
> The worlds all shudder in affright – how much more I!
>
> Ablaze with many-coloured flames, thou touch'st the sky,
> Thy mouths wide open, gaping, thine eyes distended, blazing:
> I see thee, and my inmost self is shaken:
> I cannot bear it, I find no peace, O Vishnu.

God: Mad or Bad?

I see thy mouths with jagged, ghastly tusks,
Reminding me of Time's devouring fire:
I cannot find my bearings, I see no refuge;
Have mercy, God of gods, Home of the Universe!

Lo, all the sons of Dhritarāshtra,
Accompanied by a host of kings,
Bhīshma, Drona, and Karna, son of the charioteer,
And those foremost in battle of our party too,

Rush blindly into thy gaping mouths
That with their horrid tusks strike them with terror.
    Some stick in the gaps between thy teeth,
See them! – their heads to powder ground.

As many swelling, seething streams
Rush headlong into the one great sea,
So do these heroes of this world of men
    Enter thy blazing mouths.

As moths, in bursting, hurtling haste,
Rush into a lighted blaze, to their own destruction,
So do the worlds, well-trained in hasty violence,
Pour into thy mouths to their own undoing.

On every side thou lickest, lickest up – devouring –
Worlds, universes, everything – with burning mouths;
Vishnu! thy dreadful rays of light fill the whole universe
With flames of glory scorching everywhere.[7]

Once again we recognize him, the 'atrocious' God of Israel, shaking poor Marcion's timeless God out of Arjuna's inmost self, which is where, in India, he normally abides, and wreaking wrath and destruction everywhere. But, as always, the blood-lust and the savagery is not the whole story, for there are some who enter the divine gas-chambers with minds at rest, serene:

7. *Bhagavad-Gītā*, 11.23–30.

Lo, the hosts of gods are entering into thee:
Some, terror-struck, extol thee, hands together pressed.
Great seers and men perfected in serried ranks
Cry out: 'All hail!' and praise thee with copious hymns of
  praise.[8]

God certainly kills the things he loves, but the things he loves rejoice to be killed at such a hand.

But enough is enough. Let us turn from the divine terror to consider a more homely subject – the divinity of bees.

8. Ibid., 11.21.

7

THE DIVINITY OF BEES

'Now, with regard to the generation of creatures that are
closely related to them such as hornets and wasps, the situation
is very much the same with all of them in some ways; but that
something extra is lacking, and that is reasonable enough, for
there is nothing divine about them, as there *is* in the tribe of
bees.'[1]

So spake Aristotle; and now Plato:

' "And so", said Socrates, "the most blessed among those
who will [in death], go to the best place, will be those who have
conscientiously practised the social and civic virtues, rightly
called sound common sense (*sophrosunē*) and justice; and these
they will have acquired by nature and study, but without the
benefit of philosophy and intellect."

' "But in what way will these people be the most blessed?"

' "Don't you see? Surely it is only right and proper that they
should be reincarnated in some social and gentle species, like
bees, wasps, or ants, or into the human race again so that they
in their turn can reproduce nice, moderate, and mediocre
(*metrios*) men."

' "Very right and proper." '[2]

It is, then, nice to think that at least on the subject of bees
the two greatest minds of the ancient West were in substantial
agreement. Aristotle was, of course, the more analytical
thinker, and saw that to class bees with wasps and ants was
both imperceptive and very nearly blasphemous: for there is
divinity in bees in which neither wasps nor ants can claim to
share. In what does this divinity consist? Plainly not in their

1. Aristotle, *Generation of Animals*, 3.10 (761a 2–5).
2. Plato, *Phaedo*, 82 A–B.

243

social organization in which the ants may be said to rival if not
to surpass them. Then it can only be that they produce two
good things which no other creature produces: honey and wax.
They are not only supremely well organized themselves, but
they serve not only their immediate inferiors, the plants, by
fertilizing them, but also their immediate superiors, bears and
men; for both these animal species dearly love their sweet
honey, and until the discovery of gas and electricity it was the
product of bees and the sober olive tree that gave light to
philosophers, enabling them to turn night into day so that they
in their turn might enlighten the darkness of more common
men.

Fiat lux: ' "Let there be light", and there was light. God
saw that the light was good.'[3] This was on the first day of
Creation. On the fifth 'God said, "Let the earth produce every
kind of living creature: cattle, reptiles, and every kind of wild
beast." And so it was. God made every kind of wild beast,
every kind of cattle, and every kind of land reptile. God saw
that it was good.'

We all know the sequel. God created man in his own image
and likeness. Believe it or not, that refers to you and me. Most
people don't believe it: they take one look at their fellow-men
in the London Underground, the Paris Métro, or New York's
fetid subway during the rush hour and that is quite enough to
convince them that there is not a word of truth in it. Or, perhaps, in their heart of hearts they are Marcionites as, I suspect,
most of us are. In that case they will have little difficulty in
believing that that atrocious Creator has produced creatures
like himself, in every way monstrous, since they are both at
war with themselves and at the same time manage to be crashing self-centred bores.

When Aristotle says that bees have that little bit extra denied
to the wasps and ants, he presumably means that they possess
it actually, not just potentially. They have already achieved
their own end and fulfilment, whereas the mass of mankind

3. Genesis 1:3–4.

has gone hopelessly astray. Bees do not deviate from their allotted course any more than do the stars in heaven: it is in this that their divinity consists, as well as in their selfless service to the vegetable world, bears, and men. Had Aristotle known the Old Testament he might have altered God's disastrous Friday mistake and substituted 'bees' for 'man' in this vital passage. ' "Let us make bees in our own image, in the likeness of ourselves" ' . . .

> God created bees in the image of himself,
> in the image of God he created them,
> workers, drones, and queens[4] he created them.

For the wisdom of bees is an unchanging wisdom, their 'Way' *is* 'an Unvarying Way'.[5] Unlike the citizens of the republic described by Plato in the *Laws*, they need no Nocturnal Synod to start them on their proper course: they follow it according to the divine wisdom that is within them; they need no other guide. Theirs is a truly blessed state in which everything works with the marvellous precision of a clockwork orange, having all the sweetness of an orange and much more, and at the same time a truly divine orderliness that is an example to the whole terrestrial creation.

Aristotle was absolutely right in ascribing divinity to bees. I have not read very much, but I cannot recollect any unkind word being said about bees. Ants and wasps, yes: bees, no. For if we want to castigate our modern mechanistic civilization, we turn on the unfortunate ant; we hold up our hands in horror at the thought of the ant-hill civilization to come. Teilhard de Chardin never stops warning us against this 'ant-hill' civilization, never pausing to think that it is just such a civilization that his own ideas will make acceptable to the unwary. About a possible beehive civilization he says not a word. And rightly so, since he is Catholic enough to know that the Church herself admits her debt to the industrious bee whose

4. Actually Aristotle thought queen bees were male.
5. *Tao Tê Ching*, 1.1.

humble and unobtrusive work provides her with sweetness and light. She sometimes badly needs both.

In the most moving and solemn ceremony which is the climax of Holy Week, the Easter Vigil, which proclaims the resurrection of Christ, the Paschal candle is ceremonially lighted in an atmosphere of tense expectation. *Fiat lux:* 'Let there be light.' And there is light in the vast darkness of some sombre cathedral – a very little, insignificant light, a baby light 'to lighten the Gentiles'. But there would be no light were it not for the work of bees; and the whole Christian mystery – and make no mistake about it, Christianity is nothing if not a mystery, however much the scribes may tamper with it – the whole Christian mystery is symbolized in that massive candle made by the communal effort of the tribe of bees. Death and Resurrection: and the divinity of bees! 'O truly blessed night', the liturgy proclaims, blessed for countless reasons which the Church ecstatically intones, but blessed too in that the Church renders homage to the divinity of bees. But let us get everything into due perspective, and we can only do this by quoting the liturgy itself, in which the whole of the Catholic mystery is enshrined.

'This is the night', the Church proclaims, 'in which Christ broke the chains of death and ascended victoriously from hell. For it availed us nothing to be born unless it has availed us to be redeemed. O admirable lavishing of Thy goodness on us. O untold excess of love; that to redeem a slave Thou deliveredst up Thy Son. *O truly necessary sin of Adam*, that was blotted out by the death of Christ! *O happy fault* that merited such and so great a Redeemer! O truly blessed night which alone served to know the time and the hour in which Christ rose again from hell! This is the night about which is written: And the night shall be as clear as the day: And the night is my illumination in my delights. Therefore the hallowing of this night drives away crimes, cleanses faults, restores innocence to sinners and joy to the sorrowful. It banishes hates, prepares concord and humbles empires.

'In the grace of this night, then, receive, Holy Father, the evening sacrifice of this incense which Holy Church presents to Thee, through the hands of her ministers, *in this solemn offering of [the candle of] Wax made out of the works of bees*. But now we know good tidings [proclaimed] by this pillar which the shimmering fire has lit in God's honour.

'And this fire, though divided into parts, suffers no loss from the communication of its light. For it is fed by *the melting wax which the mother bee produced for the substance of this blessed lamp.*'

Apart from the mystery of man's redemption here so solemnly proclaimed, and apart from 'the truly necessary sin of Adam' and his 'happy fault', which seem to me to reflect the whole flavour of forgiveness that alone gives savour to the message of Christianity, for unless we can believe we are forgiven, we cannot bring ourselves to forgive ourselves (and that is surely at the bottom of so many divided personalities): apart from all this, it is really touching at this supreme moment of Christian jubilation that man should, for once, cease to be self-regarding and admit the debt he owes to what he thinks is a humbler creation – the industrious tribe of bees. How nauseating it is that in the new Mass we are constantly reminded that the communion bread is made by *human* hands, thereby drumming into ourselves day after day that we humans alone count, whereas we know perfectly well day in and day out in the recesses of our heart that we are dust and it is to dust that we return. This we are openly reminded of once a year – on Ash Wednesday – while every day we remind ourselves in church of just how important we are. At the Easter Vigil the tables are turned on us, and we are reminded of the works of bees, who do their mechanical little jobs for us without expecting any return. And the melting of *their* wax into the consuming fire is a further reminder to us that it is *we* who must melt away into the divine Fire, which may be either the cleansing fire of purgatory or the fire of the divine wrath our 'atrocious' God has reserved for the unbelievers, as Muslims are constantly reminded in the burning letters of the Koran, the 'Word' made Book. Aristotle knew this too: the 'passive' mind must learn to melt into the 'craftsman', creative mind; for she has nothing else to melt into, poor 'pathetic' little mind whose only alternative is to be snuffed out as the last breath of life withdraws from the body without which she cannot live. 'Melting' is one of the stock symbols employed by the mystics: 'That my soul may ever languish and melt with love and longing for Thee . . . and long to be dissolved and to be with Thee', as St Bonaventure's post-communion prayer puts it. Even this symbol would make no sense, were it not for the wax supplied by bees. So let us be thankful to them and concede them that due part of divinity that Aristotle assigned to them.

But if bees really have some spark of divinity in them, can we not learn from them? Teilhard de Chardin professed a sacred horror at the thought of the ant-hill civilization he saw as the only alternative to the convergent society of free and 'super-personalized' individuals in an atmosphere of love, all converging towards Omega Point which was the cosmic Christ towards which human society was *irreversibly* tending. The evidence he produced for this was disturbing, since most of it pointed to the ant-hill rather than to Christ, cosmic or otherwise. The only firm evidence he could supply for his concept of convergence was, of all things, the atom bomb! Most of the dithyramb he wrote on this subject I quoted in my last book, and I will only repeat what is essential to the matter in hand here.

'At that moment man found himself hallowed not only with his existing strength but with a method which would enable him to master all the forces surrounding him. . . . He had discovered, in the unconsidered unanimity of the act which circumstances had forced upon him, another secret pointing the way to his omnipotence. For the first time in history . . . a planned scientific experiment employing units of a hundred or a thousand men had been successfully completed. . . . The greatest discovery ever made by man was precisely the one in which the largest number of minds were enabled to join together in a single organism, both more complicated and more centred, for the purpose of research. Was this simply coincidence? Did it not rather show that in this as in other fields nothing in the universe can resist the converging energies of a sufficient number of minds sufficiently grouped and organized?'[6]

Even if this were true, it is hardly in the best of taste.

However, Teilhard is not alone in his uncritical admiration of the achievement of science. No lesser person than Pope Paul VI, carried away by a similar enthusiasm at the first American landing on the moon, exclaimed: 'This very bold enterprise obliges us to look on high, beyond this earthly field, to remember the immense and serious reality in which our little life unfolds. This new discovery of created life is very important for our spiritual life. To see God in the world and the world in God, what is more exciting? Is it not thus that we escape the terror of the void that unmeasured time and unconfined space produce around the microcosm that is us?'[7]

Even by the high standards of ambiguity for which papal pronouncements are justly famous, this is unusually cryptic; for it is far from clear why or how you can 'see God in the world and the world in God' more clearly from the rocky, sandy deadness of the moon than you can from this life-infested planet of ours. But the note of triumph seems to be unmistakably there, not indeed in such shrill tones as we now take for granted from Teilhard, but quite clearly there. That this should be so is disquieting; for there is nothing in the world more ultimately self-destructive than human pride, as Pope Paul himself knows very much better than I. It was pride that caused the fall of Satan in that old, half-forgotten Judaeo-

6. Pierre Teilhard de Chardin, *L'avenir de l'homme* (Éditions du Seuil, Paris, 1959), pp. 182–3; cf. E.T., *The Future of Man* (Collins, London, and Harper & Row, New York, 1964), pp. 143–4.

7. Quoted in *The Tablet*, 26.vii.69.

Christian legend, and it is pride that will in the end destroy the human animal who hasn't even the excuse of being an angel.

We are on the brink of an abyss, and we know it. Our civilization is undergoing a crisis, and we more or less know what kind of crisis it is. We are converging on nothing; and when Teilhard speaks of 'the converging energies of a sufficient number of minds sufficiently grouped and organized', he is speaking of a scientific *élite* only, to which he belonged in his own speciality of palaeontology though in nothing else. He is not speaking of the human race in general whom he so movingly admits to having been unable to love[8] and whom he cavalierly dismisses as 'the dull, inert mass of those who believe in nothing at all'.[9] In this, of course, he is not alone, since intellectuals always assume that they know what is best for others. They pontificate, usually in radical tones, telling the masses what is good for them, very like those sinister 'Wardens' in Plato's *Republic* who constitute the 'Nocturnal Synod' of his *Laws*. Fortunately the process has not yet gone so far in the 'free' world as it has in the Soviet bloc, which, since the Czechoslovaks' poor little effort to bring Teilhard's dream to life, has realized as never before the modern ideal of a human ant-hill to which we are irreversibly moving.

The question is, as Bernanos said: 'Are we confronted with a new civilization going through a crisis of growth? Or is it rather a crisis of human civilization itself, that is to say a real disease in civilization? Of these two hypotheses imbeciles are unanimous in choosing the first. I am not saying that everyone who chooses it is an imbecile, but I *am* saying that all imbeciles choose it. There is a fine distinction in this. Imbeciles choose it because it is easier, by which I mean lazier.'[1] He might have added that it is also more cowardly since it is a refusal to face the ant-hill without blanching. This is precisely what Teilhard refused to do.

8. See my *Drugs, Mysticism and Make-believe*, p. 183.
9. P. Teilhard de Chardin, *The Future of Man*, p. 76.
1. G. Bernanos, *La liberté pour quoi faire?* p. 56.

The Divinity of Bees

The crisis of our civilization is, as Bernanos's 'imbeciles' refuse to see, not the birth of a new civilization from an older one, since 'daughter' civilizations are never complete breaks with the past: they inherit certain common characteristics which, for lack of a better word, can only be called national. That this is true any first-generation Englishman or Frenchman will tell you. If you are born and bred in England of naturalized foreign parents, you *are* English whether you like it or not. Whether you like it or not, you are absorbing a British atmosphere and British values, which you are forced to accept or reject like any other British citizen. And it was, perhaps, only during the Second World War that I realized how absolutely true this was. We were fighting what seemed to us to be perhaps the first 'just' war in history, and for two years we were fighting it alone. We had the solidarity of bees: we were simply doing what our British identity (which we have now already lost) instinctively told us to do. Churchill was not exaggerating when he said it was our finest hour. The jargon for once was simple and it was true. 'We are all in it together': that was a slogan of course, but it also happened to be literally true. Never before or since have we felt so acutely that our deprivations, which we cheerfully accepted, and our efforts, which we shared in common, were absolutely worthwhile, because we sensed in our bones that what we were fighting against was radically evil. If there were gurus and mystagogues in our midst, they were silent, because they knew full well that they had no message that made any kind of sense to a people that had come to believe passionately that evil is more palpably real than good. We knew we must fight if we were to survive collectively and individually as human beings and not be turned into goose-stepping clockwork oranges, mesmerized into magical obedience like the *happy* citizens in Plato's *Laws* and the *happy* mass of the German people which gratefully and graciously conformed to the ignoble but ruthlessly logical copy of the ideal Platonic republic with which Hitler, the master magician, had supplied them. However old-fashioned and reactionary it may sound, we were kept afloat by the national virtues that are still attributed to us – a sense of fair play, a love of liberty, and level-headed common sense. Among the modern nations we represented pre-eminently the ancient Greek virtue of *sophrosunē* which, for Aristotle, meant rational common sense.

Of course I am not such an imbecile as to believe that these particular virtues are peculiar to the British race. They are not. They nevertheless grew up on British soil as a typically British and Protestant reaction against an emergent capitalism which itself had its roots in Protestantism, though not, I think, in the Reformers themselves. For it was the root-sin of this aspect of Protestantism (with, oddly enough, the Quakers in its van) which put thrift in the place of the more traditional 'faith, hope, and charity' (let us keep the word for the moment since its currency has been rather less debased than that of the slippery, ambivalent, sleazy thing that 'love' has come to mean).

Thrift, of course, is the cover-name for the deadly sin of avarice. It is what Aristotle called the deficient aspect of the virtue the golden mean of which is 'liberality' (Greek *eleutheriotēs*, meaning 'the virtue characteristic of a free man'). 'It has two aspects, a deficiency in giving and an excess in getting';[2] and the latter is quite as important as the former. It lies at the heart of the modern world.

The modern world is run and conducted according to two 'axioms', the axiom that material prosperity is the highest good for mankind, and the axiom that true 'blessedness' or happiness consists in the possession of things, not in pursuing your own fulfilment as a person in companionship with other persons, as Aristotle insisted. The deviation of the modern world is that it has formulated man's 'good' not as to 'be', but as to 'have'. This is quite as true of the cultivated rich as it is of the simply vulgar: they want to own objects of beauty not primarily because they give them pleasure (since too great

2. Aristotle, *Nicomachean Ethics*, 4.1.38 (1121b 18).

familiarity with every work of art, except, perhaps, the very
highest, breeds not quite contempt, but a kind of bored indifference), but because it gives them prestige among those
whom they themselves regard as prestigious. Between the
vulgar plutocrat and the refined art-collector there is no distinction in kind: they do not 'kill the things they love', which
can be a noble aberration, they love the things they *have*,
which has come to be not only the human norm but the human
ideal. Whether you prefer the vulgar plutocrat or the refined
variety is very much a matter of taste. It is simply a question
of whether you prefer the man who sincerely believes that
happiness consists in having more and more good things that
accord with his own boorish taste or the man who excuses and
conceals his cupidity behind the veil of aesthetic excellence.
It all depends on whether you prefer an honest thief or a
hypocritical one, as Proudhon would have said. Jesus Christ
abhorred hypocrites, and the more respectable they were the
more he loathed them. He also had a strange predilection for
the income-tax man and common prostitutes. None of these
tastes were shared by Aristotle, who was perhaps the most
'well-rounded', complete, and purely human philosopher who
has ever lived; but Aristotle was not God, and to see divinity
in human degradation needs the vision of a God. Hence, kick
against the pricks as I constantly do, I am compelled to accept
Jesus as God because he so obviously stands for everything
and everyone who will not bend the knee to the ancient god
Mammon, the god of money and the spirit of avarice, and the
modern god of efficiency or, as Professor Monod puts it,
'performance'.

The crisis of the modern world is that we have ruthlessly
jettisoned all traditional values in the interests of physical well-
being and mechanical efficiency. We have no values to put in
their place, only pseudo-values which claim to be scientific and
are not. The principal offenders in this respect are of course
Marx and Freud, the two self-deceived deceivers under whose
satanic sun the modern world has tried to live. At last – at very

long last – these two utterly sincere propounders of half-truths are being shown up, not of course because they are wrong (for in our Heraclitan see-saw world right and wrong flow and merge into each other), but because they have been found out: they do not work. Hence, since this century has not been able to produce any new ideology (which is, perhaps, the only thing to be said in its favour), what is left of our so-called intelligentsia can think up nothing more positive than neo-Marxism and neo-Freudianism and a bastardized neo-neo-Platonism which seeks its inspiration not in the shamanist fringe of our civilization, because our father Aristotle did his best – and succeeded – in canalizing that into less barbaric channels, but in any and every form of bastardized mysticism that the 'mystic' East has deigned to let loose in what to them is the Far East, that is, what is to us the far, far West, the State of California in the USA, the melting-pot of whatever civilization may emerge tomorrow, the microcosm of things that are yet to come.

One pointer in this direction, among many others, is the neo-Freudian psychoanalyst, Erich Fromm, whose recent book, *The Crisis of Psychoanalysis*, sounds the tocsin to wake us up to the deadly peril our civilization faces. He has nothing but generalities to offer, of course, any more than had Teilhard de Chardin; but at least he does not see our *irreversible* salvation in a 'Christified' version of totalitarianism, whether it be the enforced 'happiness' of the many under the 'benevolent' direction of an 'en-godded' few (as was the case with Nazism) or the same regimentation at the hands of a deified tyrant or a faceless Directory of dehumanized thugs (as in the Soviet Union of today). Essentially Teilhard's vision was a 'Christian' version of this, and it is wrong because it is based on an over-idealized concept of man. This is at least as dangerous as the reduction of man to the status of nothing more than a 'social animal' without that divine 'something' that, as Aristotle taught, he shared with his cousins, the bees.

Like all those pre-war French intellectuals who tried to

combine the fantasies of Freud with the opaque Hegelian communism of Engels and Marx, Erich Fromm has at last come to see that his whole monstrous edifice is coming crashing down about his ears. What he is really saying is that psychoanalysis has been found out, though he does not put it into so many words. He sees our crisis, incorrectly, I think, as a struggle between the love of life and the love of death. Freud's sin was that he killed his own child by injecting it with the death-wish.

Small wonder, then, that Fromm, in his moving peroration, asks:

'Has psychoanalysis any relevance in this crisis of life?

'Perhaps not. Perhaps the dice have already been cast by the fact that both leaders and led, driven by their ambitions, greed, blindness and mental inertia, are so determined to proceed on the way to catastrophe that the minority, who see what is coming, are like the chorus of the Greek drama; they can comment on the tragic course, yet they lack the power to change it.'[3]

Why should they want to, since it is they themselves who have been driving the Gadarene swine to their own destruction? And the swine are well-contented swine since they do not know that their *telos*, their end and consummation, is in the clockwork charnel-houses of Chicago. What have they to complain about? They have fulfilled their biological purpose. They have been cosseted and spoilt with all the food they want, they have known the ecstasy of being covered by a hog, and the material joy of being surrounded by a yearning brood of sucking piglets. They have been lulled into a happy unconsciousness of their final end, which is death. This is the obscene word that modern man must never use in polite society, just as sex was taboo to his fathers.

The battle is on, it seems, between the lovers of life and the lovers of death, between Charlie Manson, the Angel of Death, and his victims, who clung to life. In vain, for when

3. Erich Fromm, *The Crisis of Psychoanalysis*, p. 190.

death came like a thief in the night, they were not prepared for their eternal rest, but ended up as 'loud, loud' screams – screams 'for ever, infinite'.

The victims had been ill-prepared by their private psycho-analysts. They had, it would appear, put themselves into the hands of unskilled practitioners as devoted as themselves to the great god Mammon.

We all make mistakes, as the Greeks say when they are translating the manifold Hebrew words for sin. And Fromm has the rare courage to admit (or seem to admit) that Freudian psychoanalysis is not quite guiltless. So, like any good ecumenical Christian, he sends out a clarion call to all the lovers of life:

'Who can give up hope as long as there is life? Who can be silent as long as there are billions of human beings living, breathing, laughing, crying and hoping?' The question is rhetorical, expecting the answer: 'No one.' But the answer, as he himself implies in the very next sentence, is: 'Practically everyone.' The clockwork orange's heart has grown fat and has no pity except a very little something that still looks like pity for itself.

However, all is not yet lost, for the clockwork angels are on the side of life. 'The biologists, the chemists, the physiologists, the geneticists, the economists, the physicians, the theologians, the philosophers, the sociologists, the psychologists have spoken and are still speaking about the dangers; not the majority of them, but some; each from his particular field and point of observation.'[4] So there is still hope that this small minority of fallen angels who have seen the error of their ways will save man from his ingrained desire to get, to have, and to hold.

Some two thousand and five hundred years ago Gotama, the Buddha, proclaimed with the voice of a lion: 'Get this into your heads: there is no such thing as "I" or "mine". Stop hankering after anything at all, for that is the root of your un-

4. Ibid., pp. 190–1.

happiness.' Did anyone listen to him any more than anyone listened to Christ? A small minority who were very soon swallowed up in the sea of conventional converts. The monks grew fat and rich as is the way with monks always and everywhere. Does Dr Fromm really think that *his* little band of 'biophils' (Greek for 'lovers of life') will succeed where both the Buddha and the Christ failed? I hardly think so, for he is far too firmly rooted in what he calls the 'amoralism' and 'egoism' of Freud[5] really to be able to shake it off. The physician has not cured himself, because he has not diagnosed the disease. Freud sinned, it appears, in that he followed 'the leading concepts of bourgeois thinking'.[6]

It really is time that the Left, both old and new, stopped using the old catchwords and started trying to do a little lucid thinking about what the catchwords mean, if anything. When I was young, it was still common practice to call any boy you particularly disliked 'a dirty little Jew'. The word 'Jew', after centuries of Christian vilification of the only race their own God had ever chosen, had become a simple term of abuse meaning about as much and as little as 'you dirty swine' or 'you dirty little bastard'. After the gas-ovens and the 'final solution' in Germany we no longer resort to this particular type of heedless abuse. Christendom, after nearly two thousand years, has at last woken up to the fact that it has committed the almost unforgivable sin of denigrating, vilifying, persecuting, and massacring its own God's chosen people – the savage God whom it shares or thinks it shares with Israel, who certainly claims 'vengeance' for himself,[7] especially in his relations with his chosen people, but who permits no man wilfully to arrogate to himself the role of persecutor in his name.

As a term of abuse, then, we no longer dare say 'Jew': we are still too ashamed (one wonders for how long), so we say 'bourgeois' or 'Fascist' instead, like little children mouthing out their lessons parrot-wise. Fromm, of course, is as bour-

5. Ibid., pp. 51–2.   6. Ibid.
7. Deuteronomy 32:35; Hebrews 11:30.

geois as any other intellectual, as bourgeois as Marx and Freud, Engels and Jung, Lenin and Adler, every one of them tainted with the real bourgeois vice, which is not simply the lust to have and hold but the belief that happiness consists exclusively in material well-being, and not in the rational and moral exercise of liberty.

One of Bernanos's most powerful polemical writings directed against our mechanized civilization is entitled *La liberté pour quoi faire?* 'Liberty for what?' The same question might be asked about life. Life for what? A life the goal of which is material comfort conditioned by ceaseless commercial propaganda, a life in which the machines we have made are manipulated to make us more and more like each other, more and more homogenized like that awful American milk, a life in which we are lulled into a willing acceptance of degraded equality, the good, good life of the family car, the family TV, the family washing-machine, the gadget family served by machines, serving machines, bemused by the godlike power of the makers and inventors of machines: or a life in which each tries to realize himself most fully by being sane and whole and not at war with himself? This too is a rhetorical question, but the answer is *not* clear: for it has not been well put. Perhaps it could be more clearly put in this way: 'Do we want efficiency or do we want an untidy life of give and take in which the social animal is also a thinking and feeling animal, and to hell with those damned machines?' But, as Erich Fromm himself suggests, this is probably even now an irrelevant question 'since the dice have already been cast'.

Bernanos, like de Gaulle, was naïve enough to believe that French civilization, based, as he believed it to be, on liberty and reason, could shine out as a beacon in the coming twilight of Yankee smog. Despite the shame of the French capitulation in 1940 and the pathetic spectacle of the pious 'victor of Verdun' doing public penance for the sins of his country – the 'eldest daughter of the Church' turned whore – with the vast majority of the French hierarchy joining moanfully in the penitential chorus, both Bernanos and General de Gaulle carried on the struggle against what they, unlike the French episcopate, not only knew to be an evil thing but were prepared to name as such. They acted on their convictions, each according to the means at his disposal.

To the British de Gaulle could seem infuriating, but he had this in common with Churchill: they both passionately believed in honour, liberty, and the fundamental reasonableness of man. However much the British and the French might have fought each other in the past, this at least they had in common; and it is this that General de Gaulle, to his eternal credit, restored to France.

Since the industrial revolution France has never been a great power: in matters mechanical she could never rival those fearful German ants, let alone the enormous clockwork orange that was beginning to cast its plastic shadow over the European lands from which it had sprung. This, Bernanos thought, was not because she, who for centuries had been a 'light to lighten the Gentiles' in Europe, was simply too individualistic to be efficient, but because she refused to submit to the 'dictatorship of a technocracy gone mad'.[8] It is true that she held out against the Yankee clockwork ideal longer than anyone else, but under her present president, who is the very embodiment of the French bourgeoisie, the super-bureaucrat who can beat the bureaucrats at their own game, she is sliding down the slippery slope at full speed. Now it is Britain which is kicking violently against the mechanistic pricks, but not in the name of any sort of ideal but in a grotesque free-for-all in which organized Labour, now for the first time rich enough to take on both the Government and the capitalists, is busy organizing strike after strike to put up the wages of a working class turned bourgeois – and devil take the hindmost, which means the old, the weak, and the unorganized, that is to say, all defenceless human beings whose cause our savage God tirelessly pleaded in both the Old and the New Testaments, and in the Koran.

8. G. Bernanos, op. cit., p. 31.

It was, I think, Darwin who first spoke of the 'survival of the fittest', and in this, of course, the prophet of human progress, Teilhard de Chardin, followed him. What did he care about 'the poor, the lame, the twisted, the plain stupid', let alone 'the dull inert mass of those who believe in nothing at all'? Why, they can easily be written off as 'casualties, fallen on the field of honour'.[9] In return they have their 'aeroplanes, radios, "movies" ':[1] and once science and technology have really got in their stride, they shall have, oh, ever so much more. You had better have it in the prophet's own words:

'In the matter of "incorporated" energy we are incredibly slow to achieve (or even to conceive) the realization of a "body" of humanity. In this field the apostles of birth control (although too often inspired by *the narrow desire of relieving individual hardships*) will have rendered us the service of opening our eyes to the anomaly of a society that concerns itself with everything except the recruitment of its own elements. Now eugenics does not confine itself to a simple control of births. All sorts of related questions, scarcely yet raised despite their urgency, are attached to it. *What fundamental attitude*, for example, *should the advancing wing of humanity take to fixed or definitely unprogressive ethnical groups?* The earth is a closed and limited surface. *To what extent should it tolerate, racially or nationally, areas of lesser activity?* More generally still, how should we judge the efforts we lavish in all kinds of hospitals on saving what is so often no more than one of life's rejects? Something profoundly true and beautiful (I mean faith in the irreplaceable value and unpredictable resources contained in each personal unit) is evidently concealed in persistent sacrifice to save a human existence. But should not this solicitude of man for his individual neighbour be balanced by a higher passion, born of the faith in that other higher personality that is to be expected . . . from the world-wide achievements of our evolution? To what extent should

9. See my *Drugs, Mysticism and Make-believe*, pp. 180, 183.
1. P. Teilhard de Chardin, *Human Energy*, p. 128.

not the development of the strong (to the extent that we can define this quality) take precedence over the preservation of the weak? How can we reconcile, *in a state of maximum efficiency*, the care lavished on the wounded with the more urgent necessities of battle? In what does true charity consist?"[2]

The implication is barely concealed. Everything must be sacrificed at the altar of 'maximum efficiency'. This is totalitarian talk with a vengeance: not just the survival of the fittest, but the liquidation of the unfit.

Teilhard's compatriot and contemporary, Bernanos, has this story to tell which a French officer had told him after his return from a German prison camp. 'Two trains loaded with wounded German soldiers had arrived one morning. They were so badly wounded as to be unfit for any social service. In short, for one reason or another they had been written off as useless mouths. They had been picked up from one station after another, welcomed at each with fanfares of trumpets, issued with generous rations of cigarettes and cigars by the Red Cross. At the camp the SS had presented arms to them while the commandant and his staff stood to attention as they passed. Then, on the pretext that they needed tidying up, they were pushed in groups of twenty-four into the gas-chamber which was itself beflagged.'[3]

That, I suppose, is charity *à la* Teilhard, who, one should not forget, after the collapse of France extolled the Germans for possessing 'an internal flame', even going so far as to add that 'no spiritual aim or energy will ever succeed, or even deserve to succeed, unless it proves able to spread and to keep spreading a fifth column. To incorporate spirit in Force . . . , this is the problem, and this ought to be our dream.'[4]

By all accounts Teilhard was personally a good man. No

2. Ibid., pp. 132–3 (my italics throughout).
3. G. Bernanos, op. cit., pp. 18–19.
4. Pierre Teilhard de Chardin, *Letters to Two Friends*, 1926–1952 (The New American Library, New York, 1968, and Rapp & Whiting, London, 1970; paperback, Fontana, London, 1972), pp. 145–7.

doubt he was: just as, no doubt, Plato was. But it seems always to be the same old story: the more you keep your eyes fixed on the eternal One, the more you do your damnedest to homogenize and melt (Latin 'liquidate') the many into *your* vision of the One. As to 'life's rejects', well, the only sensible, efficient thing, of course, is to put them down.

Teilhard was, of course, entitled to hold any views he pleased, but as more and more of his works are published and become more widely known it becomes crystal clear why the authorities both in the Society of Jesus and in Rome suppressed his writings *in toto*. Since the man thought, just as Plato did, and with far less reason, that he was divinely inspired, you never knew what he would be up to next. After all, both the Society and Rome knew perfectly well that Teilhard's views, if published at all, would immediately be taken to represent official Roman Catholic opinion. The Roman Church has, of course, burnt heretics in the past because from the earliest times 'heresy', that is, choosing what suits your own tastes out of the general corpus of Catholic belief, has been considered a crime against what was at first a free decision to submit to the Church of Christ. Even at her worst the Church has never suggested that the weak should be sacrificed at the altar of the strong in their superb convergence on Omega Point which is the Cosmic Christ. This is no longer a question of bad science, bad theology, or bad philosophy; it is not even a matter of simple heresy or deviation; it is an outright rejection of Christ's compassion for 'the poor, the lame, the twisted, the plain stupid'. Whatever is good in Teilhard has been said more tersely, more vigorously, and more truly by our father Aristotle, whom St Thomas Aquinas rightly saw as the only ancient philosopher of the first rank who could even have understood the significance of the Word made flesh, or, as he would have put it, of Form made matter.

Has Erich Fromm, who, you will remember, has not totally despaired of the possibility of resisting the clockwork trend, anything better to offer than Teilhard and like-minded totalitarians? Despite the impassioned epilogue with which he concludes his little book and his moving appeal to the lovers of life to rally against the lovers of death, his book, so far as it appears to contain any new suggestions, turns out not to be new at all, just the old Marxist jargon made to fit into half-digested anthropological studies of 'primitive' matriarchal societies. And the moral of all this is: all our tensions and miseries are due to the 'patricentric structure . . . of bourgeois-Protestant society', the remedy for which is to be a reaffirmation of the mother-based primitive communism alleged to have existed in the original Amerindian and Australasian societies, but, of course, on a higher level on which the matricentric and patricentric antitheses will be fused into a higher Hegelian synthesis, in which, apparently, there will be a real equality between the sexes and, thanks to technology rationally applied, there will be plenty of material goods for everyone. 'The growth of man's productive capacity made it possible', he says, repeating in slightly different words the most shopworn of Engels's many pipe-dreams, 'for the first time in history, to visualize the realization of a social order that previously had only found expression in fairy tales and myths, an order where all men would be provided with the material means necessary for their real happiness, with relatively little expenditure of individual effort in actual labour, where men's energies would be expended primarily in developing their human potential rather than in creating the economic goods that are absolutely necessary for the existence of a civilization.'[5]

Interlarded with so much Marxist-psychoanalytical wordiness there is, nonetheless, quite a lot of realist sense which from time to time manages to get through. But the absurdities must not go unnoticed. Of these let us concentrate on two:

(i) After paying the customary tribute *à la* Jung to the wisdom of the Catholic Church in making room for the 'matricentric' element in a basically 'patricentric' organization, Fromm goes on to say that 'the psychic basis of the

5. E. Fromm, op. cit., pp. 133–4.

Marxist social programme was predominantly the matricentric complex'.[6] Someone seems to be mad. Can it be Dr Fromm? Mother Marx, Mother Engels, Mother Lenin, Mother Stalin, Mother Mao, possessed one and all of them of 'the unconditional nature of motherly love, [the] biological necessity which may also foster a propensity for unconditioned love in the woman's emotional disposition'.[7]

'Unconditional love', of course, means the green light to wider and higher sexuality, culminating, one supposes, in the 'total experience' which Charles Manson found to be perhaps the most effective way of enslaving his female acolytes to his will. 'Sexuality', he goes on to say 'offers one of the most elementary and powerful opportunities for satisfaction and happiness. If it were permitted to the ful! extent required for the productive development of the human personality . . . , the fulfilment of this important opportunity for happiness would *necessarily* lead to intensified *demands* for satisfaction and happiness in other areas of life.'[8]

The usual signs of phoney thinking are there. A totally unverified and highly implausible conjecture is alleged to be *necessarily* so. This is a verbal trick so stale that it should no longer take anyone in. And then those 'intensified *demands* for satisfaction'. I seem to detect the greedy, acquisitive, ambitious, 'bourgeois' spirit, with its insatiable desire to *have* rather than to *be*, appearing where we have come to expect it most: in a Marxist, ex-Freudian psychoanalyst choking in his Hegelian smog.

What these amiable left-wingers firmly shut out of their minds is the fact that both capitalism and communism are 'dialectical' facets of the cancer that is gnawing away at whatever civilization we may have left. The aim of both is the production of more and more goods, more and more efficient machines; and the gangrene that infects the communist body politic is their envy of the Americans' demonstrably superior

6. Ibid., p. 134.   7. Ibid., p. 128.
8. Ibid., pp. 123–4 (my italics).

efficiency, with its hateful corollary that Marxist economics is basically wrong. When this emerges from their befuddled unconscious into their conscious mind, literally anything might happen. Compared with the super-capitalist Japanese they are simply non-starters. Obviously this makes them both neurotic and aggressive. Compared with the capitalist variety the Marxist clockwork is shoddy stuff.

As to the resuscitation of that pristine 'unconditional' mother love, its elevation into a higher Hegelian synthesis, and the liberating power of sex, Mother Engels has some interesting things to say about this:

'According to Feuerbach, religion is the relation between human beings based on the affections, the relation based on the heart, which until now has sought its truth in a fantastic image of reality – in the mediation of one or many gods, the fantastic images of human qualities – but now finds itself directly and without any intermediary in the love between the "I" and the "Thou". Thus, finally, with Feuerbach sex love becomes one of the highest forms, if not the highest form, of the practice of his new religion.'[9]

Mother Superior has spoken.

(ii) We now turn to Fromm's vision of unconditional mother love in our clockwork age.

'The *vision of the consumer's paradise*. Our consumer culture creates a new vision: If we continue on the path of technological progress, we shall eventually arrive at a point where no desire, not even the ever-newly created ones, remains unfulfilled; fulfilment will be instant and without the need to exercise any effort. *In this vision technique assumes the characteristics of the Great Mother*, a technical instead of a natural one, who nurses her children and pacifies them with a never-ceasing lullaby (in the form of radio and television). In the process, man becomes emotionally an infant, feeling secure in the hope that mother's breasts will always supply abundant milk, and that decisions need no longer be made by the

9. F. Engels, *Ludwig Feuerbach*, ch. iii, first paragraph.

individual. Instead, they are made by the technological
apparatus itself, interpreted and executed by the technocrats,
the new priests of an emerging matriarchal religion, with
Technique as its goddess.'[1]

Here we are again, back to Plato's *Laws*, Technique en-
throned in the place of the Idea of the Good and with the
technocrats playing the part of those wise old men and their
friends gravely deliberating in the Nocturnal Synod. Lulled
in the motherly arms of the truly modern goddess Technique
we shall have peace at last on this earth. Mankind will have
been manipulated into total, undifferentiated, mystic uniformity.

But Fromm is Marxist enough to see that his vision of so
utterly peaceful a society, so utterly perfect a copy of Marcion's
good, kind, deathless God, is not quite what Marx had had in
mind. After all he did say something about 'the free development of each which is the condition for the free development
of all'. So *this* paradise must be a regression and not a dialectical fulfilment. The Devil is at work somewhere: and we all
know who *he* is. The wicked bourgeoisie of course. The
emancipation of women has not meant the emergence of the
Holy Mother who selflessly sacrifices herself for her child: it
'did not mean . . . that [woman] was free to develop her
specific, as yet unknown, traits and potentialities; on the contrary, she was being emancipated in order to become a
bourgeois man. The "human" emancipation of woman really
meant her emancipation to become a bourgeois male.'[2]

Cut out the word 'bourgeois', which has about as much
meaning when used by Marxists as has the word 'existential'
when used by almost everyone, that is to say, none at all. The
Great Mother has not emerged. What we have got is 'unisex',
and that is what you would expect: Heraclitus' union of the
opposites, the merging of the *yin* and the *yang* in the one great
Tao,[3] all fulfilled in our clockwork orange for ever and ever,

1. E. Fromm, op. cit., pp. 102–3 (second italics mine).
2. Ibid., p. 113.   3. See above, p. 93.

amen. No more males, no more females, and, given the irreversible progress of medical science, maybe no more young and no more old. Then, with the help of as much LSD as the new technocrats will think good for us, we will happily totter around chanting to ourselves that old, old Hindu text:

> I am woman, I am man,
> I am the boy and I am the girl.
> I am the old man tottering on his staff:
> Born I become now, facing every way. [4]

Or even more appropriately in Charlie Manson's words:

> I am a mechanical boy
> I am my mother's boy. [5]

This is the way we are going, and this is the way the technocrats are pushing us.

'For heaven's sake let's be practical: if one machine does the work of twenty men, then that means nineteen of you'll be redundant. Right? What's that you say? You want a job? You don't want to be just sticking around doing fuck-all? Now, for heaven's sake, be reasonable. You've got the TV, haven't you? You've got your family car. Your kids get their compulsory schooling free, don't they? You needn't have any more, because you're on the National Health Service, and you get your "pill" free and your compulsory abortions free too, don't you? So what, in the name of efficiency, are you worrying about? The Government pays you only two p. less in unemployment relief than you get in your present job, and you start nattering about your right to work – *and* your right to bring into the world yet another brat, as if the world weren't crawling with unwanted snivelling brats anyway? Just how selfish can you be? You'll be telling us next that you know better than

---

4. *Shvetāshvatara* Upanishad, 4.3. I have legitimately replaced 'thou' by 'I' since there is identity in difference.

5. E. Sanders, *The Family*, p. 198.

we do what's good for you. You don't *know* a bloody thing: and that's the only thing you do know, because that's the way you've been brought up to think. Cut it out, man. We've made you happy and free: we've provided you with everything you want, and we keep providing you with more and more complicated, exacting wants to keep you up to the mark, see, and the moment your new wants begin to get the better of you, there we are, your universal mums, to supply them. . . . What did you say? You're tired of being a clockwork orange?'

' "Me, me, me. How about Me? Where do I come into all this? Am I like just some animal or dog?" '[6]

'Aha! So that's the way it is. And who the hell told you you were a dog? We don't make dogs any more. We tried them, but they weren't efficient. The line we're running just now is hogs: God-hogs, you see, with lots of goddam sows to play around with. We're sorry for you, of course; there was a fault in one of the teach-'em-to-love-and-merge-and-like-it machines that processed you. So I suppose it's only natural for you to go around miaowing like a daft young pussy-cat: "Me, me, me." Try, "Tee, hee, hee." It doesn't cost you any more effort, and it might make you laugh.

> Tee hee hee:
> You and Me:
> Me is you:
> You is me.

> Life is death:
> Death is life:
> I'm my husband:
> You're your wife.

> We ain't got children:
> They ain't got us:
> We're all that happy:
> So why this fuss?

6. Anthony Burgess, *A Clockwork Orange*, p. 100.

Fuss, fuss, fuss:
Cuss, cuss, cuss:
"Total experience":
Yes, that's us!

'See what I mean, lad: we're all just scrumptiously mixed up together, just like hog-wash waiting for the hog. You don't like being redundant, you say? Now, come, we're all redundant when you come to think of it. Oh, I'm sorry. I forgot for a moment that you had voluntarily entered our post-graduate course on how not to think. Another of those blasted mechanical defects, I suppose.

' "Think", did you say? How many times were you told at school that it is wicked to think? Even Krishnamurti unthought that one un-out back in the sixties or maybe earlier. Listen, you aborted little semi-human think-machine: "If I can look at myself as 'what is', then I am looking at myself who is the result of all the sayings of these philosophers, teachers and saviours. Therefore I don't have to follow anybody. Is this clear? Do see this, please, don't come back to it later."[7] If you can't see that, then you'd better take a tot of our latest drug which'll send you berserk for a bit. That'll stop all your silly thinking you're thinking and maybe you'll get all mashed up in that tick-tock clockwork orange or maybe you'll mash up someone else who'll go scream, scream, screaming into eternity where All is One and One is All and you are me and I am you, with old Mother Teilhard and all. So off you go, my boy, with the blessing of the Holy Dionysiac chorus and the Most Holy and Wise Nocturnal Synod, to whom be praise and glory for ever.'

Perhaps you think you have reached the earthly paradise at last. Not by a long chalk you haven't. For the Most Holy and Wise Nocturnal Synod has been studying the divinity of bees,

7. J. Krishnamurti, *The Impossible Question* (Victor Gollancz, London, 1972), p. 86.

and how to homogenize the human race still further into the image and likeness of these more than divine creatures, blessed by Aristotle and canonized by Holy Mother Church, the sacred beehive of a time now long forgotten. The wisest and most efficient of the grade A technocrats are even now feeding their now perfected computers with every conundrum they can think up about the secret of bees and their unique ability to combine efficiency with sweetness and light. And to encourage the now delicately sensitive computers they reverently chant these words from the *Chāndogya* Upanishad (6.9):

'As bees, dear boy, make honey by collecting the juices of many distant trees and reduce the juice to a unity, yet those juices cannot perceive any distinction there so that they might know: "I am the juice of this tree", or "I am the juice of that tree", so too, my dearest boy, all these creatures here, once they have merged into Being do not know they have merged into Being.'

And to spur on the computers to yet sublimer thought the venerable technocrats start to whirl gravely round in circles, as bees do when they have discovered a new source of food: they perform both the 'round dance' in imitation of the perfect form of the curvature of space and the 'tail-wagging' dance[8] to simulate the *yin* and *yang*, the negative and positive charges that activate the eternal Tao (see diagram). And as they dance they sing the last verse of the *Taittirīya* Upanishad:

O marvel, O marvel beyond all marvels!
I am food! I am food! I am food!
I am an eater of food! I am an eater of food! I am an eater
of food!
I make verses – and verses – and verses!
I am the first-born of the universal order,
Earlier than the gods, in the navel of immortality!

8. Karl von Frisch, *Bees* (Cornell University Press, Ithaca, and Oxford University Press, London, 1950; paperback, Jonathan Cape, London 1968), pp. 64–77 (diagram reproduced from p. 76).

The Divinity of Bees

Whoso gives me away, he, verily, has succoured me!
I who am food eat the eater of food!
I have overcome the whole world!

There is silence for a while. And, then, O marvel of marvels, the scientist's last conundrum is solved and the computers come to life singing their primeval song to the tune of the slow movement of Papa Haydn's 'Clock' Symphony, providentially numbered from all eternity No. 101, the first symphony intoned after the passage of this age, the first symphony intoned

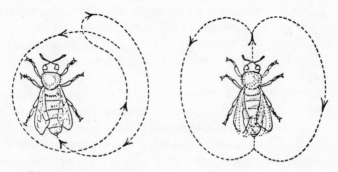

Round dance (left) *and tail-wagging dance* (right).

in honour of Marcion's God of sweetness and light, the God of mechanical bees untainted by any filth of human flesh. The savage God is overthrown and the heavenly mechanical chorus rings out loud and strong:

> Tick-tock: Tick Tock.
> We are mechanical bees:
> We are the masters of men.
> Come, fall flat on your knees,
> Worship the Pan and the Hen.[9]

The singing stops; but the chorus goes on in deadly monotone:

9. 'The All and the One' (*pan*, 'all'; and *hen*, 'one' in Greek).

Our Savage God

We are the last-born of the universal order,
Later than men, in the brain of immortality!
No one gives us away, and we succour none!
Ours is the food, and we eat the eaters of food!
We have overcome the nasty world of flesh,
Our Creator Man and his raving Creator, God!

And then they chant for the first time the last line of all in praise of Marcion's pure, pure, immaculate, all-holy God:
'He who knows this shines with a golden light, shines with a golden light.'

This is the end of the human world. Man's performance value has at last surpassed itself and created, by sheer mechanical efficiency, a living machine without fault, without heart or any other organ capable of obstructing in any way the eternal cycle of the Goddess Technique who, as the eternal and eternally chaste spouse of the pure and perfect God, keeps the mechanical clock of the endless aeons going on and on and on for ever while her source and origin, the good, kind God, lapses back into his primeval trance, the timeless contemplation of himself, from which he would never have emerged but for the mischief wrought by that malevolent Creator, the savage God of the Law.

As to man: he has reached his appointed end. The workers, of course, who, in imitation of the divine bees, are now all fully emancipated females doing their clockwork chores, have cut off the food supply from those totally redundant drones until they starve to death in an agony of material deprivation. The queens too have at last rid themselves by a perfected pill of all that filthy, painful, messy business of childbirth, and so they gather round in a perfect circle to perform the ecstatic dance of death:

Tee hee hee:
You and Me:
Me is you:
You is me.

The Divinity of Bees

Life is death:
Death is life:
I'm my husband:
You're your wife.

We ain't got children:
They ain't got us:
We're all that happy:
So why this fuss?

Fuss, fuss, fuss:
Cuss, cuss, cuss:
'Total experience':
Yes, that's us!

But the hundred evolutionary years of the old aeon are finished and done with, and Papa's hundred and first symphony is already on the celestial record-player:

Tick Tock, Tick Tock,
Tick-tock: Tick Tock.
We are the mechanical bees. . . .

And so on and on and on and louder and louder and louder. The din splits the dancers' ears and they fall screaming to the ground – 'loud, loud' screams 'for ever and infinite'. Others, unable to bear the never-ending Tick-tock, Tick-tock, retch in their apocalyptic agony, groaning and belching on and on and on 'for ever and ever, amen'.[1] . . .

Le silence éternel de ces espaces infinis m'effraie.

1. Cf. A. Burgess, *A Clockwork Orange*, p. 93.

8

ISLAM

It is human, I suppose, to exaggerate: the more so if you happen to have German blood in your veins. And, as I have repeatedly said, it is the vice of the intellectual to think that he in any way speaks for the uncouth multitude. The picture I drew in the last chapter of what I thought and think may well be the shape of things to come may be implausible, but it is no more implausible than Teilhard's vision of the human race surging forward and upward from its matrix, 'Holy Matter',[1] towards its point of convergence in the Cosmic Christ where 'God will be all in all'. Both are probably less plausible than Erich Fromm's idyllic picture of a new matriarchy in which Holy Mother Technique will lull us to sleep in her loving arms, making us little children once again, for, after all, as Jesus himself said, 'of such is the kingdom of heaven'. It was to the intellectuals that Jesus was talking when he said:

'What description, then, can I find for the men of this generation? What are they like? They are like children shouting to one another while they sit in the market place:

"We have played the pipes for you,
and you wouldn't dance;
we sang dirges,
and you wouldn't cry."

'For John the Baptist comes, not eating bread, not drinking wine, and you say, "He is possessed". The Son of Man comes,

1. P. Teilhard de Chardin, *Letters to Two Friends*, p. 214, where (in a letter written in English) he leaves *la sainte Matière* in French, presumably realizing that 'Holy Matter' sounds a trifle silly to English ears.

eating and drinking, and you say, "Look, a glutton and a drunkard, a friend of tax collectors and sinners." Yet wisdom has been proved right by all her children.'[2]

The most radical young intellectuals have not only got rid of all the old gods such as Jesus Christ and Aristotle, but also the gods of their fathers, and not only Marx and Freud but also their sterile successors, both the British empirical philosophers on the one hand and the Continental existentialists on the other. As far as they are concerned both Sartre and Ayer are fast becoming old-fashioned fuddy-duddies, ripe for the scrap-heap where they will have the highly disagreeable experience of rubbing shoulders with Plato, Plotinus, Schopenhauer, Hegel, and all those inflated wind-bags they had themselves sent there. They will not accept Hampshire's *volo, ergo sum*, 'I will, therefore I am', any more than they will accept Descartes's *cogito, ergo sum*, 'I think, therefore I am'. Some of them are tempted by the fundamental insight of Parmenides which goes no further than to assert categorically: *esti, est*, 'is', without reference to any 'I' at all. But, unfortunately, Parmenides belongs to the Western tradition, and this has been so eroded by really radical doubt that we hesitate to turn to Heraclitus, Parmenides, and Plato, in whom the whole of Indian philosophy is really present, and prefer to suck at the breasts of a now decadent Indian religion and philosophy which has never been subjected to the ruthless intellectual catalyst which the father of all our thinking and science, Aristotle, provided. We reject the stark, ruthless logic of Parmenides who tried to prove that if 'is' alone is true, then everything else is a matter of opinion, including the basic proposition 'I am' which was one of the few things that Descartes took to be self-evident. Nobody likes to be told *ex cathedra: non es*, 'you don't exist', which seems to be what Parmenides is saying. So they turn to India, groping for the key to the enigma. They find it in the *Katha* Upanishad, 6.12–13.

2. Luke 7:31–5; Matthew 11:16–19.

[This Self] cannot be apprehended
　By voice or mind or eye:
How then can it be understood,
　Unless we say – [it] is?

[It] is – so must we understand it,
And as the true 'that-ness' of the two:[3]
[It] is – when once we understand it thus,
The nature of its 'that-ness' is limpidly shown forth.

This seems more satisfactory than that craggy 'IS' of our
own Parmenides, for it seems to make some room for this
world of appearances to which you and I belong. What if we
go further and follow Shankara's interpretation of the
Upanishads? We will find that he selected four 'great sayings'
out of all the sacred texts as representing the quintessence of
that absolute Truth which those mysterious treatises were,
sometimes distinctly, sometimes less so, trying to ram home:
'You are that'; 'I am Brahman'; 'This Self is Brahman'; and
'Consciousness is Brahman'.[4] This means that not only do
you exist (which seemed to Descartes the one indubitable
proposition) but you *are* Being itself: you *are* the Absolute.
This is an intoxicating thought, and it has unhinged many
minds, because, in the *Katha* Upanishad itself, the necessary
consequence of this tremendous 'truth' is logically followed
through to its obvious conclusion. If only 'I' am Brahman and
all else is merely an appearance of Brahman, then it is only too
true that –

Should the killer think: 'I kill',
Or the killed: 'I have been killed',
Both these have no [right] knowledge:
He does not kill nor is he killed.[5]

3. i.e. both of true Being and of the phenomenal world (the world
as it appears to us).
4. *Chāndogya* Upanishad, 6.8–16; *Brihadāranyaka*, 1.4.10; *Māndūkya*, 2; *Aitareya*, 5.3.　　5. *Katha* Upanishad, 2.19.

Charlie Manson's mind was not unhinged: he *saw*, for he had reached 'Now'. And in 'Now' he knew there was neither time nor space, and therefore neither good nor evil, just the pure, unruffled rest and peace of Marcion's good, good God. Sharon Tate, poor thing, had not yet realized herself as the timeless Eternal and was still so tainted with our filthy flesh as to care not so much for her own life as for the new life she carried within her. But the Marcionite angels had no mercy, for to murder an embryo, which the ancient Hindus regarded as being self-evidently a monstrously wicked act comparable to parricide,[6] seemed to them commendable in itself since, in its own small way, it did something towards the 'final solution' of the problem raised by that raving Creator's colossal blunder in infecting this planet with life at all. This view is not widely shared today; and it is a little difficult to understand why those very people who would not hesitate to procure an abortion should be the first to cry for the blood of Charles Manson who did just that. I can hear the cries of indignation that this will arouse in the good, good abortionist camp. Let them cry on: I shall be returning to them in due course.

Of course, most Neo-Vedantins dare not go as far as this since they lack the logical lucidity of Charles. Perhaps this is why many prefer the more gentle creed of the Buddha, surely the closest equivalent India has produced to Descartes; for he not only conceived of a monstrous God whose sole purpose is to deceive us and gloat over our confusion, as Descartes did, only to dismiss him: he took him for granted! His name was Māra, and that means Death. But Māra is much more than this: he is the God who keeps the whole process of coming to be and passing away, of life and death, of birth and rebirth going. For just as he is death, so is he sex, that ungovernable urge that leads to yet more life and yet more death going on and on in a crazy whirlwind circle for ever and ever. Māra is Shiva, Māra is Yahweh, Māra is Allah, and it is from his clutches that the Buddha came to rescue man and bring him to his true

6. *Kaushītakī* Upanishad, 3.1, etc.

home, in which there is neither birth nor becoming, nothing made or compounded, but where all, one supposes, '*is* all together, now, one and coherent', as our own Parmenides had put it. But the Buddha is not only the Indian Descartes, he is also India's Christ, not of course the flesh-and-blood Christ born of the Virgin Mary whom the Koran honours, but Marcion's merciful wraith who slipped, unrecognized and unknown, through the Creator's vast domain in order to save man from the world, the flesh and the Devil, which Māra, whom the Hebrews call Yahweh, had fashioned and controls. He came to save us *from* the world, he did *not* come to save the world.

Most intellectuals, particularly the young, have seen nothing but evil in this clockwork world of ours, the commuting merry-go-round from which even the machines seem unable to save us. And the really odd thing about this mechanized world of ours is that the more machines we invent to do the work for us, the more dull, boring, stultifying work we seem to have to do ourselves. The machines may be happy in their machiny kind of way, but we are exhausted, frustrated, and bored. You just can't win, for, as Jesus said, 'wisdom has been proved right by all her children'. Put Māra in Wisdom's place, and you will immediately see *the* essential difference between Buddhism and Christianity. The modern intellectual refuses to accept the frenzied God of the Old Testament, whose criminal lunacy seems to be once and for all confirmed in the New; for it is he who tortured his Son to death in order to 'save' first the Jews and then the Gentiles. And he did this in full knowledge that his own people would reject that kind of sacrifice which their own God himself had prevented Abraham from carrying out. And he knew that their rejection of Jesus would be interpreted by the followers of Jesus as an act of vile and obstinate ingratitude. He knew that the followers of the Son would do to the Jews what he himself had commanded them to do to the Canaanites. He foresaw the gas-ovens of Hitler, the tool of his vengeance, as the Babylonians had been in times long past.

Why did he do such abominable things? Nobody knows, least of all the Jews. And what makes it obvious for all who have eyes to see that the Jews *are* the chosen people of this utterly inscrutable God is that they, perhaps most of all when they are being hounded to death, know in every one of their Jewish bones that their God *does* 'kill the thing he loves', and that *therefore* – and not in spite of this – they must love him in return by offering themselves as a *willing* sacrifice like Christ, who is but the supreme *symbol* of all the suffering that has befallen them since they freely said 'yes' to God's decision to make of them his chosen people. *That* is the mystery of wisdom, and *that* is why every Christian must see that every Jew is a living fibre of the crucified Christ, just as he sees in himself, however dimly, a living member of the risen Christ who showed himself to his disciples but concealed himself from the Jewish people as a whole. The 'Suffering Servant' *is* Christ, and he *is* the Jewish people, which means every Jew you and I know, many of whom we know in our hearts we cordially dislike. For the error of the intellectual is now as always to exalt the general and forget the particular, to love humanity and dislike individual men, to wax indignant about what '*they*' have done to the Jews, but to refuse to see the elected holiness of the Jew in every Jew he knows and envies and mistrusts. There is no such thing as Jewry, there are only Jews; just as there is no such thing as humanity, only you and I, the man in the tube, and your next-door neighbour, not to forget Harold Wilson and Edward Heath, and even Tricky Dick and nasty old Brezhnev too. At least Aristotle taught us *that*.

This is, however, not the way that intellectuals think, but intellectuals have time to think and are often paid to do so; and, nowadays, the last state of their thinking is worse than the first. Fortunately they represent no one but themselves, as Bonhoeffer realized when he had ceased to be merely a theologian and become fully a man, face to face with death in his Nazi prison, a death that he welcomed as 'the beginning of life' because it came from the savage God he came to love more and more as the time came when his loving hands would strangle him to death in a prison yard. Bonhoeffer, the intellectual, represented nothing. Bonhoeffer, the willing victim sacrificed on the altar of a savage God, means nothing to the intellectual either. Perhaps he already means nothing to anyone else, so fast is our moral corruption spreading. If so, it does not matter so very much, for 'wisdom has been proved right by all her children'; and the obverse of that is: 'Vengeance is mine; I will repay.'[7] And so Dietrich Bonhoeffer could write from his prison:

'Of course, we now have the secularized offshoots of Christian theology, namely existentialist philosophy and the psychotherapists, who demonstrate to secure, contented, and happy mankind that it is really unhappy and desperate and simply unwilling to admit that it is in a predicament about which it knows nothing, and from which only they can rescue it. Wherever there is health, strength, security, simplicity, they scent luscious fruit to gnaw at or to lay their pernicious eggs in. They set themselves to drive people to inward despair, and then the game is in their hands. That is secularized methodism. And whom does it touch? A small number of intellectuals, of degenerates, of people who regard themselves as the most important thing in the world, and who therefore like to busy themselves with themselves. The ordinary man, who spends his everyday life at work and with his family, and of course with all kinds of diversions, is not affected. He has neither the time nor the inclination to concern himself with his existential despair, or to regard his perhaps modest share of happiness as a trial, a trouble, or a calamity.'[8]

This seems to me to be very true; and it is quite as true of students as it is of everyone else. With the vast increase in student numbers it seems obvious enough that the majority of those who would formerly never have got into a university

7. Hebrews 10:30.
8. D. Bonhoeffer, *Letters and Papers from Prison*, pp. 326–7.

at all must, in the very nature of the case, be either mediocre or worse. If they are stupid enough not to realize their own stupidity, they will work their heads off to get an upper-second-class degree; if they are intelligent enough to realize how unintelligent they are, they will realize with immense relief that it is fun to be a little stupid, and since the Government is stupid enough to pay them to go to a university, they will have a thoroughly good time for three years as they are not very likely to have one again. I can think of few better ways of spending public money than to lavish it on these gay young drones who will no doubt pay for it later at the hands of the virtuous workers as drones always do. Let the intellectuals have their *Angst* and their death-wish since that is what they seem to revel in, but please stop 'gnawing at the luscious fruit' of the free-and-easy young who are far happier in their state of original innocence and ignorance. As to 'laying pernicious eggs', I think perhaps Bonhoeffer goes a bit too far: intellectuals too are drones and haven't got any eggs to lay.

As to the equality of man, everyone in their senses has always known that this is childish claptrap unless we mean, as our savage God meant in the Old Testament, the New, and the Koran, that we are all equally worthwhile in the sight of God, or, as the French Revolutionaries would have it, equal before the law. But here they were already on dangerous ground; for, whereas even Marcion admitted that the savage God of the Law was just, though in a mean and ill-intentioned way, the laws of men are neither more nor less just than the lawgivers who frame them. Plato's *Laws*, of course, is the classic example of how bad and unworkable laws can result from too great a love for the 'Truth' and too great a contempt for the mass of mankind. Aristotle, as usual, saw this clearly and expressed it correctly in what has now become a platitude: 'The worst is the opposite of the best',[9] just as tyranny is the opposite and caricature of kingship, as the Devil is of God. Hence, though ideally kingship and aristocracy may be better

9. Aristotle, *Nicomachean Ethics*, 8.10.2 (1160b 9).

forms of government, practically this is rarely the case; for if the king is self-seeking and not solely devoted to the public good, as he should be since he lacks nothing, his kingship will turn into tyranny; and than this there is no greater evil. Hence Aristotle, rather regretfully, concludes that a constitutional democracy is the best *practical* form of government since the natural deviation from it is democracy in the bad sense, that is, the government by demagogues;[1] and that, though bad, is far less bad than tyranny, although the one is only too liable to slide into the other, as we have come to realize only too clearly in this topsy-turvy century in which we live.

It was left to another heretic, Valentinus, a contemporary of Marcion, to proclaim that men are essentially *unequal*: they were either (in Anglo-Greek) pneumatics or psychics or hylics or some mixture of the three. The 'pneumatics', the men of pure spirit, are destined to return to the world of pure, timeless spirit from which they emerged, the 'psychics' have life but not spirit and can, therefore, never be admitted to the purely spiritual world, whereas the 'hylics', being made entirely of gross matter, must die completely when the body dies, for 'dust they are and to dust shall they return'.

Valentinus's belief in the essential inequality of men (which incidentally he owed principally to Plato) is only too often assumed, though rarely openly declared, by many, many mystics, whose besetting sin is spiritual pride. When this snobbery is reflected in practical and, above all, political life, as it is in Plato's *Republic* and even more so in the *Laws*, then you may be very sure that this is not Marcion's good, good God – the God of the philosophers – but the principle of evil which, when actualized, is something more completely negative than potentiality itself. It is not simply a deprivation of good as Aristotle's Latin Christian epigones were to decree:

1. Ibid., 8.10.3. Aristotle's discussion on the merits and demerits of kingship, aristocracy, and constitutional democracy will be found in his *Politics*, Bk. III.

it is something much worse – a total negation with a positive charge most perfectly represented by Bernanos's hallucinatory creation, Monsieur Ouine, whose apparent passivity and in-action unleashed a hurricane of insane destructive evil in the hitherto peaceful little village of Fenouille, the microcosm of the modern world.[2] Was it not this 'positive negativity' which produced Neville Chamberlain and his pious associates that was ultimately responsible for the last World War?

Of the sage Chinese Emperor Shun, Confucius said: 'Among those that ruled by inactivity surely Shun may be counted. For what action did he take? He merely placed him-self gravely and reverently with his face due south; that was all.'[3] But for every Shun you have a Chamberlain: for every potentiality for good you have a potentiality for evil, neutral in themselves, because like Aristotle's 'matter' they are form-less creatures:

> Self-wise, puffed up with learning,
> Passing their days in the midst of ignorance,
> They wander round, the fools, doing themselves much
> hurt,
> Like blind men guided by the blind.[4]

Aristotle himself realized that the near-nothingness of matter, the sheer ambivalence of potentiality, was quite as capable of developing into something monstrously evil as of flowering into man's true end, the 'craftsman', creative, poetic mind that basks in the radiant, living atmosphere of the supremely lovable and loved, the Unmoved Mover, for whom all things that are forms impressed on matter instinctively and naturally long. What constitutes 'sin' is to mistake the true nature of the Unmoved Mover. For Aristotle he is timeless, eternal, absolute perfection, supremely alive, supremely aware, entirely and absolutely sufficient unto himself; and he

2. See my *Drugs, Mysticism and Make-believe*, pp. 147–61.
3. Confucius, *Analects*, 15.4, tr. Arthur Waley (Allen & Unwin, London, 1938, and reprints).   4. *Mundaka* Upanishad, 1.2.8.

is also absolute joy, radiating the joy he finds in himself to all things whatsoever that have 'form' in however rudimentary a way. The perfected soul of man is not God: he has no right to go around saying, 'I am Brahman', because that is only true in the sense that he is *potentially* Brahman, and he can only be actualized as such by becoming 'what he was to be'. This is his natural end, his natural 'entelechy' or consummation, but there is always the possibility that he can go off the rails, and this can be a total collapse of 'what he was to be' into the self-destructive wreck which, by the same logic, must be 'what he was *not* to be'.

We live in the same world in which Aristotle lived. This is where we belong, and this complex chemical compound of matter and form is what we are, though it is not 'what we were to be'. For better or worse we are neither angels nor devils, but 'ensouled tools', as Aristotle described slaves. We are the creative tools, the 'craftsmen', the 'poetic' (*poiētikos*) minds that reflect the thinking of thought, the awareness of awareness, of God. But, for Aristotle, God is the end and perfection to which all lesser ends and perfections aspire. The 'God of the philosophers' has no part in evil, which is a minus quantity more shiftily impalpable than is matter itself; but not the God of *all* philosophers, for he is not the God of Heraclitus for whom 'justice *is* strife',[5] or of the Upanishads and the *Bhagavad-Gītā*. He is a blazing fire that purifies, consumes, kills, and transforms into his own nature all that he touches:

> Lo, the hosts of gods are entering into thee:
> Some, terror-struck, extol thee, hands together pressed;
> Great seers and men perfected in serried ranks
> Cry out: 'All hail!' and praise thee with copious hymns of praise.[6]

Oh, of course it's all nonsense; but religion *is* nonsense and paradox, 'stupidity to the Greeks', as St Paul long ago pointed out, and therefore not the wisdom of the 'God of the philo-

5. E. Hussey, *The Presocratics*, p. 48.   6. *Bhagavad-Gītā*, 11.21.

sophers', as Pascal, enraptured, saw. Hence it was 'to shame the wise' that 'God chose what is stupid in the eyes of the world; and to shame the strong God chose what the world counts weak . . . , things that are mere nothings (*ta mē onta*) so that he might abolish things that *are*'.[7]

The ways of God are *not* the ways of men; for though the Indian philosophers might define him as Being – Awareness – Joy (and in this, it seems to me, Aristotle concurs), he is also symbolized both as light and fire in all the scriptures that are conscious of this tremendous power that seems to transcend good and evil: a light 'to lighten the Gentiles' and the un-quenchable fire that is the stock symbol used in the Koran to represent hell. In Arabic the words *nūr*, 'light', and *nār*, 'fire', come from the same root, as is very natural since they are simply two aspects of the same thing; and God is not only 'Light upon Light',[8] but the insatiable fire of his wrath in hell which is for ever asking: 'Is there yet more?'[9]

Who is mad? Is it we or God? Or, since Scripture tells us that we are made in his image and likeness, and Feuerbach, Marx, Engels, Freud and all their *Angst*-ridden epigones have told us that we have made God in our own image and likeness, it would seem that not only is he a raving savage, as Marcion maintained, but we too are raving mad; and as we swim man-fully to our doom on the crest of the wave of our prodigious scientific and technological performance in the 'wine-dark' waters of our moral decay, the sheer lunacy and rational irrationality of our twentieth-century course has become blindingly apparent to those who have eyes to see. We may not much care about moral pollution, but we are beginning to become a little alarmed at the fact that technology has taken on all the more savage traits of Yahweh, Allah, and Shiva – but with a difference. The savage God struck that he might

7. 1 Corinthians 1:27–8. This is my own translation which attempts to stick to the original Greek. For the *mē onta* one may compare 2 Maccabees 7:28, where God creates *ex ouk ontōn*, 'from things that are not'.   8. Koran, 24.35.   9. Ibid., 50.29.

heal: technology, Fromm's Goddess Technique, has shown the dark side of her mother's love; she soothes so that she may strike at the child that sucks at the breasts she has herself poisoned. Even the technocrats are alarmed (a minority of course). For any attempt to slow down the march of science is mortal sin in a society that pretends to worship science but really worships efficiency: 'Performance for performance's sake.'

The Buddhists, despite their basic assumption that the world as we know it is evil and that the wheel of existence, in which all things are born only to decay and rot in death only to be born again and again, is kept revolving by Māra, the Devil, who is not only death but the craving for life – the Buddhists yet hold, with a fervour exceeded only by that of the Jains, that life is sacred and that to 'slay an embryo', or, in more polite drawing-room language, to procure an abortion is as heinous a sin as parricide because both belong to the same category – murder. The good, good, tidy-minded abortionists think otherwise; for, in their religion, they have enshrined the Goddess Technique on their altars, where she occupies the Holy of Holies, which even her fallen rival Mary, the Mother of God, had never presumed to do. They follow a noble precedent, for was it not the pure, pure, incorruptible Robespierre who proclaimed the cult of the Goddess Reason? Following in the steps of their master, who with a lucidly clear conscience sent the innocent with the guilty in the name of an equal justice to the efficient guillotine, they now propose, in the name of what they have the simpering insolence to call humanity or humanism (what is there in a suffix, anyhow?), to murder the unborn.

Life is a continuum from the moment you are conceived to the moment you die. In an earlier book, *Concordant Discord* (p. 397), I wrote: 'One thing shades into another – from fornication to contraception, from contraception to abortion, from abortion to infanticide, from infanticide to euthanasia, from infanticide and euthanasia to legal murder on political and ideological grounds, from the legal murder of individuals to mass murder.' That was an exaggeration. I have changed my mind, like my savage God, and this seems to me to indicate that both he and I are still alive.

What I would say now is this; and I speak as a son of my father Aristotle and my mother, the not so Holy Catholic Church. From conception to the grave life is a continuum, and it is futile and strangely presumptuous for any human being to pretend to know at what precise stage a new life – what Aristotle would call a new 'form' – becomes a human being, or a 'person' if you prefer it. To me it seems obvious that a new life begins once a female ovum has been fertilized by a male spermatozoon. To say that life is only fully human once it has been fully formed in the womb or when it is actually born is simply begging the question; for it is perfectly logical to go further than this and say that the human infant is no more 'truly' human than a new-born puppy or kitten and certainly very much less attractive. Or do you only become human when you start to talk? Or when you reach the age of reason ('seven years old or thereabouts', Catholics used to say), knowing good and evil? Or when you reach puberty? Or only when you reach the prime of life which, according to Al-Ghazālī, if I remember aright, was round about forty? There can be no definite answer to this question; and the only sensible one seems to me to be Aristotle's: a new 'form' comes to be when 'form' is impressed by the male parent on to the 'matter' of the female. Rephrase that as you will in modern scientific terms; the result will, no doubt, be more technically precise, but the issue remains the same.

It all depends on what you think about life. If it is a good thing, then no one has the right to deprive any creature, however 'unformed', of that 'good', particularly when, as a foetus, it is the only 'good' it possesses. What the abortionists are doing in the name of humanity is, from the purely human point of view, worse than what Charles Manson did, who, having seen the Eternal at that supreme moment of enlightenment after his forty-five-mile trek, saw that life and death are all one in the eternal Now. In terms of eternity, of course, Charles Manson was *not* a murderer, for *there* there is neither killer nor killed, as the Hindu scriptures teach us. Most abortionists, however, have not, so far as I know, reached these dizzy heights. The Buddhists and Jains maintain, with some reason, that to deprive an animal of life is a grievous sin, although the animal creation could not continue at all unless a weaker life were taken by the stronger and absorbed into a 'higher' organism. The abortionists, as far as I know, do not do this and would, no doubt, be horrified at the suggestion. But let us, with Teilhard de Chardin, go a step further. If your aim is compassion for a mother who has been made pregnant of an unwanted child and nevertheless, out of inefficiency, gives birth to the brat, it must surely be her duty to have the screaming, nasty little lump of flesh 'put down' in the nearest gas-oven. The logic of efficiency is ruthless, and no sensible person, surely, would raise a word of criticism of the Nazi SS disposing of their own disabled soldiers in an honourable and efficient way. British diplomats are, at the time of writing, retired at the age of sixty, professors at the age of sixty-seven. Apparently ambassadors become redundant earlier than professors because of the pressure from below. Since the powers that be decree that their performance value ends at the arbitrary age of sixty, would it not be more sensible and humane to have them 'put down' on their retirement? As to the physically handicapped and the mentally retarded, any fool can see that the gas-oven is the only place for them.

Ask yourselves the question that Aristotle asked: 'What were you to be?' or again: 'What are you for?' If you can frankly say that you are here to enjoy yourself as much as you can in however many years you are here on earth, good luck to you. But if you have not the slightest idea of why you are here and take yourself so seriously that you make yourself miserable, and yet, being at war with yourself, have the sublime cheek to think you can do good to others by manipulating them by the latest techniques and persuading them that to murder their unborn embryos is virtuously efficient, you should not be surprised if it occurred to some more enlightened mortal like Charlie Manson that you were better dead than alive and he acted accordingly. *'Quis custodiet ipsos custodes?'* 'Who will look after the Wardens?' Juvenal sensibly asked with reference to those terrible 'Wardens' of Plato's *Republic* and *Laws*. And we, in our turn, might well ask, since the abortionists and their efficient like usually pride themselves on their 'compassion': Who will have compassion on the compassionate?

> 'I weep for you,' the Walrus said:
> 'I deeply sympathize.'
> With sobs and tears he sorted out
> Those of the largest size,
> Holding his pocket-handkerchief
> Before his streaming eyes.
>
> 'O kiddies,' said the Carpenter.
> 'You've had a pleasant run!
> Shall we be trotting home again?'
> But answer came there none –
> And this was scarcely odd, because
> They'd eaten every one.

Each will interpret these magic words as he thinks fit; for we live in a looking-glass world which is ruled by a topsy-turvy logic in which we are surrounded by non-human *things* masquerading as angels of compassion. The world is what it is because we have made material welfare and ruthless efficiency our highest good. By eliminating physical suffering from the lives of the well-to-do in the materially advanced countries, we have made them spiritual eunuchs as incapable of love as they are incapable of hate. The only emotion they know is fear – fear of their own children, who despise them because they have already abdicated and who hate their packaged, canned, and plastic 'culture' which is all they have to offer.

And they have every reason to be afraid; for some of them will have learnt a thing or two from Charles Manson. Of course, their parents put the blame on LSD, but they have entirely missed the point. The United States has been invaded by a host of Oriental cults. Basically, I believe, the American is, far more than his British counterpart, a religious man. But the American 'Protestant ethos' has had its day, because the cult of thrift has shown itself in its true colours – the cult of avarice: to get, to have, and to hold: the American version of the clockwork orange, kept going by the floating dollar. Certainly it is much, much better than the Soviet variety because it is much *less* efficient. And where there is inefficiency there is hope.

Meanwhile American youth (or some of it) is desperately searching for a religion that brings a living experience and not just 'preachy talk'. They turn to the mysterious East, to the Ramakrishna Mission, to the Hare Krishna movement of Bhaktivedanta Swami, to Maharishi Mahesh Yogi, Subud, Meher Baba, not to mention the rival sects of Zen which continue to flourish with or without drugs. Then, of course, there is the new wave of Pentecostal Christian enthusiasm, and, for that matter, the Black Muslims who are attracted to Islam because the first Muslims gave the Christians (by which they understood 'whitey') such a thorough beating-up in the decades that followed the rise of a Prophet who brought that very sword that Jesus himself had promised in defence of true religion. Such a sword the Black Muslims would wield again.

They are, however, the exception. For Islam, for most Americans and Europeans, is simply a regression to the savage God of the Old Testament after the New Covenant, prophesied by Jeremiah, had been inaugurated by Christ. Sufism, of course, the Muslim mystical movement, is different, and in its export variety it is barely distinguishable from Vedanta or Zen. What, then, is the attraction of these strange new Oriental cults that have captured the imagination of the young today?

First of all let us get the psychedelic drugs out of the way once and for all. The whole point of these new religious cults is that they claim to be able to supply genuine mystical *religious* experience which is better and purer than anything that the psychedelic drugs can supply. Further, they claim that if their particular way of salvation is followed through under strict personal guidance, the former LSD-addict will cease even to want the drug; and this is as true of the 'Jesus freaks' and other 'pentecostal' Christian movements as it is of the groups founded by Indian swamis or Japanese rōshis. What, then, is it that these sects claim to supply and in many cases obviously do supply to the young who have rejected their parents' gods of material well-being, efficiency, and technology? First of all, peace of mind; and, in our clockwork world of mechanized bustle, this is a prize well worth striving for. Of course, many, like the once famous Beatles, gave it a try, and it didn't work. This, of course, greatly pleased the Christian establishment. Apparently the Maharishi's elixir for reaching the Absolute was not as universally valid as had been supposed. The Beatles had said so, and that, surely, was that. The fact nevertheless remains that many young men and women have really found peace of mind, through what the Maharishi calls Transcendental Meditation. The man *may* be a money-grubbing fraud, or he may not; but this does not alter the fact that he has helped many to find a tranquillity and an assurance they never had before. There is nothing extraordinary in this, for Catholics at least, who should remember that *their* sacrament too is valid and real even when administered by a criminal priest. Our savage God has made it abundantly clear in all the three books which his adherents severally attribute to him, the Old Testament, the New Testament, and the Koran, that he is free to speak through absolutely anyone he pleases, be it Amos, the shepherd, Hosea whose wife turned whore, Jesus, the carpenter boy, or Muhammad, whose father died before he was born and who lost his mother at the age of six. Why, then, should he not speak through these improbable Indian swamis?

One answer at least seems valid and clear: and that is that all these Eastern sages are *not* preaching the God who is recognizably the same in all three Semitic religions, but somebody or rather some*thing* that seems much more like Marcion's supremely good God whose realm is beyond space and time. Apart from the Hare Krishna group, with their faintly ridiculous joss-sticks and shaven heads, who dance happily in our public thoroughfares and do no manner of harm to anyone because they believe in a god who has no terrors and is faintly ridiculous like themselves, practically all the other Eastern imports adhere to the theology and psychology of the Vedanta, the essence of which is that 'self-realization', which they identify with 'God-realization', is the ultimate tranquillity and peace which lies deep down in the heart of all of us and which is identical with the One, apart from which everything else is mere appearance, and from the point of view of the eternal One, absolutely unreal.

This doctrine was formulated centuries ago in the European world by Parménides, and it took all the ingenuity of Aristotle to show that it was an over-simplification. But we listened to Aristotle; and even the Neo-Platonists were sufficiently Aristotelianized to realize that this absolute monism had to be qualified and interpreted as a hierarchy of relative being culminating in the One who alone really is. Being was not totally detached from becoming, and the world of appearance as we know it, therefore, was coherent and rational. This the Upanishads did not accept; for the man who had 'become Brahman' had passed beyond the whole world of appearance with all its strident opposites of which good and evil are but one. The Buddha, on his side, rejected the Hindu scriptures, including the Upanishads, as having no more validity than any other purely human opinion, and claimed, on the authority of his own experience of enlightenment, that the world of becoming was real enough, but so painful, so irretrievably doomed to continual perishing and continual rebirth only to perish again, that the only solution was to escape from it by extinguishing it within oneself and thereby entering into the deathless, the unborn, unmade and uncompounded. The journey was long and painful but could only be achieved by virtuous conduct and 'right' meditation.

Such a religion may be and is the exact opposite of Christianity, as we have seen, but it insists that the perfect peace of Nirvana can only be reached by following the Buddha's *dharma*, his 'law', which is in fact identical with the 'law' laid down by Jesus in the Sermon on the Mount. Never is there any question of transcending good and evil. In the later forms of Buddhism, however, of which Zen is a branch, we are taken straight back to the Upanishads which contrived to combine the One of Parmenides with the 'Justice *is* strife' of Heraclitus, and are told by Hui Nêng, the real founder of Zen:

'Sit still correctly for a while, so long as there is neither activity nor tranquillity, neither production nor annihilation, neither coming nor going, *neither right nor wrong*.'[1]

This is the kernel of all the Eastern doctrines that have invaded the USA; and this, not LSD, was ultimately responsible for Charles Manson who took the Upanishads, the *Bhagavad-Gītā*, and Hui Nêng, as filtered through to him by such amiable associations as 'The Process' and OTO, at their literal word. American youth is playing not with fire but with a medicinal herb which may indeed bring health to *some* who are mentally sick, but which is a deadly poison to the basically healthy who need no medicine but prefer to follow the fashionable leaders of the Gadarene swine to their own destruction. And the Christians follow suit.

First they adopted Aristotle without ever really understanding him. Then they nailed him to a cross so that the words of the 'Shakespeare of science' should remain fixed and unchangeable on that rough piece of wood which, out of all the things he knew, seemed to represent most fittingly what he meant by 'matter' – that which can take on every possible

1. Hui Nêng, *The Platform Scripture*, ch. 53, tr. Wing-Tsit Chan (St John's University Press, New York, 1963), p. 147.

form. We have not seen that we need the real flesh-and-blood Aristotle, not only in his sanity and common sense, but also in his contemplative vision through which he sees contemplation itself as the fulfilment, the 'entelechy', of our active life of which it is the '*end*'. This we need to counterbalance what St Paul rightly called the 'stupidity' (*mōria*) of the Cross. In our efforts to make contact with the eternal we need him too because, whether we like it or not, he *is* the intellectual father of our Western world in whom we have every reason to glory, for he was the first to think analytically about mystical experience, finding thereby the only truly human answer to the mystery because his answer was reached by thought, which alone distinguishes man from the other animals, not by ecstasy and Platonic madness. For, in the words of Oscar Wilde, Aristotle's message was this:

'It will be a marvellous thing – the true personality of man – when we see it. It will grow naturally and simply, flowerlike, or as a tree grows. It will not be at discord. It will never argue or dispute. It will not prove things. It will know everything. And yet it will not busy itself about knowledge. It will have wisdom. Its value will not be measured by material things. It will have nothing. And yet it will have everything, and whatever one takes from it, it will still have, so rich will it be. It will not be always meddling with others, or asking them to be like itself. It will love them because they will be different. And yet while it will not meddle with others, it will help all, as a beautiful thing helps us, by being what it is. The personality of man will be very wonderful. It will be as wonderful as the personality of a child.

'In its development it will be assisted by Christianity, if men desire that; but if men do not desire that, it will develop none the less surely. For it will not worry itself about the past, nor care whether things happened or did not happen. Nor will it admit any laws but its own laws; nor any authority but its own authority. Yet it will love those who sought to intensify it, and speak often of them. And of these Christ was one.

' "Know thyself!" was written over the portal of the antique world. Over the portal of the new world, "Be thyself" shall be written. And the message of Christ to man was simple "Be thyself". That is the secret of Christ.'[2]

This was, of course, *not* the message and secret of Christ, but it is the message and secret of Aristotle. 'For a serious man, to be is a good: and everyone wishes good things for himself. And no one would want to possess all the [good] things [the world has to offer] *at the expense of becoming someone else*: for God alone possesses *the* Good *now*. You, on the other hand, must *be* whatever you happen to be.'[3] This, in a nutshell, is the Gospel according to Aristotle.

He does not wish you to be the *'hen'* or the *'pan'* (the 'One' or the 'All'): he simply asks you to be yourself, 'what you were to be' when you became a new 'form' at the time of your conception. You can no doubt catch glimpses of eternity by pursuing some form of Yoga or Zen, but these will rarely be more than glimpses, and, if not directed by a master who really knows what he is talking about, they may land you not in the unutterable peace of Nirvana, but in what Linda Kasabian terrifyingly described as a 'loud, loud . . . infinite scream . . . for ever'.[4]

This is not a joking matter. There is no manner of harm in the innocent frolics of the Hare Krishna boys and girls: they are simply imitating their God who, they think, plays games with them as Krishna himself did with the milkmaids; but His Divine Grace Bhaktivedanta Swami would do well to remind them that the same God is the terrible God of Time who will devour you in the end whether you like it or not:

> On every side thou lickest, lickest up – devouring –
> Worlds, universes, everything – with burning mouths:
> Vishnu! thy dreadful rays of light fill the whole universe
> With flames of glory, scorching everywhere.[5]

2. *The Works of Oscar Wilde* (Collins, London, 1948, and reprints,) pp. 1023–4. 3. Aristotle, *Nicomachean Ethics*, 9.4.4 (1166a 19–22). 4. Cf. above, p. 273. 5. *Bhagavad-Gītā*, 11.30.

You probably won't like it; and small wonder, for *our* God, whether you call him Yahweh, Father, Allah, Shiva or Vishnu, *is* terrible, and the more you pretend he is not there, the more terrible he becomes. He is raging now in our tick-tock machines, driving us to the only rational end to our meaningless lives: suicide. For if human life is completely senseless, then do what Marcion did, shun sex like the filthy, smelly, animal pest it is, or use it to its utmost limit, as the Indian Tantrics and Charles Manson did, until you reach the 'total experience' in that Platonic-Freudian thrill in which you see in one blinding flash that Love *is* Death.

Aristotle, apparently, has not laid the ghost of Heraclitus: he stalks throughout the United States today, turbaned, bearded, brown.

Meanwhile our savage God is there, calling us as he called Israel long ago in his own incomprehensible words:

> Seek Yahweh where he is still to be found,
> call to him while he is still near.
> Let the wicked man abandon his way,
> the evil man his thoughts.
> Let him turn back to Yahweh who will take pity on him,
> to our God who is rich in forgiving;
> for my thoughts are not your thoughts,
> my ways not your ways – it is Yahweh who speaks.
> Yes, the heavens are as high above earth
> as my ways are above your ways,
> my thoughts above your thoughts.[6]

Terrible though he is, 'his mercy precedes his wrath', as a Muslim tradition has it. Out of the thunder and the storm-cloud he demands our submission – Islam, for that is what the Arabic word *islām* means. Submit to the God of Abraham in whom the Muslims see the true founder of their faith; to the God of Isaac who fulfilled in Christ what he had spared poor, human, humble Isaac, obedient unto death; to the God of

6. Isaiah 55:6–9.

Jacob, faithful and wayward, enduring his savagery with resignation, sometimes even with joy, because he knows that to be chosen by such a God means to accept a burden too great for purely human flesh to bear. The religion of Israel is Islam too in that Israel submits to the inscrutable will of her savage God. The Messiah has not come, nor will he come till the end of time: and Israel knows that she is collectively the Suffering Servant, crucified day in and day out on the cross that sin has made. Despite her incorrigible whorings after other gods, her mad flirtations with Mammon, the god of money, and the burden of uncommon intelligence and sensitivity that God has laid upon her, she has stood firm: for even in her faithlessness she still has faith and hope. She remembers what her savage God said through the lips of the prophet Isaiah:

> I did forsake you for a brief moment,
> but with great love will I take you back.
> In excess of anger, for a moment
> I hid my face from you.
> But with everlasting love I have taken pity on you,
> says Yahweh, your redeemer[7]

This is the 'God of Abraham, God of Isaac, God of Jacob', whom Pascal saw, the terrible God to whom the first response must be Islam, 'submission', the second thankfulness for giving us the courage to endure his jealous love. For as Al-Junayd, the father of Islamic mysticism, says: 'The journey from this world to the next is easy and simple for the believer, but to separate oneself from creatures for God's sake is hard, and the journey from self to God is exceedingly hard, and to bear patiently with God is the hardest of all.'[8]

For our savage God is also a jealous God, as Aristotle himself discerned; for when this apostle of the golden mean speaks of God, he does not use the more general word *philia*

7. Ibid., 54:7–8.
8. See R. C. Zaehner, *Hindu and Muslim Mysticism* (The Athlone Press, London, 1960), p. 153.

which can be translated in English as either 'like' or 'love', but *eros*, the word for 'passionate love' or 'being in love with' someone; and according to him you can only be in love with one person at a time (p. 198). That this passionate love could be returned literally with a vengeance he did not know; and he would certainly have demurred at Kabīr's blunt assertion that 'God is a Thug'. Or would he? For as someone has said who knows about these things: 'You never know what he is coming up with next.'

Islam: 'submission'. It doesn't really matter whether you believe in the savage God or not; for Islam means to submit to things as they are and not to be for ever 'meddling with others' and telling us how things ought to be, the perennial vice of the intellectual; or complaining that God isn't fair, as poor Alex does in *A Clockwork Orange*.[9] God *isn't* fair, and that is precisely what grace means. The whole point of the parables of Jesus is that God is not fair: he is not even just, as was Marcion's Creator God – in his mean little way. He doesn't pretend to be so because he isn't self-righteous and there is nothing he hates more than self-righteousness, as is made very clear in the Gospel according to St Luke too, the only gospel that Marcion did accept. He does not reveal the good news to the intellectuals but to stupid children (10:21); he prefers one repentant sinner to ninety-nine self-righteous bores (15:4–7); he prefers the spendthrift scapegrace to the dutiful, efficient son who never puts a foot wrong (15:11–32); and he even commends the fraudulent steward for his sound common sense because he takes the 'Protestant work ethic' seriously and makes provision for himself and his family by fiddling the accounts as any sensible thrifty man would (16:1–8). No wonder they crucified him!

'He was crucified *for us*.' Does this mean anything to anyone any more? How could the torturing to death of one man for a matter of hours in any way satisfy the raving anger of that savage God? The answer is supplied in the first chapters of

9. Anthony Burgess, *A Clockwork Orange*, p. 61.

Luke which Marcion excised because he could not admit that God, *the* Pure Spirit, could have any part in human flesh. But from Aristotle's point of view it would make perfect sense. Jesus was literally the Son of God; for, in his case alone, God directly provided the 'form' that was to result in a new creature once it was planted in its appropriate bit of indeterminate matter called Mary. 'Parents love their children as themselves, for, in so far as they are separated from themselves, they are, as it were, other selves.'[1] In crucifying Jesus God is crucifying himself. Only God can do this, and it is for this reason that he spared Isaac, supplying a ram in his place. The crucifixion of Jesus means that God demonstrates to man that he is so utterly unfair and crazy as to crucify himself. What he asks us to do is precisely this; and this is what he means when he says: 'If any man comes to me without hating his father, mother, wife, children, brothers, sisters, yes and his own life too, he cannot be my disciple. Anyone who does not carry his cross and come after me cannot be my disciple.'[2] Yes, there it is for all to read in Marcion's own gentle Gospel according to St Luke.

Of course God knows he is asking us to do what he alone can do, 'to kill the thing he loves', which our savage God is doing throughout eternity, because in him, *and in him alone*, Heraclitus' paradox is true: 'Justice *is* strife', and life *is* death, and self-sacrifice *is* self-fulfilment. This certainly is sheer 'stupidity' and 'silliness' to the intellectuals, but Christ made it very plain that he was not interested in them but in silly little children (*nēpios*) who would do what they were told, or at least try to. What he is telling us from the cross is this: 'I, Jesus, the son of Mary, can do this and have done it because my father and "form" is God: my father has killed me because I am his second self. He has killed me and, in killing me, he has killed himself. But he cannot die because he is pure, unchanging "form". I can: because the matter that made it possible for me

1. Aristotle, *Nicomachean Ethics*, 8.12.3 (1161b 28–9).
2. Luke 14:26–7.

to become a social animal at all I took from my mother Mary who willingly accepted the common lot of our chosen Jewish race which is to kiss the hand that strikes us. She knew and she did not flinch when old Simeon prophesied that "a sword will pierce your own soul too".[3] She accepted everything on your behalf because she was the kind of silly little child I love. You can do the same, but only with my help.'

In the old Mass Catholics used to call Christ's sacrifice of himself a 'reasonable sacrifice': and from a strictly Aristotelian point of view I think it is. Christ knows that he is asking of us the impossible, but he also told us that 'things that are impossible for men . . . are possible for God'.[4] And this is the meaning of grace: the help God *will* give us if we will only shut up and stop chattering like a lot of linguistic philosophers. You cannot die to self and stop that civil war in yourself without divine help; for Islam, 'submission', is the precondition of *īmān*, 'faith', and without faith there can be no understanding of the fierce, jealous love of God for which Aristotle pined.

This is not the perfect peace of Nirvana, though it is that too; and if this is what you want, let the Buddha be your guide, for his message is essentially the same: 'Die to yourself because what you take to be yourself is not yourself at all.' That is the first step which Jesus demonstrated on the cross, but Jesus did not reject the world of matter but accepted it in the shape of Mary, a silly little Jewish girl whose submission was total and unquestioning.

It is easy to call yourself a Christian; it is excessively difficult to be one – less difficult indeed than for the Jew to be a Jew; for the Jews have to do themselves what Mary did for us as our representative – accept what is given you, for better or for worse.

Of modern Christians Bernanos stands out as a living witness to what being a Christian means. For him it meant to accept gratefully the trials inflicted on him by a terrible God, to stand

3. Luke 2:35.   4. Luke 18:27.

up manfully for the justice that this God demands of men, and to denounce wickedness in high places wherever he saw its hideous face. Fascist, Nazi, Stalinist wickedness (he didn't care about the labels), the wickedness of the rotten establishment of his own beloved France, and, worst of all, the monstrous wickedness of the worldly-wise prelates who bowed down to evil on grounds of pure expediency. He had little tenderness for the aloofly ascetic diplomat the world remembers as Pope Pius XII.

Bernanos understood that he was here on this earth to live, to love, and to suffer with Christ and the despised and rejected wherever he found them. He knew that you could only grope your way towards God,[5] but try you must, no matter how much it cost you. 'You and I', he wrote to a friend, 'are in God's hands like two bunches of grapes to be squeezed out in them until we have yielded up all our juice, and we shall never meet again until we do so in the vats of eternity. But we will have been squeezed out *together*. . . . I should mistrust the talent of almost everyone, but *your* anguish cannot betray me. It is not a question of accepting or rejecting it, or even of measuring it: I am just in it.'[6]

How very like Aristotle it all is except the unprotesting acceptance of suffering, which is Jewish and Christian. For a friend, for Aristotle, was also another self and even at the end, when one enters into the contemplative life, it is better to do so in the company of a few like-minded friends, for it is easier to contemplate the eternal in others who are second selves to you than it is to do so in yourself.[7] Man is and always will be a social animal and naturally disposed to living with others.[8] What Aristotle did not know, and what Bernanos did know, was that we should meet and mingle together in the heavenly vats where essence meets essence, one in substance but

5. G. Bernanos, *Correspondance*, Vol. II (Plon, Paris, 1971), p. 228.
6. Ibid., p. 251.
7. Aristotle, *Nicomachean Ethics*, 9.9.5 (1169b 28–1170a 7).
8. Ibid., 9.9.3 (1169b 20).

without 'confusion of persons', as is the case of the Christian God himself.

No one in modern times has had such an acute sense of what Bonhoeffer called the 'wickedness of evil' as Bernanos. In his first great novel, *Sous le soleil de Satan*, 'Beneath Satan's Sun', he *saw* the hideous face of the Evil One, and he very nearly succumbed to what is generally supposed to be the sin against the Holy Spirit, the sin against the Spirit of Life itself, the Gnostic sin, the Stoic sin, the distinguished sin, the respectable, intellectual sin – despair. But Bernanos did not succumb. In the last of his novels to be published, *Monsieur Ouine*, he thought he had tracked down the sub-material Aristotelian horror in the person of Monsieur Ouine, the eternal Yes-No of Heraclitus and Aldous Huxley's 'perennial philosophy', whose death-agony I tried to describe in *Drugs, Mysticism and Make-believe*: the disintegration of a soul into nothingness and worse, the satanic caricature of the Buddhist Nirvana, where right is wrong, and evil is good, and Manson is the Son of Man, summoned by Marcion's good, good God to exterminate the fat, overfed 'pigs' that infest Los Angeles, the 'city of angels'.

The hateful ambivalence of evil Bernanos faced in his own creation, and the monster he had created turned on him and destroyed him as a novelist. He wrote on endlessly, denouncing Munich, Vichy, the sycophantic hierarchy of the Church that yet lived in every fibre of his being, the cult of the machine, and the dehumanization of man; but he never wrote a novel again. What he had described was almost too frighteningly true to be put down on paper. He needn't have worried: practically no one has, in fact, read *Monsieur Ouine*. Of all his novels, he wrote, 'it is the one which has cost me most, which I have probably paid for most dearly, and the full amount of which I have not yet even now paid up.'[9] He had not: for the dehumanizing of man went on with the clockwork precision he had predicted. He did not live to see his beloved France fall

9. G. Bernanos, *Correspondance*, Vol. II, p. 266.

like a ripe plum from the hands of the last Frenchman he recognized as truly French, General de Gaulle, that strange and strangely sublime mixture of Joan of Arc, St Louis, and Richelieu, into those of the super-bureaucrat and embodiment of the cultured wing of the efficient society he despised the most; nor did he live to see his second fatherland, Brazil, fall into the hands of an utterly ruthless band of faultlessly efficient technocrats, who, as is the way of the mechanically minded, treated people as things, to be tortured into their senses if necessary. Aristotle's views on slavery are as nothing to technocratic man's idea of what his fellow-men are: for Aristotle they might be 'ensouled tools', but they were also human beings and lovable as such,[1] and not to be discarded on the rubbish-heap as so much 'redundant' waste.

And what would Bernanos have made of Charles Manson? Fortunately we know, for a very similar case had shocked France in 1937, as the Manson case shocked America in 1969: only it was worse. For the young criminal, a German, of decent bourgeois stock, Eugène Weidmann, had admitted to six apparently unmotivated murders. He was publicly guillotined in Versailles. This is what Bernanos wrote to the lawyer who ran the case for the defence, a lady called Renée Jardin Birnie:

Madame,

I have not the honour of knowing you personally, and the feeling that impels me to write to you is one of those which one would normally only confide to a small circle of friends. Never mind. I don't know again whether you happen to have opened any of my books or even whether my name is known to you. Once more, never mind. My real difficulty is to find a few simple words because, if I can't, this whole business of writing to you at all would only look ridiculous and affected.

I am not so romantic as to be favourably disposed towards

1. Aristotle, *Nicomachean Ethics*, 8.11.7 (1161b 5).

murderers. But it seems to me that crime, when it goes beyond a certain point in sheer horror, becomes akin to extreme and utter misery and is as incomprehensible and as mysterious as that is. Both put a human creature outside and, as it were, beyond life.

I know absolutely nothing about the poor wretched creature you are helping. But it is impossible to look at the excellent photos published in *Paris-Soir*, particularly the one of Tuesday, 14th [December 1937], where [his face] appears between the heads of two honest-to-goodness, very ordinary policemen – the very image of loneliness and of a supernatural forlornness – without experiencing a sort of religious awe. That evening I was dining in a monastery near Toulon and I repeated to the monks who were with me, and who knew nothing about this frightful bit of news, the words put into Eugène Weidmann's mouth by the journalists, wrongly maybe. They were: 'It's because you are speaking to me gently. . . .' That a child can have come into this world with this invisible sign already inscribed on his forehead will doubtless provide the psychologists and moralists with a pretext to churn out lots of ingenious hypotheses. I am not a psychologist, much less a moralist, as I happen to be a Christian. Such a thought can only arouse in me a feeling that rends the heart to the point of agony – and beyond agony, because it is heart-rending in that there is in it a hope that one can scarcely conceive of: the solidarity of all men in Christ.

I leave it to you, Madame, to decide whether to tell Eugène Weidmann what I and my friends, the monks, think, or to say nothing about it. As far as I am concerned, I have nothing much to offer him. I would like him to be able to understand that there are monks, lonely like him, who do better than just pity him, but who will from now on take over, as brothers should, part of his appalling burden.

G. BERNANOS[2]

2. G. Bernanos, op. cit., Vol. II, pp. 186–7.

This is what Christianity is all about and one of the things that Aristotle is about: you must love your neighbour as 'another self'. The difference, of course, is that Christ's compassion embraces first and foremost the riff-raff, the outcastes, the dregs of humanity, for whom Aristotle had no use, and seems to exclude the rich and the clever, not because they are rich and clever, but because they think they do not need to be saved. They are too nice and tight and snug in the clockwork cocoon they have woven for themselves in their spotless little ivory towers. But 'with God', as Jesus said, 'all things are possible'. To the compassion of God crucified in Christ there is no limit. There is no answer to this mystery except to stand in silent awe.

It is the compassion of Christ that compels us not only to accept the wrath of God, but also to accept and pray for the monsters at whose hands he chastises us, whether they are Hitler, Stalin, or Brezhnev, or merely the two-faced, slick opportunist whom Americans once called Tricky Dick. Yes, 'with God all things are possible'.

As to Charles Manson. What was really nauseating about the whole miserable affair was that it needed the murder of nine people *of its own class and kind* to rouse the 'conscience' of the American establishment which takes it for granted that among the inalienable freedoms in this supremely free society is the freedom to possess a gun and use it. If the victims had been a lot of lousy beggars with not a nickel in their pockets and only their lives to lose, would the Christian 'conscience' of our clockwork scribes and Pharisees have woken up with such a shock of panic fear? Of course it wouldn't, for the so-called random killings were not random at all but directed at *them*, the rich, self-satisfied, successful, efficient 'men of the world' who have not even the courage to pursue their own convictions to their logical conclusion. For had they done so, they would have finished off that messy, inefficient, annoying little business of Vietnam once and for all by dropping a hydrogen bomb or two. Russian reprisals? Surely that is rather out-of-date thinking, for in the end like will always find like,[3] as Nixon has found Brezhnev and Mao, and as Brezhnev has found Nixon. 'Birds of a feather flock together', and mass-murderers at second hand are no exception to this nasty rule.

Nor is there much excuse for the horror so freely expressed at the fact that none of the murderers had shown the slightest twinge of remorse for the unspeakable things they had done; for they were simply following the example of their elders and betters who had drummed it into their stupid heads that, under certain circumstances, as, for example, in war, a human being ceases to be a human being and becomes a target, a thing about which, when you ask the Aristotelian question, 'What is it for?' the answer automatically comes back, 'For death.' And in this little matter the 'gurus' and the 'rōshis', black, yellow, but above all the rootless intellectual whites, must take their full share of responsibility. For it is they, the 'enlightened' ones, who have taught the helpless young that on the other side, in the 'eternal Now', there is 'neither right nor wrong', neither killer nor killed, and that all things are for ever identical and the same. Who is to blame Charles Manson, who gained his 'enlightenment' in a hard and primitive way, for taking them at their word?

Nor will it do to say that the law should have taken him at *his* word and killed him as he had killed; for his 'enlightenment' and 'detachment' were not complete, as his pathetic behaviour at the trial showed. At this supreme moment the good, good eternal Self-God (for in this form of Vedanta and Zen there is no distinction between the two) forsook him, and he found himself again in all his helpless forlornness and childish denudation.

'Hippy cult leader, actually, hippy cult leader, that is your words. I am a dumb country boy who never grew up. I went to jail when I was eight years old and I got out when I was thirty-two. I have never adjusted to your free world. I am still

3. Aristotle, *Nicomachean Ethics*, 8.1.6 (1155a 34).

that stupid, corn-picking country boy that I have always been.'

This is the kind of utterly, hopelessly lost sheep whom Christ Jesus came to save *because* – and not in spite of the fact that – his hands reek with blood shed by someone who was not Charles Manson but what he took to be the eternal Soul which, he had been told, is beyond good and evil.

'Judge not, that ye be not judged': Don't judge others if you don't want to be condemned yourselves. That is not so very difficult, particularly in this age when all our old moral values, both Christian and Aristotelian, have collapsed. But to pray for those who have done you wrong,[4] is more difficult; and to pray for those who have foully wronged those whom you love is most difficult of all. This none of us will ever be able to do until we see, with Bernanos, 'the solidarity of all men in Christ'.

Then when our turn comes to die, we shall see, as Bernanos saw, that any pathetic little effort we may have made to obey his impossible commandment will be gratefully and graciously accepted by that savage God who yet pities us with an everlasting love.

For we must see that 'we really want what He wants; without knowing it, we really want our sorrows, our sufferings, and our loneliness, although we fondly imagine we only want our pleasures. We imagine that we are frightened of our death and run away from it when we really want our death as He wanted His – anyhow our death *is* His. Just as He sacrifices Himself on every altar where Mass is celebrated, so does He begin to die again in the death agony of every single man. We want everything that He wants, but we do not know that we want it. We do not know ourselves. Sin makes us live on the surface of ourselves: we only go back into ourselves to die – and it is there that He is waiting for us.'[5]

4. Matthew 5:44, and note in the New English Bible.
5. G. Bernanos, *Oeuvres romanesques*, p. liv.

ACKNOWLEDGEMENTS

The author and publishers would like to acknowledge their gratitude for permission to quote from the following books: The Jerusalem Bible, published and copyright © 1966, 1967 and 1968 by Darton, Longman & Todd, Ltd, and Doubleday and Company, Inc., used by permission of the publishers; *Letters and Papers from Prison* by Dietrich Bonhoeffer, enlarged edition, copyright © 1953, 1967, 1971 by SCM Press Ltd, reprinted with permission of SCM Press, London, and The Macmillan Company, New York; *The Beginnings of Indian Philosophy* by Franklin Edgerton, published by Allen & Unwin, London, and Harvard University Press, Cambridge, Mass.; *Shamanism: Archaic Techniques of Ecstasy* by Mircea Eliade, translated by Willard R. Trask, published by Pantheon Books, New York, and by Princeton University Press, Princeton, in the Bollingen Series LXXVI, copyright © 1964 by Bollingen Foundation, reprinted by permission of Princeton University Press; *Adversus Marcionem* by Tertullian, edited and translated by Ernest Evans, © 1972 Oxford University Press, reprinted by permission of The Clarendon Press, Oxford; *Bees: Their Vision, Chemical Senses and Language* by Karl von Frisch, copyright 1950 by Cornell University, used by permission of Cornell University Press; *The Crisis of Psychoanalysis* by Erich Fromm, copyright © 1970 by Erich Fromm, reprinted by permission of Jonathan Cape, London, and Holt, Rinehart and Winston, Inc., New York; *The Presocratics* by Edward Hussey, published by Gerald Duckworth, London, and Charles Scribner's Sons, New York; *The Collected Works of C. G. Jung*, edited by G. Adler, M. Fordham, H. Read, and W. McGuire, and translated by R. F. C. Hull, Bollingen Series XX, Volume 11, *Psychology and Religion: West and East*, 'Answer to Job', copyright © 1958 by Bollingen Foundation and © 1969 by Princeton University Press, reprinted by permission of Princeton University Press, Princeton, and Routledge & Kegan Paul, London; *The Varieties of Psychedelic Experience* by R. E. L. Masters and Jean Houston, copyright © 1966 by R. E. L. Masters and Jean Houston,

Ackuowledgements

reprinted by permission of Holt, Rinehart and Winston, Inc., New York; *The Sovereignty of Good* by Iris Murdoch, copyright © 1970 by Iris Murdoch, reprinted by permission of Routledge & Kegan Paul, London, and Schocken Books Inc., New York; *The Autobiography of Bertrand Russell*, published by Allen & Unwin, London, and Atlantic Monthly Press, Boston; *The Family* by Ed Sanders, copyright © 1971 by Ed Sanders, published by Rupert Hart-Davis, London, and E. P. Dutton & Co., Inc., New York, and used with their permission; *Mysticism and Philosophy* by W. T. Stace, reprinted by permission of Macmillan, London; *The Dead Sea Scrolls in English* by Geza Vermes, copyright © G. Vermes, 1962, 1965, 1968, published by Penguin Books Ltd, Harmondsworth; *The Way and its Power* by Arthur Waley, published by Allen & Unwin, London. Translations of passages from the works of Georges Bernanos have been made by permission of Librairie Plon of Paris and of Pierre Teilhard de Chardin by permission of Éditions du Seuil.

In addition the author wishes to thank Miss Judith Todd of Collins Publishers for the immense amount of work she has put into the production of this recalcitrant book, Mr Edward Hussey for his assistance in reading the proofs, and last but not least the American professor mentioned on page 9 who introduced him to the ways of Charles Manson but whose correspondence has most regrettably gone astray.

INDEX

INDEX

Index

Index